GREAT CITYMAPS

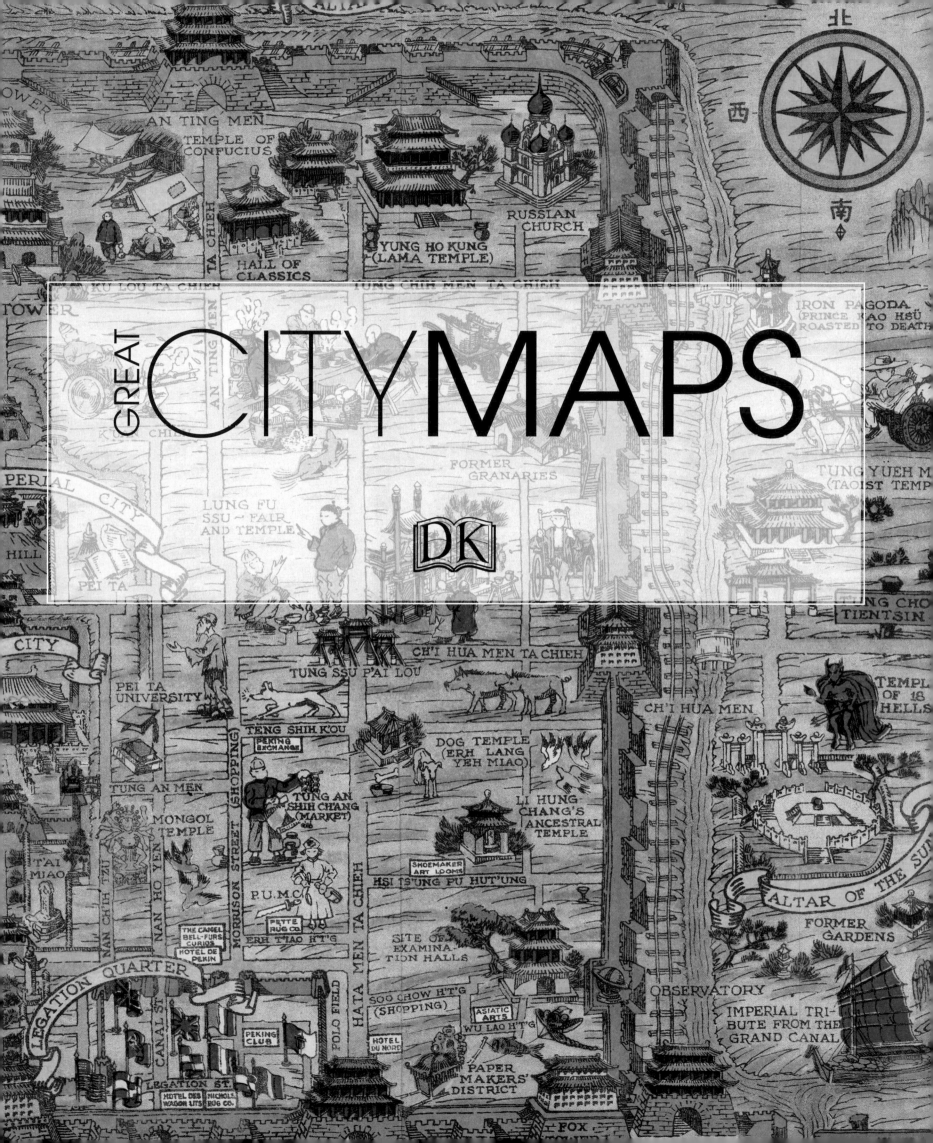

GREAT CITYMAPS

DK

Penguin Random House

Senior Editor   Sam Atkinson
Editors   Victoria Heyworth-Dunne, Ruth
O'Rourke-Jones, Debra Wolter
US Senior Editor   Shannon Beatty
US Editor   Margaret Parrish
Senior Art Editors   Gillian Andrews, Gadi Farfour
Designer   Ray Bryant
Senior Producer, Pre-Production   Nikoleta Parasaki
Senior Producer   Mandy Inness
Picture Research   Sarah Smithies
Jackets Design Development Manager   Sophia MTT
Jacket Editor   Claire Gell
Managing Editor   Gareth Jones
Senior Managing Art Editor   Lee Griffiths
Publisher   Liz Wheeler
Art Director   Karen Self
Publishing Director   Jonathan Metcalf

DK INDIA

Senior Art Editor   Chhaya Sajwan
Assistant Art Editor   Roshni Kapur
DTP Designers   Syed Mohammad Farhan
Jacket Designer   Suhita Dharamjit
Senior DTP Designer   Harish Aggarwal
Managing Jackets Editor   Saloni Singh
Managing Art Editor   Arunesh Talapatra
Production Manager   Pankaj Sharma

SMITHSONIAN ENTERPRISES

Product Development Manager   Kealy Gordon
Licensing Manager   Ellen Nanney
Vice President, Education and Consumer   Brigid Ferraro
Products
Senior Vice President, Education and   Carol LeBlanc
Consumer Products
President   Chris Liedel

First American Edition, 2016

First published in the United States by
DK Publishing, 1450 Broadway, Suite 801,
New York, NY 10018

 Smithsonian

Contents

ANCIENT CITIES

MEDIEVAL TRADING CENTERS

IMPERIAL CAPITALS   COLONIAL CITIES   IDEAL CITIES   MEGACITIES

Contributors

Jeremy Black, General Consultant
Professor of History at Exeter University
in the UK, Jeremy Black graduated from
Cambridge University with a Starred First,
and did graduate work at Oxford University
before teaching at the University of Durham,
and from 1996 at Exeter. His two major fields
of scholarship are military history and the
history of cartography. Recent books include
War and Technology, *Rethinking World War
Two*, and *Metropolis*. He has held visiting
chairs at a number of American institutions,
including West Point, and received the Samuel
Eliot Morison Prize from the Society for
Military History in 2008.

Andrew Heritage
As editorial director at Time Books, Andrew
Heritage oversaw the reinvention of *The
Times Comprehensive Atlas of the World* and
many authoritative historical and thematic
atlases. At DK, he created the first entirely
digital world mapping system, and built a list
of innovative contemporary and historical
atlases. He has continued to be involved in a
range of historical and cartographic projects.

Andrew Humphreys
An award-winning travel writer, Andrew
Humphreys is the author of two books on the
golden age of travel. He has written for DK,

National Geographic, and Lonely Planet, and
his journalism has appeared in the *Financial
Times* and *The Sunday Times* newspapers in
the UK. He has a passionate interest in maps.

Thomas Cussans
A freelance historian and author based in
France, for many years Thomas Cussans
was a publisher responsible for a series
of best-selling history atlases, among them
The Times Atlas of World History, *The Times
Atlas of World Exploration*, and *The Times
Atlas of the 20th Century*. He has contributed
to numerous DK titles, including *History: The
Definitive Visual Guide*.

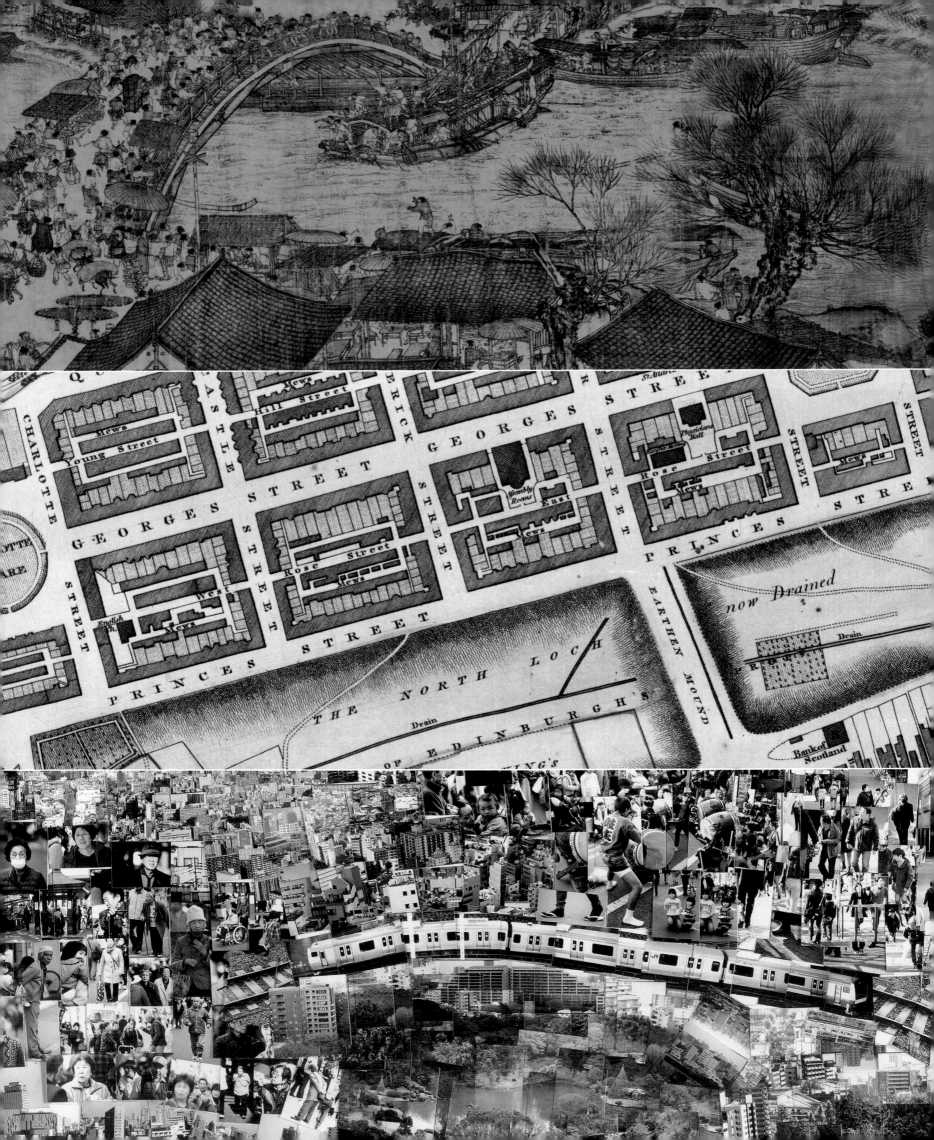

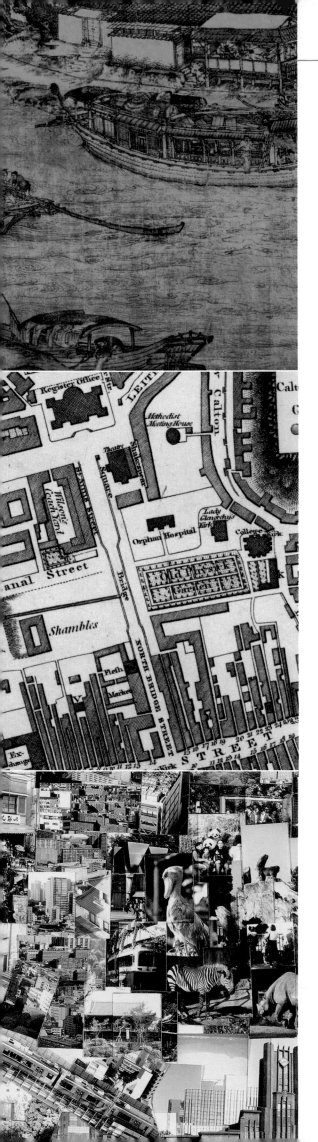

Preface

Beautiful as well as useful, historic as well as contemporary, city maps record the molding of the environment as humans create the key places in which they interact and seek to determine their development. Often these urban plans define their environment in ways that the inhabitants and even the patrons or sponsors of the maps could not recognize.

As this excellent collection makes clear, cities are centers of political, economic, religious, and cultural power. Maps of urban centers reflect the aspirations of humankind and yet also the realities of life—whether they portray slums or arrays of rich buildings fronting grand boulevards.

Maps can show the reshaping of long-established cities such as Beijing, Baghdad, Constantinople, Paris, and London, all of which have been superbly depicted in this book, but they also record the rapid creation and shaping of new cities in alien lands: for instance, Rio de Janeiro, San Francisco, Sydney, and Washington, D.C. Different cartographic techniques and concerns can be seen in the very contrasting maps of post-Columbian Tenochtitlan (now Mexico City), Madrid, Barcelona, Cairo, Kyoto, and Seoul. Indeed, the cultural significance, aspirations, and splendor of individual national traditions can be shown to great effect in a map.

Maps can also focus on key events, such as the Turkish siege of Vienna or the American War of Independence from the perspective of New York. Cities can be shown changing with reference not only to political events but also to technological changes. Thus, these maps record developments such as the spread of the railroads and the introduction of the steamship and, eventually, trans-global flight. The maps included in this book demonstrate how cities have continued to evolve, and have adapted to new and often threatening challenges. An abundance of human history is here.

PROFESSOR JEREMY BLACK, GENERAL CONSULTANT

The Earliest City Plans

The first cities came into existence more than 7,000 years ago as the production of an agricultural surplus, the emergence of craft industries and trading, and the need for administrative systems developed largely independently across Eurasia. Urban growth was focused on the major river valley systems, such as the Nile in Egypt, the Tigris and Euphrates in Mesopotamia (southwest Asia), the Indus in South Asia, and the Yellow River in China, because early societies were reliant on fertile land for farming.

Over time, these first cities became magnets for people from outlying agricultural areas. Higher levels of literacy, technological progress (notably in metals), and increasingly complex forms of social organization all distinguished cities from smaller ancient settlements. As they grew, these citiescreated an enduring, and largely unchanged, template for the numerous vast metropolitan areas that characterize much of our globe today.

Çatal Hüyük

Planning and accommodating an organically growing urban environment was a major problem, and mapping became, albeit gradually, a vitally important tool of urban administrators. However, few maps of ancient city areas have survived. One of the earliest plans discovered to date is a wall painting found at Çatal Hüyük (c.7000 BCE), now in modern Turkey, which predates the first substantial metropolitan developments on the Nile and in Mesopotamia by several thousand years. It clearly shows an urban entity comprised of linked multistoried buildings and courtyards, accessible by ladders mainly from the rooftops (*see below*).

Mesopotamian mapping

An important ceremonial and trading city (now in southeastern Iraq) dating back to the 3rd millennium BCE, Nippur grew, layer upon layer, in the lower Mesopotamian valley. Fragments of city plans that were incised on clay tablets in about 1400 BCE have been excavated from the site (*see right*). Although they are clearly part of a larger city map or plan, they prove to be remarkably accurate when compared with modern archeological surveys.

Annotated in cuneiform (the writing system used in ancient West Asia) and drawn to scale, these fragments reveal a depth of urban planning that included the delineation of temple complexes, the Tigris and Euphrates rivers, some housing plans, and the new city walls that

▲ **ÇATAL HÜYÜK** This reconstruction of the wall painting of the settlement and trading center of Çatal Hüyük emphasizes the towering volcano of Hasan Dag above the town, probably the source of the obsidian its citizens traded widely.

▲ **MOHENJO-DARO** Still only partly excavated today, this large city extended over an area of around 60 hectares (150 acres). It was divided into a raised governmental and ceremonial citadel area, and a lower residential precinct.

> For those who **pass it without entering**, the city is one thing; it is another for those who are **trapped by it** and never leave. There is the city where you arrive for the first time; and there is another city which you leave **never to return** "

ITALO CALVINO, *INVISIBLE CITIES*, 1972

▲ **NIPPUR MAP FRAGMENT** The function of the map made of Nippur–the religious center of the Sumerians–remains unclear, but its creation seems to have coincided with a rejuvenation of the city with new buildings and fortifications.

were built at the time. The use of an overhead ground plan, orientated approximately northwest to southeast, is clearly based on a grid approach. Similar, but less accurate, plans for the Mesopotamian centers of Uruk–a major city dominated by monumental mud-brick buildings–and Sippar in Babylonia, have also been discovered.

Planning and the city

It is likely that the city planners of Mesopotamia and the Nile Delta in Egypt–where in 3000 BCE, Memphis was founded as the capital of the new, unified Egyptian state– used accurate measurement systems to build their

monuments, walls, and cities, but these are largely lost to us today, like lines in the sand. However, it is apparent from excavations of very early cities, such as the Indus Valley settlement of Mohenjo Daro (c.2500 BCE), which had a population around 40,000 and carefully constructed street, drainage, sewage, and bathing systems, that architectural and urban planning techniques were already becoming highly sophisticated by the 3rd millennium BCE. The age of the city–and city mapping–had begun.

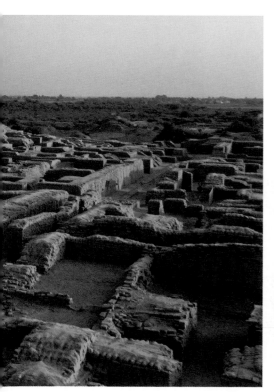

▲ **ATHENS** Unfortunately, as is the case with many of the early great cities, no maps from the ancient era survive of Athens. Later archeologists have had to piece together maps of the city in Classical times based on surviving remnants and structures such as the Acropolis.

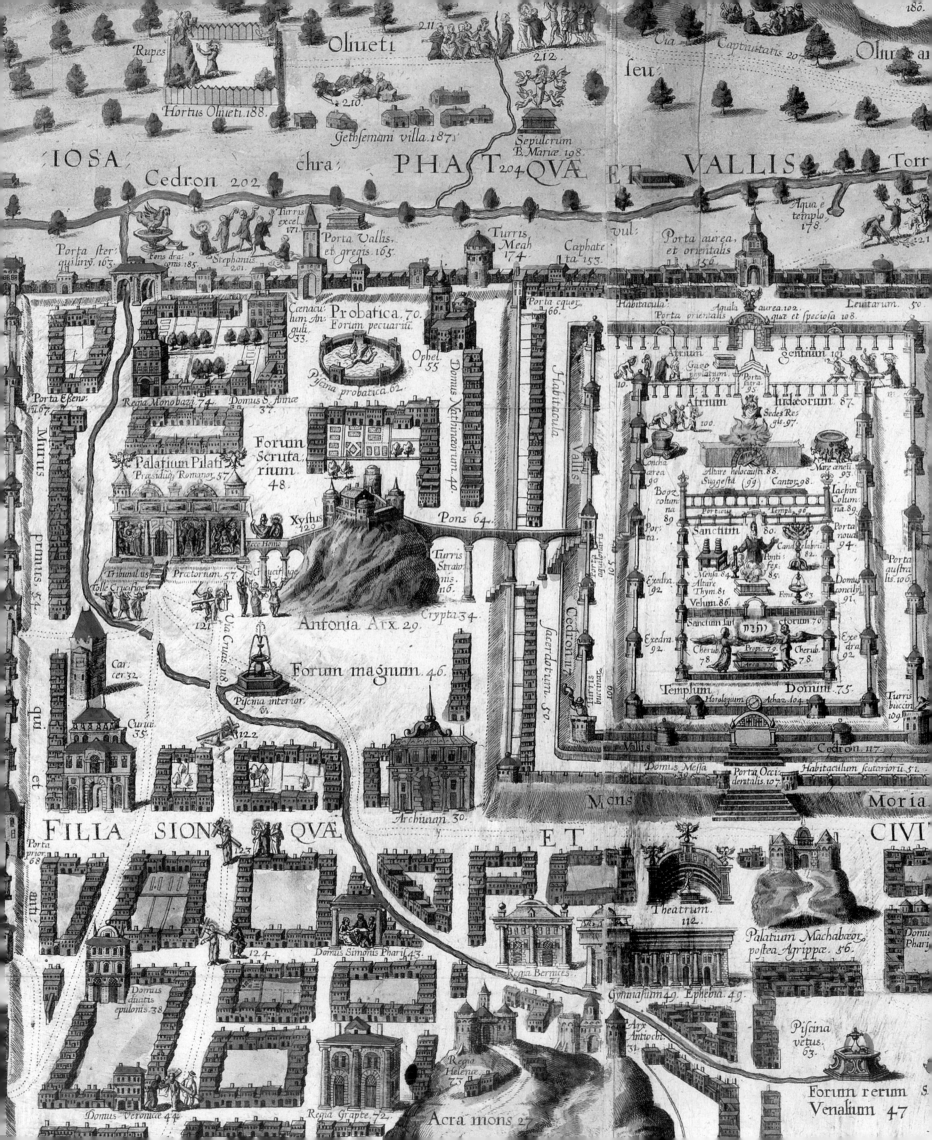

Oliueti

211.

212.

Via Captiuitatis 20

Olix ai

feu

Rupes

Hortus Oliueti. 188.

210.

Gethsemani villa. 187.

Sepulcrum
B. Mariæ. 198.

IOSA,

chra,

PHAT, T 204 QVÆ

ET

VALLIS

Torr

Cedron 202.

Aqua e
templo
178

221.

Porta ster'
quiliny. 163.

Fons dra'
gonis. 185.

Stephanus.
201.

Turris
excel.
171.

Porta Vallis,
et gregis. 165.

Turris
Meah
174

Caphate
ta. 153.

vul:

Porta aurea,
et orientalis.
156

Porta equor
66.

Habitacula'

Porta orientalis.
aurea. 102.

Leuitarum. 50

Porta Essen.
67.

Regia Monobazi. 74.

Domus S. Annæ.
37.

Cænacu'
lum An'
guli.
33.

Probatica. 70.
Forum pecuarii.

Ophel.
55

Piscina probatica. 62.

Domus Nathinæorum. 40.

Habitacula

Aquila
aurea. 102.

quæ et speciosa 108.

Atrium
Gazo
phylatium.
103

Porta
sera.
95.

Centrum 101

10.

Atrium

Iudæorum. 87.

Murus

primus. 54.

Palatium Pilati
Præsidiis Romanor. 57.

Forum
Scruta'
rium
48.

Ecce Homo

Xystus
129.

Pons 64.

Vallis

Sedes Re:
gia. 97.

100.

Concha
ærea
90.

Booz
colum
na.
89.

Altare helocausti. 88.

Suggesta (99)

Cantor. 98.

Mare æneii
93.

Porticus

Temple. 96.

Iachin
Colum
na. 89.

Porta.

Sanctum
80.

Candelabria
82.

Ponti
fex.
85.

Porta
noua
94.

Tribunal. 115

Tolle Crucifige

Prætorium. 57.

Crucifige
116

Turris
Strato'
nis.
116.

Porta
aquilonaris
105.

Cedron.

Exedra
92.

Mensa 84.
Altare
Thym. 81.
Velum. 86.

Porta
austra
lis. 106.

Domus
concilii.
91.

Sacerdotum. 50.

Fons 83.

121

Via Crucis. 118.

Antonia Arx. 29.

Crypta 34.

Exedra.
92.

Sanctum san'
ctorum. 70.

יהוה

Cherub
78.

Propic. 79.

Arca 77.

Cherub
78.

Exe
dra
92.

Car:
cer. 32.

Forum magnum. 46.

Turris
buccinat.
109

Templum

Domini. 75.

Turris
buccinat.
109

Piscina interior.
61.

Horologium
Achaz. 104.

Curui.
35.

122.

Vallis

Cedron. 117.

Domus Messa
39.

Porta Occi'
dentalis. 107.

Habitaculum scutariorū. 51.

Mons

Moria

FILIA SION, QVÆ

Archiuum. 30.

ET

CIVI

Porta
prior.
68.

123

Domus
ditatis
epulonis. 38.

124.

Domus Simonis Phari. 43.

Theatrum.
112.

Palatium Machabæor.
postea Agrippæ. 56.

Domus
Phari.

Regia Bernices.
71.

Gymnasium 49. Ephebia. 49.

Domus Veronicæ. 44.

Regia Grapte. 72.

Regia
Helenæ.
73.

Acra mons 27.

Arx
Antiochi.
31.

Piscina
vetus.
63.

Forum rerum s
Venalium 47

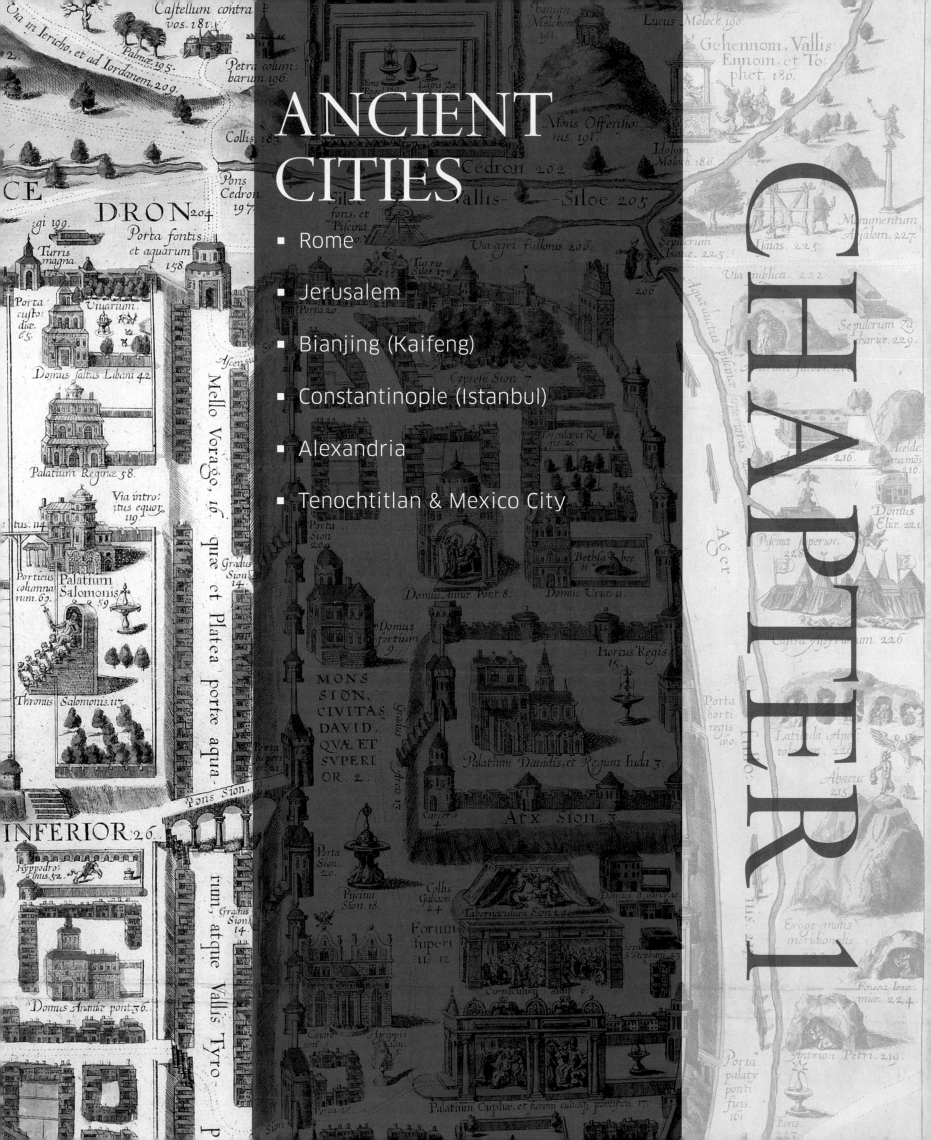

ANCIENT CITIES

- Rome
- Jerusalem
- Bianjing (Kaifeng)
- Constantinople (Istanbul)
- Alexandria
- Tenochtitlan & Mexico City

CHAPTER 1

Ancient Cities

Historians and historical cartographers of city planning are confronted by a major obstacle when conducting research on the layouts of the cities of the ancient world: very few contemporary records of their street plans have survived. What is known is largely the result of digging, deduction, and reconstruction by archeologists. Some clues have been gleaned from later medieval maps, although these can offer misleading visions of cities in ancient times, since early cartographers often drew on popular legend rather than firsthand observation.

The city plans that have been excavated, or rather the broken fragments of the originals—among them the marble tiles of the Forma Urbis Roma map of ancient Rome (*see pp.14-15*) and the Madaba mosaic map that shows Jerusalem (*see pp.26-27*)—have raised perhaps unanswerable questions about their intended purpose and the motivations of their creators. While it is evident that

the siting and layout of cities such as el-Armana in Egypt, Athens in Greece, and Mohenjo-Daro in the Indus Valley required careful planning and civic administration, how these factors were implemented remains a mystery. The volcanic-ash-covered small cities of Pompeii and Herculaneum beneath Mount Vesuvius in southern Italy are almost unique in providing us with a "snapshot" of the structures in which both rich and poor ancient Roman citizens lived, worked, ate, drank, and bathed.

Reinventing the past

Historically, many cultures have attempted to impose their own, often ideological, interpretations on the pasts of the cities they have conquered. For example, in the 16th century, Spanish Catholic soldiers in Mexico and the "New World" tore down Native American cities such as Tenochtitlan (today's Mexico City) and rebuilt them to

> A map is the greatest of all epic poems. Its lines and colors show the realization of great dreams.

GILBERT H. GROSVENOR, EDITOR OF *NATIONAL GEOGRAPHIC*

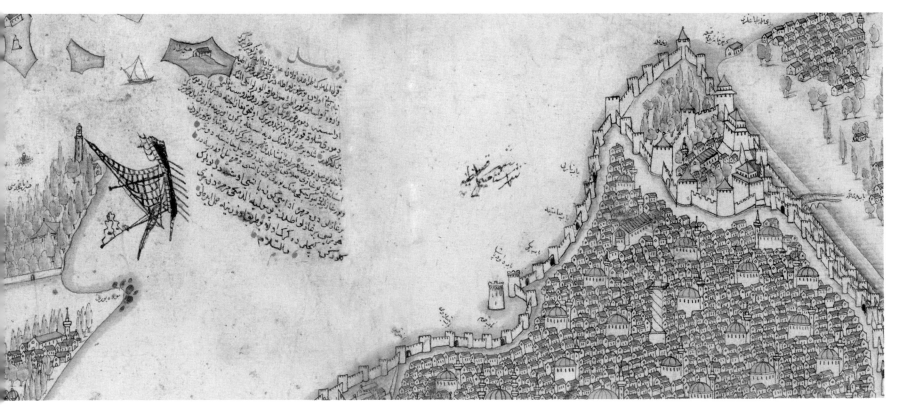

▲ **CONSTANTINOPLE, 1521–26** The former capital of the Christian Byzantine Empire fell to the Ottoman Turks in 1453; Ottoman depictions of the city highlight the newly constructed Muslim mosques.

their own cultural and religious requirements. These impositions are also evident on maps: the so-called Hague Map depicts Jerusalem, the city venerated by Christians, Jews, and Muslims, as filled with churches and containing roadways that together formed a cross—subtly reinforcing the idea that it was Christianized territory (*see pp.28–29*). In much the same way, maps of Constantinople (today's Istanbul) that were created after the Muslim conquest of 1453 (*see pp.42–45*), fill the city with mosques, and confine churches to one well-defined foreign quarter.

Ancient cities in the modern world

The cities of the ancient world that have survived to this day are characterized by a strong sense of continuity—they have often retained their spiritual and cultural significance even as their political or economic clout has waxed and waned. Today, we continue to investigate and probe their long histories, and we are constantly adding to and expanding our knowledge of them. Some of the earliest maps of these cities were drawn thousands of years ago, but we are still referring to them today, using them as source material to assist in the creation of new and more detailed maps of these ancient metropolises.

▲ **JERUSALEM, c.1190–1200** Medieval interpretations of the holy city, such as the round Hague Map seen here, were not accurate in cartographic terms, but they were true to the Christian idea of it being the "Navel of the world."

▲ **TENOCHTITLAN, 1524** This jewel-colored map was the first view Europeans had of the exotic Aztec capital; once published, it became a means of justifying Spain's brutal conquest of the Aztec Empire.

Rome, c.205 CE

UNKNOWN ARTIST ▪ CARVING IN MARBLE ▪ THE CAPITOLINE MUSEUM, ROME

SCALE

FORMA URBIS ROMAE

This extraordinarily detailed and enormous city plan of Rome was created in around 205 CE, under Emperor Septimius Severus (who ruled from 193 CE to 211 CE). Carved onto 150 carefully measured marble slabs, the Forma Urbis Romae was mounted in the Temple of Peace on the wall of a side hall. This hall may well have been converted to accommodate a municipal planning office following a fire in the temple in 192 CE; however, the illusion of this being in any sense a usable map for administrative purposes is belied by the medium in which it was carved. The marble map could not be adjusted, amended, or updated. It seems likely that it was primarily a vision of the scale and complexity of the Roman capital, designed to awe the viewer.

Only fragments of the map now remain, but these pieces reveal a carefully managed city, of which the ground plans of every public building and most private dwellings were known. The map itself remains a remarkable piece of public publishing, centuries before the advent of printing or mass media.

IN **CONTEXT**

During Rome's decline, this magnificent marble map was gradually broken up to create materials for other buildings. It was only in the mid-16th century that antiquarian investigators began to recover the surviving pieces. To date, it has only been possible to reconstruct about 10 percent of the original map.

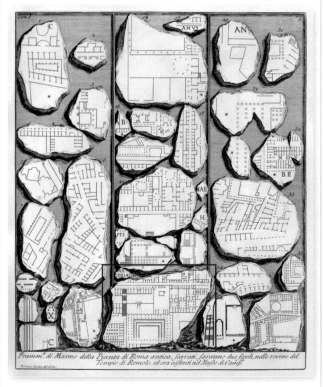

▲ **One of Giovanni Piranesi's etchings** from 1756 showing pieces of the wall that had been found by the 18th century

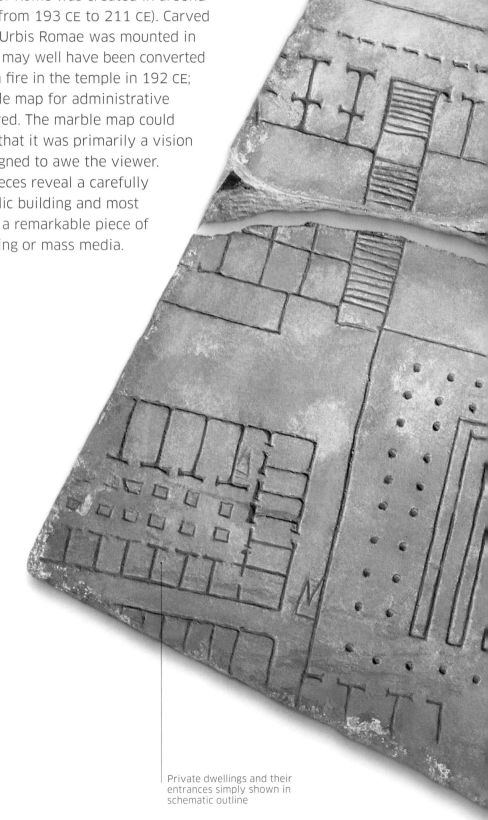

Private dwellings and their entrances simply shown in schematic outline

I found a **Rome** of bricks; I leave you one of **marble.**

EMPEROR AUGUSTUS ON HIS DEATHBED, 14 CE

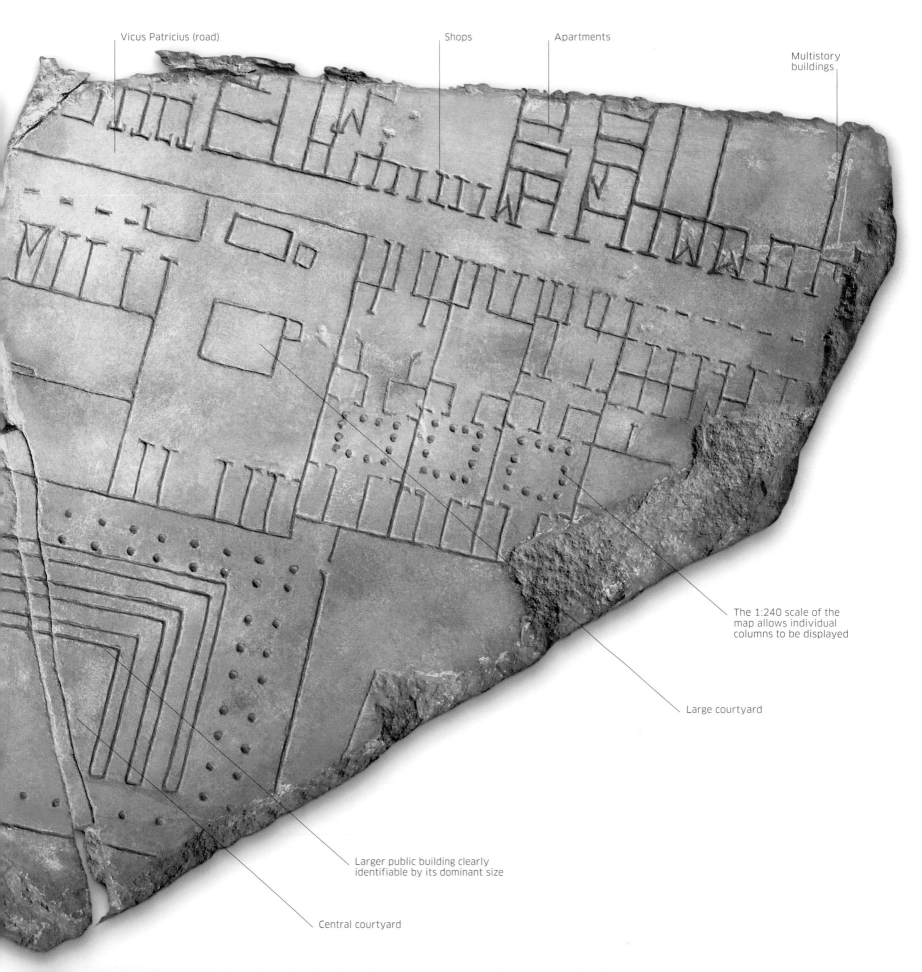

Vicus Patricius (road)

Shops

Apartments

Multistory buildings

The 1:240 scale of the map allows individual columns to be displayed

Large courtyard

Larger public building clearly identifiable by its dominant size

Central courtyard

Rome, 1413–14

TADDEO DI BARTOLO ▪ FRESCO ▪ PALAZZO PUBBLICO, SIENA, ITALY

MAP OF ROME

UNKNOWN

The creator of this view of early Renaissance Rome, Taddeo di Bartolo (c.1363–1422), was an artist who produced notable altarpieces and frescoes for the Church. However, the fresco that contains this image was created for a more secular location—it was painted above an archway in an antechamber of Siena's Palazzo Pubblico (town hall), where it can still be seen today.

It is not known for certain whether Bartolo visited Rome before embarking on his painting, although it is probable, since Sienese artists were in considerable demand across Italy at this time, and they traveled extensively to fulfill clients' commissions. The work's intricate detail does seem to bear the hallmark of firsthand experience. Bartolo's inclusion of so many realistic, recognizable monuments of Rome is impressive. But the distribution of major buildings is askew in places, and they are all crammed inside a more fanciful interpretation of the city walls and gates. The topography is also sketchy: while the configuration of the Tiber River is reasonably accurate, Rome's famed seven hills are not shown.

Visual tour

KEY

▶ **GOLD LEAF TITLE**
The name of Rome, rendered in gold leaf (gilding was a speciality of the Sienese school), hovers above part of the three-dimensional (but largely imaginary) representation of the Aurelian Wall.

1

2

▲ **ENGINEERING** The artist was careful to include practical aspects of the city as well as individual monuments. One of the architectural innovations that enabled Rome to survive and prosper during the classical period was a complex of aqueducts, threaded through the hilly topography, which fed water into the heart of the city.

3

◀ **ISOLA TIBERINA**
The Tiber River's shape, and the positioning of its only island (Isola Tiberina), indicates that the orientation of the view is from the north, looking south, although the placement of buildings is confusing. The depiction of the bridges that connect the island to both sides of the river is relatively accurate.

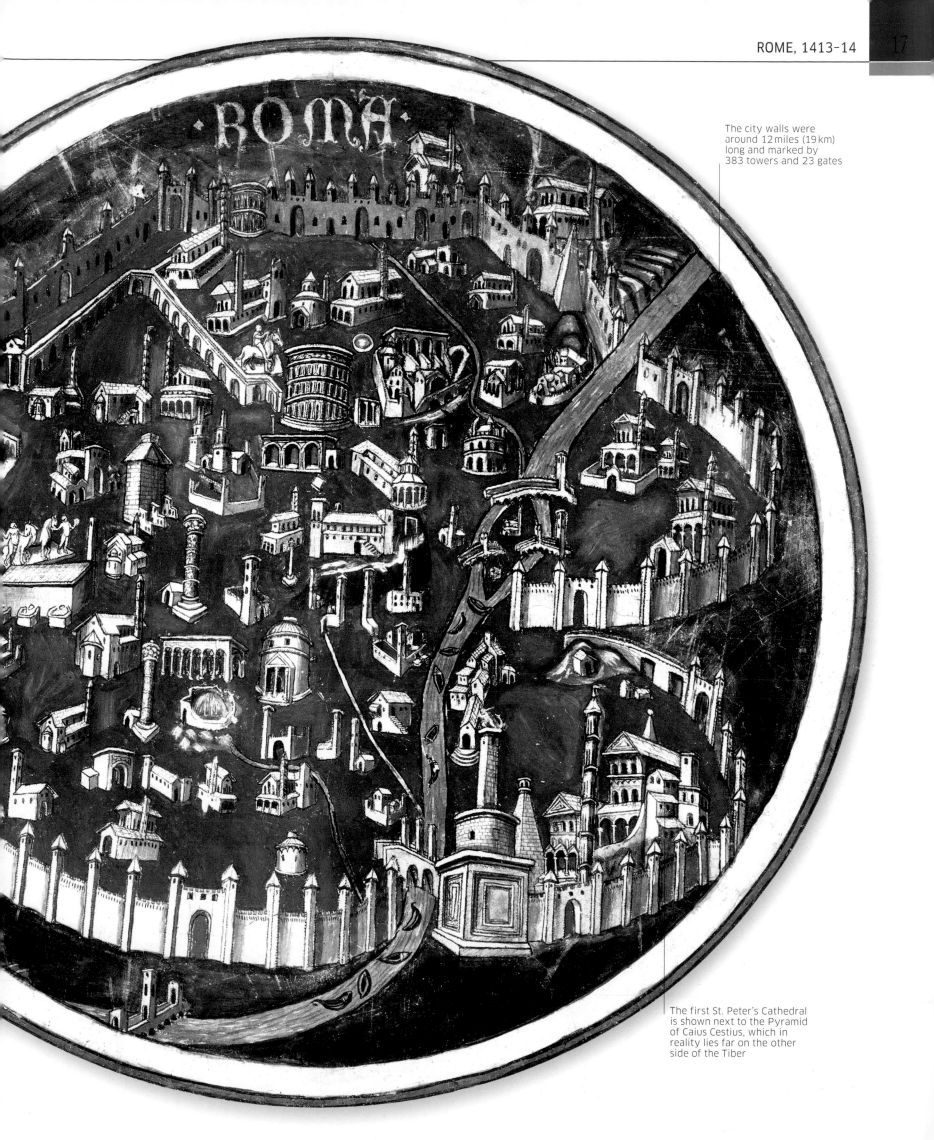

ROMA

The city walls were around 12 miles (19 km) long and marked by 383 towers and 23 gates

The first St. Peter's Cathedral is shown next to the Pyramid of Caius Cestius, which in reality lies far on the other side of the Tiber

Rome, 1493

MICHAEL WOLGEMUT AND WILHELM PLEYDENWURFF ▪ HAND-COLORED WOODCUT ON PAPER ▪
NUMEROUS COPIES EXIST

SCALE

MAP FROM THE NUREMBERG CHRONICLE

This arresting view of Renaissance Rome is only one of numerous city views from among the 645 original woodcut illustrations included in the *Liber Chronicarum*, or *Book of Chronicles* (more commonly known as the *Nuremberg Chronicle*). It is clear that the principal author, Hartmann Schedel—himself an avid cartographer—worked

closely with the illustrators Michael Wolgemut and Wilhelm Pleydenwurff on the plans, which came from a number of sources. Some were the product of original research by Schedel, some were copied from earlier works, and some were pure fabrications. This depiction of Rome is at least a recognizable view of the city, showing its walls, river, and major monuments, and it is certainly more accurate than the map produced by Bartolo some 80 years earlier (*see pp.16–17*). However, like almost all of the city views in the book, the scale of the monuments is exaggerated, and the placement of buildings has more to do with artistic effect than with a strict verisimilitude.

HARTMANN **SCHEDEL**

1440–1544

An outstanding polymath, Nuremberg-based Hartmann Schedel was a physician, bibliophile, and historian. He was also one of the first cartographers to use the printing press, introduced to Europe by Johannes Gutenberg in around 1440.

Schedel studied under the Italian philosopher and physician Matheolus Perusinus in Perugia, Italy. He was an assiduous scholar, carefully researching his material—although literary analysis suggests that only 10 percent of the text in the *Nuremberg Chronicle* is a result of his original research and observation, with the rest being drawn from secondary sources. Schedel would have had firsthand knowledge of the German and Central European cities that are included as city views, but for representations of cities that were farther afield he would have had to rely on his library and his imagination.

Visual tour

KEY

▶ **OLD ST. PETER'S BASILICA** Set in the Vatican area north of the Tiber, the first St. Peter's was demolished in the early 16th century. Schedel's representation of the cathedral and its cloisters provides an interesting insight into the shape and dominance of the earliest seat of the Popes.

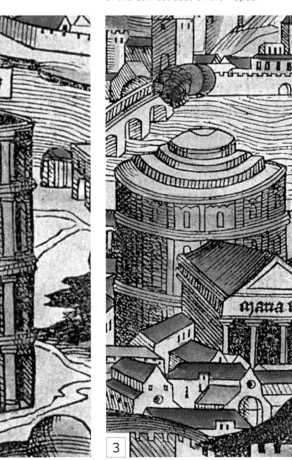

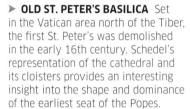

▲ **THE COLOSSEUM** The Flavian Amphitheater, more widely known as the Colosseum, is shown here as if intact; however, by early medieval times, it had fallen into disuse and disrepair. It was substantially quarried for new building elsewhere, and was also used to house shops and workshops.

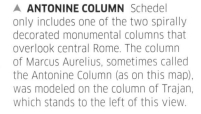

▲ **THE PANTHEON** Completed under the Emperor Hadrian in c.126 CE, the Pantheon is shown with reasonable accuracy; despite the shrinking of its dome and the foreshortening of the buildings in front of it, Schedel and the illustrators managed to include its elaborate Corinthian portico.

▲ **ANTONINE COLUMN** Schedel only includes one of the two spirally decorated monumental columns that overlook central Rome. The column of Marcus Aurelius, sometimes called the Antonine Column (as on this map), was modeled on the column of Trajan, which stands to the left of this view.

Palacium pape

Castellu s. Ageli

5

8

◀ **PAPAL PALACE** Spread across the hills behind the old basilica of St. Peter's, the Papal Palace was remodeled over the century or so following Schedel's view of the city.

▲ **CASTEL SANT'ANGELO** The monumental mausoleum of the Emperor Hadrian was refortified throughout the Middle Ages, becoming a safe retreat for the papal court in times of attack.

6

◀ **PONTE SANT'ANGELO** The Tiber River was crossed by only three main bridges at the time of this map. The Ponte Sant'Angelo, originally known as the Bridge of Hadrian, was built in 134 CE to connect Hadrian's Tomb (later called the Castel Sant'Angelo) to Rome's city center.

▼ **CITY WALLS** Schedel was at pains to convey the impression of Rome as a walled and fortified city, placing the major Porta Pia gateway in the foreground and emphasizing the walls' towering height, their castellations, and their many embedded forts.

IN **CONTEXT**

Published in both Latin and German in 1493, the *Nuremberg Chronicle* was commissioned by two Nuremburg merchants, Sebald Schreyer (1446–1503) and his son-in-law Sebastian Kammermeister (1446–1520). It was an enormously daring undertaking, aiming to outline the story of history through biblical sources. Organized chronologically, it included illustrated surveys not only of biblical texts, but also of notable European rulers, saints, and cities. The *Nuremberg Chronicle* is one of the most extensive books to have been printed before the year 1500 that still survives.

Work began on the text and illustrations in around 1487, although formal contracts with the printer and publisher Anton Koberger only date to 1491. The original woodcut illustrations (more than 300 were reused with different captions) were in black and white, although many editions were hand-tinted in watercolor. Due to its popular success, several pirated editions were created, and the more spectacular woodcuts were often sold as unbound colored prints.

▲ **The illustration of Rome** as it appears in this surviving hand-colored edition of the *Nuremberg Chronicle*

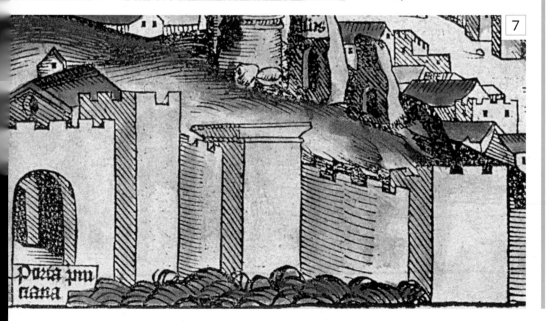

7

Porta pin nana

Rome, 1748

GIAMBATTISTA NOLLI ▪ 12 COPPERPLATE ETCHINGS ON PAPER▪
PALAZZO DELLA CALCOGRAPHIA, ROME, ITALY

SCALE

NUOVA PIANTA DI ROMA

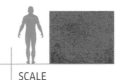

Giambattista Nolli (1701–56) began his *Nuova Pianta di Roma* ("New Plan of Rome") in 1736. This major work, published in 1748 and partly funded by the Vatican, accurately demarcated the new 14 rioni (or "districts") of Rome, and became a best-seller with tourists on the "Grand Tour" (*see below*). Its popularity was in part due to Nolli's collaboration with painter Stefano Pozzi (c.1699–1768), printer Giuseppe Vasi (1710–82), and antiquarian and printmaker Giambattista Piranesi (1720–78), who was beginning to find a lucrative tourist market for his evocative etchings of Italy's ancient sites and ruins. Nolli's map, although embellished with ornate decoration added by his collaborators, reflected the important replanning programs of the previous two centuries, and remains an authoritative map of the city.

The Nolli Map is one of the most influential urban maps in existence, and its ichnographic representation of the city (combining accurately plotted ground plans with selected elevations of building façades) remained in use for further city planning in Rome until the 1970s. Nolli also reoriented his view of the city from the traditional eastern perspective to the more modern north/south view, partly because he had used a magnetic compass to achieve his astonishingly accurate plotting.

IN **CONTEXT**

The fashion for upper-class young men of northern Europe to experience the grandeur of Classical and Renaissance culture firsthand through an extended trip to Italy was known as the "Grand Tour." The tradition was in full swing by 1748 when Nolli published his map of Rome, which was effectively an early tourist's guide—carefully annotated, with a numerical key. Among the many Italian artists who benefited from the fashion was Giambattista Piranesi, who produced hundreds of souvenir prints of Rome, and collaborated with Nolli on a smaller and cheaper version of his large original map.

▲ **A "capriccio" oil painting** by Gian' Paolo Panini (1691–1765) that combines improbable assemblages of historic monuments, produced for the tourist market that the "Grand Tour" brought to Rome

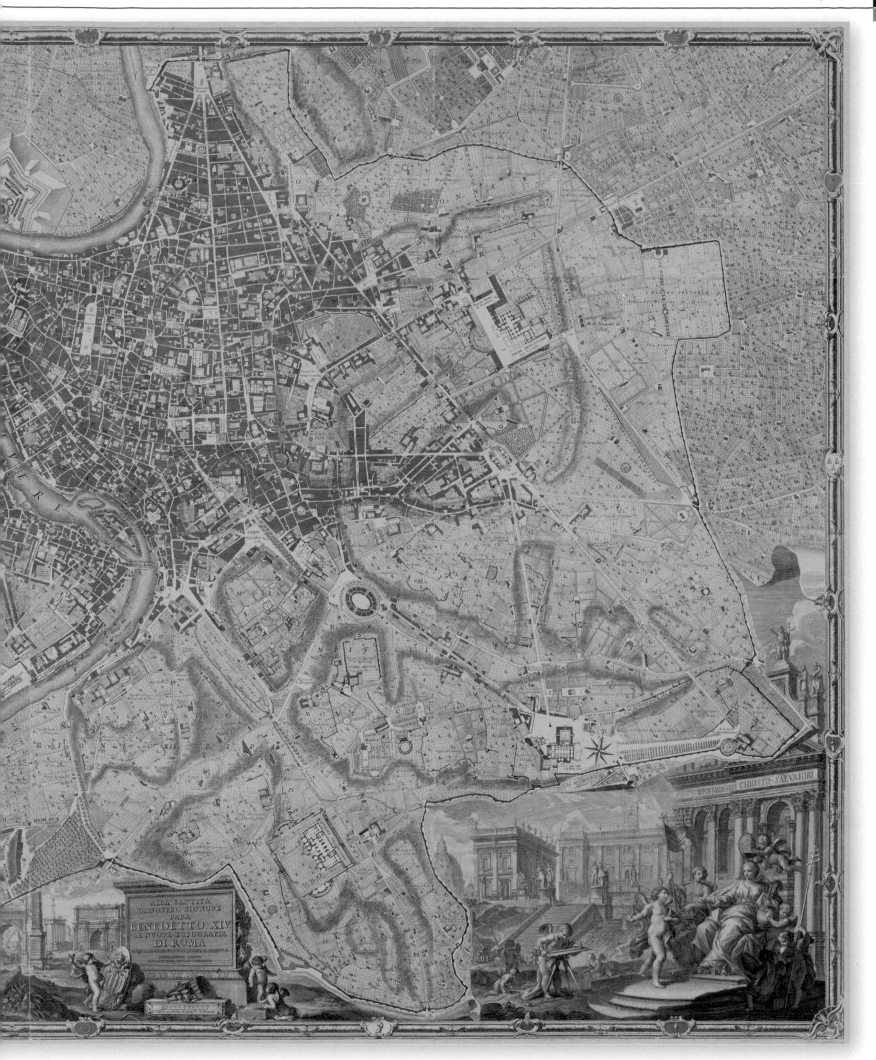

Visual tour

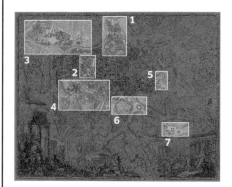

KEY

▶ **AROUND THE PIAZZA NAVONA**
The oldest area of Rome, which included the huge Piazza Navona, had been considerably remodeled by Nolli's time. A string of major new institutions and churches had been built, including the Chiesa Nuova ("New Church"), the Sant' Andrea della Valle church, and the Palazzo della Cancelleria ("Palace of the Chancellery").

▼ **VATICAN CITY** Nolli was able to represent the newly completed Vatican in all its glory, including Bernini's gigantic, all-embracing piazza and colonnade in front of St. Peter's basilica, and the avenue leading pilgrims from the Castel Sant'Angelo to the east.

▶ **THE NORTHERN ENTRANCE** The main routes into the city center from the north focused on the Porta del Popolo, an ancient gate in the Aurelian Walls. In the 17th century the Piazza del Popolo, just inside the gate, was replanned to provide a magnificent triumphal entry to Rome. The three main roads leading from the Piazza to the heart of the city were also rationalized.

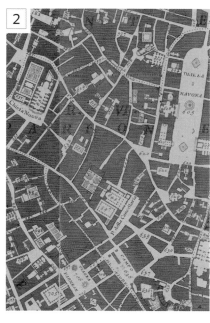

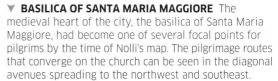

▼ **TRASTEVERE** In Nolli's time the suburb of Trastevere still retained its medieval character. Among its small cobbled streets sat the important early churches of Santa Maria and Santa Cecilia. The bridges across Tiber Island (Isola di San Bartolomeo on the map) linked the suburb to the main city.

▼ **BASILICA OF SANTA MARIA MAGGIORE** The medieval heart of the city, the basilica of Santa Maria Maggiore, had become one of several focal points for pilgrims by the time of Nolli's map. The pilgrimage routes that converge on the church can be seen in the diagonal avenues spreading to the northwest and southeast.

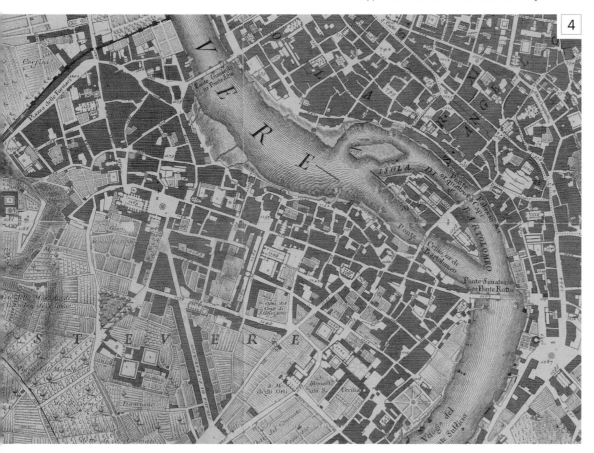

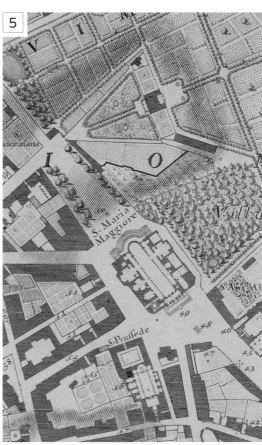

◀ **THE FORUM** By the mid-18th century, the ruins of the main Roman forum, as well as the fora complexes farther south, were gradually being excavated. In his map, Nolli attempted to reconstruct the ancient city from the evidence available at the time.

IN **CONTEXT**

Mapping the Holy City involved meeting the needs of urban administrators, pilgrims, and archaeologists alike. The plan of the city by Leonardo Bufalini (produced between 1551 and 1560) was a precursor to Nolli's map, and combines a number of ambitions. Conceived as a functional street plan, it accurately displays the topography of the area, and combines the modern layout of the city with the archaeological traces of ancient Rome.

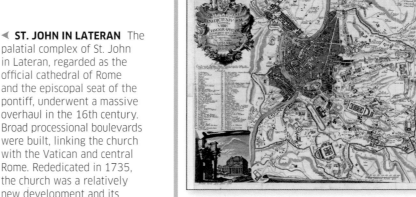

▲ **Nolli's 1748 reproduction** of the Bufalini map, published in the same year as his own, original vision of the city

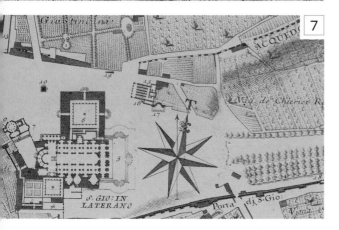

◀ **ST. JOHN IN LATERAN** The palatial complex of St. John in Lateran, regarded as the official cathedral of Rome and the episcopal seat of the pontiff, underwent a massive overhaul in the 16th century. Broad processional boulevards were built, linking the church with the Vatican and central Rome. Rededicated in 1735, the church was a relatively new development and its inclusion was a coup for Nolli.

Jerusalem, c.560 CE

UNKNOWN ARTIST ■ FLOOR MOSAIC ■ ST. GEORGE'S CHURCH, MADABA, JORDAN

SCALE

MADABA MOSAIC MAP

Ambitious mosaic floor maps have been discovered across both the classical Roman and Byzantine worlds, but the function of such maps is obscure, since they could hardly be used for route planning. Historians suggest that they were probably conceived as illuminating reference resources, or as objects intended for contemplation and instruction, much like European medieval stained-glass windows.

One of the finest and earliest examples of Byzantine mosaic mapmaking is the so-called Madaba Map, created long before the high point of the medium in the 7th century. What remains of this artwork is relatively accurate in its rendering of individual locations and topography, and it is also carefully annotated, physical features and place names being identified in Greek but using Palestinian spellings.

The focus of the Madaba Map is, not unnaturally, the city of Jerusalem, the key site of Christianity that at this time was part of the Byzantine Empire under Justinian I (ruled 527–65). This area of the mosaic remains largely intact, and despite the limited space for detail available within the representation of the city walls, the mosaic contains a number of recognizable features and buildings. Among them are the Damascus Gate, north in reality but shown to the far left of the city here, and the Church of the Holy Sepulcher, at the center of the lower half of the city.

IN **CONTEXT**

▲ **The remaining mosaic** on the floor of St. George's Church, Madaba

This mosaic of the Holy Land was constructed in an ancient building on the present site of St. George's Church in Madaba, Jordan. Its original dimensions have been estimated as 23 ft by 69 ft (7 m by 21 m); however, much of the mosaic has been lost over time, and only about a quarter remains. Under the Umayyad Caliphate's occupation of Jordan from 614, some parts of the mosaic were deemed to be offensive, and destroyed. The mosaic was then severely damaged by an earthquake in 746. It was excavated in 1884, but suffered various degrees of damage between its rediscovery and the 1960s, when work was undertaken to conserve and restore its surviving parts.

> The mosaic has loosened… by change of temperature, by influence of moisture… and by sinking of the soil, to such an extent that it reacts even upon pressure by hand.

GERMAN SOCIETY FOR THE EXPLORATION OF PALESTINE ON THE STATE OF THE MOSAIC, 1965

The Lion's Gate in the east of the city is shown here at the top

The colonnaded road known as the Cardo Maximus dominates the plan

▲ **THE HOLY LAND** The remaining quarter of this extensive floor mosaic demonstrates that it was intended to show the entire Holy Land from the Jordan Valley to the Nile Delta.

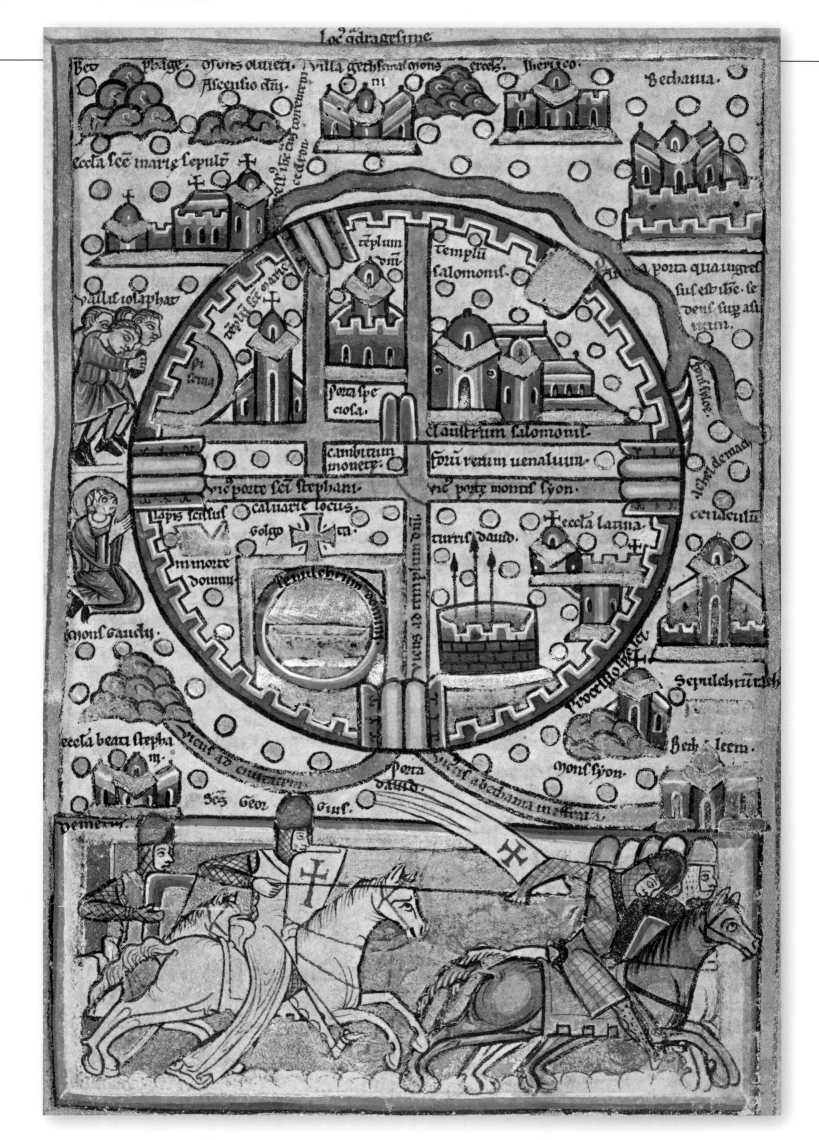

Jerusalem, c.1190–1200

UNKNOWN ARTIST ▪ ILLUMINATED MANUSCRIPT ON VELLUM ▪
NATIONAL LIBRARY OF THE NETHERLANDS, THE HAGUE

SCALE

THE HAGUE MAP OF JERUSALEM

The era of the Crusades began in 1095, when an alliance of Western Europeans attempted to "recapture" the Holy Land, and specifically Jerusalem, from Muslim occupation. For the next four centuries, various Crusades had the object of "liberating" the Holy City from Muslim hands.

This relatively early map, with its beautiful coloring, concise design, and supporting vignette of crusading knights, presents an image of Jerusalem as a valuable prize worth fighting for. Known as the Hague Map for the city in which this particular version of the manuscript is now held, it is schematic rather than topographic, using the "T-O" mapping principle (*see right*). The cartographer (who had probably never visited the city) has attempted to fit in as many features of its geography as possible, including details of the walls, gates, and holy shrines.

IN **CONTEXT**

Early Western European styles of mapping were largely conceptual rather than practical, and were hardly recognizable (or usable) as "road maps" as we would understand them today. European views of the world, such as the famous Hereford Mappa Mundi (c.1300), tended to present a non-geographical view of the world based on the idealized "T-O" system—essentially dividing the area mapped into three easily identifiable but schematized portions (which form the "T") within a circular or global outer schema (which forms the "O"). Jerusalem, with its walls and various quarters (Greek, Armenian, Jewish, Muslim), ideally lent itself to this style of representation.

▲ **The Hereford Mappa Mundi**, split into a "T" by the three continents of Asia (at the top), Europe, and Africa

Visual tour

KEY

▶ **GOLGOTHA** Beyond the city walls, the important Christian area of Golgotha is emphasized in the bottom left corner of the map. The hill is traditionally considered to be the site of the crucifixion of Christ, although today there is considerable debate concerning the actual location of the event.

| 1 |

◀ **ROADWAYS** The map's depiction of the major cross-sections of processional avenues from west to east is largely correct, although the north to south roads become exaggerated due to the confining strictures of the map plan.

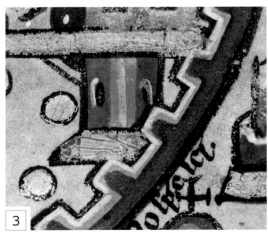

| 3 |

▲ **WALLS** The artist's view of the city walls, with their blue coloring, could lead them to be mistaken for waterways. Also, the walls of Jerusalem were not circular; the artist is conforming to the tradition of "T-O" mapping (*see above*) in which the Holy City is enclosed symbolically by a circle.

Jerusalem, 1584

CHRISTIAN KRULK VAN ADRICHEM ▪ HAND-COLORED COPPERPLATE ENGRAVING ▪ NUMEROUS COPIES EXIST

SCALE

JERUSALEM AT THE TIME OF CHRIST

The vision of Jerusalem laid out in Christian Adrichem's map is one of an idealized City of Christ. This ideal is presented in a carefully organized and detailed representation of the layout, buildings, and shrines of Jerusalem. There are 270 sites identified, each of which is annotated; the story of Christ's last days (known as the Passion) is woven through these locations.

The map is a brilliantly realized fantasy of the Biblical city, rather than a realistic portrayal of contemporary Jerusalem. Even the overall shape of the city, which is viewed from the west, and presented as an oval neatly framed by fortified walls, is misleading; the real city would have been irregular in shape, following the lie of the land on which the city perched. Adrichem had to make assumptions about the layout of the city, as Jerusalem had been in Muslim hands since its conquest in 1244, and it was therefore difficult and dangerous for Christian pilgrims to visit. Instead Adrichem had to rely on the accounts of the Gospels, as well as other ancient texts and descriptions of the city provided by the many Jewish scholars who had fled the Holy Land to Europe in previous centuries—many of whom settled in Adrichem's homeland of the Netherlands.

Depiction of the Passion

An interesting aspect of Adrichem's treatment of the city, however wildly imaginative, is his addition in minute vignettes of a narrative recording Christ's last days. This follows Jesus from his entrance to the city on Palm Sunday (upper right) to his crucifixion on Golgotha (lower left). The vignettes can be interpreted as an instructive sermon about Christ's Passion in pictures, played out against the backdrop of Jerusalem. Taken as a whole, the map is a clever mixture of imagination, scholarship, and storytelling. On its publication it proved to be enormously successful and influential, as it provided Bible readers, scholars, and preachers with a rich, visual context against which to interpret the Gospels.

CHRISTIAN KRULK VAN **ADRICHEM**

1533–85

A Catholic priest and theologian, Adrichem was born in Delft (then part of the Spanish Netherlands) during the period of the Reformation, when Protestant Christians broke away from the teachings of the Roman Catholic Church. Adrichem wrote a life of Jesus Christ (1578) and an illustrated survey of the Holy Land (1590).

During the European Wars of Religion that dominated the late 16th and early 17th centuries, the Catholic Adrichem was ousted from his position as director of the Convent of St. Barbara in Delft. He then founded a sanctuary in Cologne (in modern-day Germany) just across the Rhine River. Cologne was in the province of Berg, which tolerated mixed Catholic and Lutheran (Protestant) populations, and Adrichem remained there until his death in 1585. He had never visited the Holy Land, and his reconstructions of the city were based on biblical texts, travelers' accounts, and often picturesque hearsay. Adrichem also compiled a chronological encyclopedia of biblical lives from Adam to St. John the Apostle.

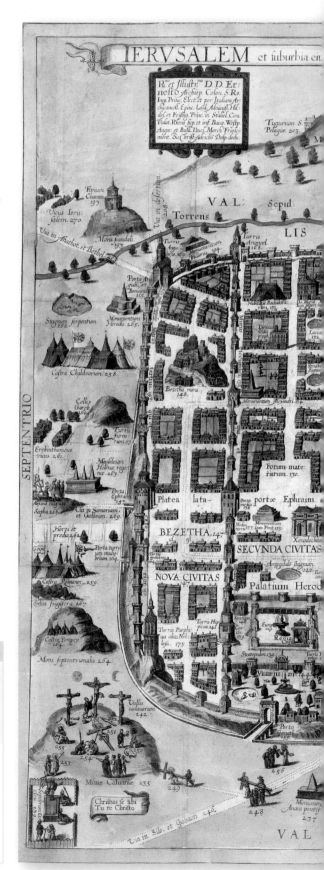

See, we are going up to Jerusalem, and the Son of Man will be handed over to the chief priests and scribes, and they will condemn Him to death.

ASCRIBED TO JESUS CHRIST, *THE GOSPEL ACCORDING TO ST. MATTHEW, 20:18–19*

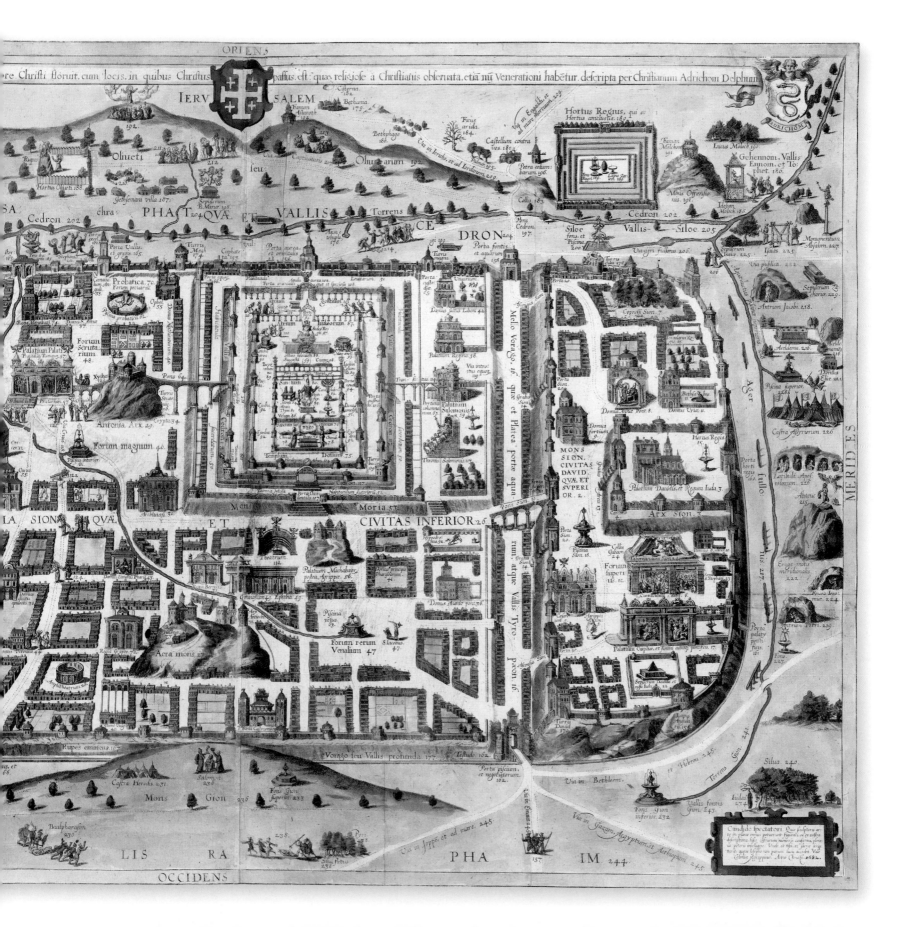

Visual tour

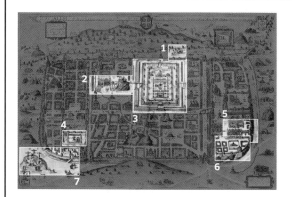

KEY

▼ **ENTRY TO JERUSALEM** Christ is depicted riding a donkey toward the Golden Gate accompanied by selected disciples on Palm Sunday. This provides the opening scene of the journey of the Passion that zigzags through the map of the city, ending at the cross at Golgotha.

▼ **PONTIUS PILATE'S PALACE** The palace of the Roman Governor, Pontius Pilate, is presented as a colonnaded structure within which the interrogation and scourging of Christ takes place. In reality, as the seat of Roman power in the city, it would have been much larger, but in Adrichem's imaginative composition it is just a convenient location to refer to a focal point of Christ's journey to his crucifixion.

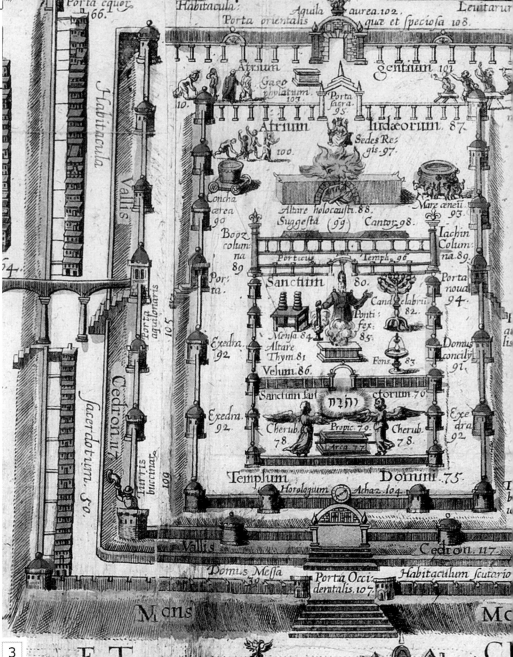

▲ **TEMPLE MOUNT** The representation of Temple Mount is overemphasized in its scale, but beautifully detailed. It appears to be almost a walled city within the city of Jerusalem, with its own bridges and gates linking it with the southern (Jewish) quarter and Pontius Pilate's palace to the north. Within its walls various historical and sacred events, some involving angels, are seen to occur.

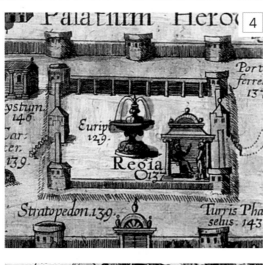

4

◄ CHRISTIAN QUARTER Adrichem gives as much detail to the more obscure parts of the city as he does to well-known areas, as if he is keen to fill in spaces with imaginative detail. This area of the Christian Quarter is almost entirely a work of fantasy.

▼ SANHEDRIN HEADQUARTERS The headquarters of the Jewish judges, or Sanhedrin, and the Jewish High Priest Caiaphas's palace, are less architecturally splendid than Pilate's. They include scenes of Christ's interrogation, trial, and condemnation by his conspiring peers. Pilate handed over the decision to condemn Christ to the Jewish authorities, which they duly did.

5

IN CONTEXT

For pilgrims from Western Christendom, visits to the Holy Land, and specifically Jerusalem, were lengthy, expensive, and potentially hazardous in the medieval and early modern periods. From 1244 Christians were unwelcome in the Muslim-controlled city, a situation that was only reversed in the early 16th century, when the Islamic but more tolerant Ottoman Turks took control of West Asia. As historical cartography developed during the Renaissance in Europe, the city of Jerusalem and its environs remained something of a blank space on the European world map, one that could only be filled by scholarly guesswork based on the Gospels and the writings of ancient historians such as Josephus (37–100 CE).

Adrichem's detailed map is a prime example of this imaginative activity, and in the Western world it remained the most widely disseminated and influential vision of Jerusalem as it was during the time of Christ until archeological surveys of the city began in the 19th century.

▲ Imaginative drawing of Jerusalem (c.1862) by the German artist Adolf Eltzner

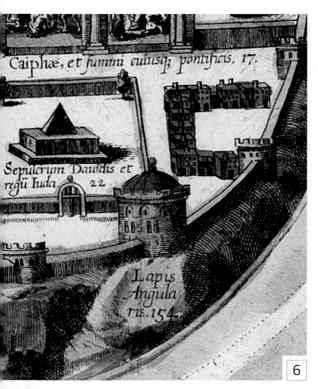

6

7

◄ SEPULCHER OF DAVID The tomb of the legendary king of the Israelites is an entirely imaginary feature of the map. No archeological evidence exists of such a structure, which the cartographer positions prominently in the Jewish Quarter of the city.

▲ GOLGOTHA The actual location of the crucifixion on Golgotha remains a matter of debate. While it was likely to have been in the vicinity shown on the map, it probably overlooked a quarry. In Adrichem's time the site of the crucifixion was believed to have been on the southwest of the city, and in this map Christ is seen dragging his cross outside the city walls.

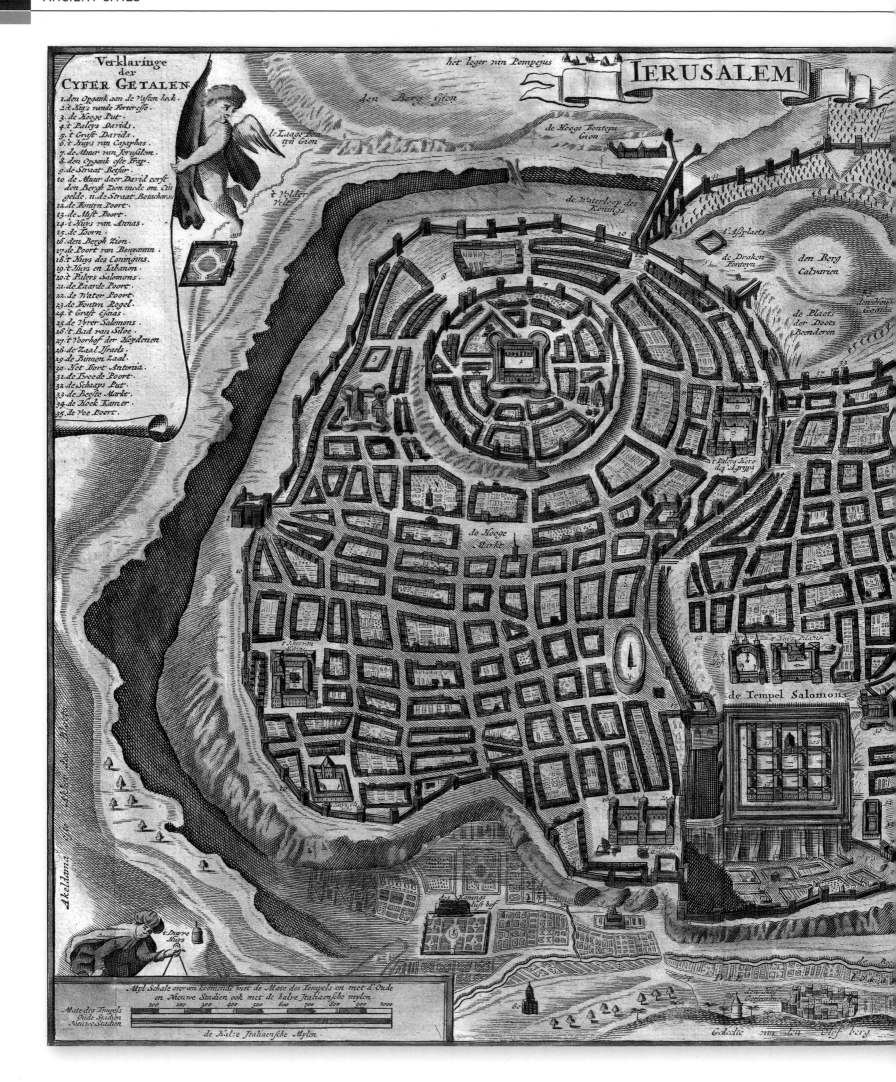

IERUSALEM

Verklaringe der CYFER GETALEN

1. den Opgank aan de Visten hoek.
2. 't Kus'rende Fortoresse.
3. de Hooge Put.
4. 't Paleys Davids.
5. 't Graff Davids.
6. 't Kuys van Caiaphas.
7. de Muer van Jerusalem.
8. den Opgank ofte Trap.
9. de Straat Bethar.
10. de Muur daer David eerst den Bergh Zion mede om Cu gelde.
11. de Straat Betacharam.
12. de Fontyn Poort.
13. de Mest Poort.
14. 't Kuys van Annas.
15. de Toorn.
16. den Bergh Zion.
17. de Poort van Benjamin.
18. 't Kuys des Conings.
19. 't Kuys en Libanon.
20. 't Pilers Salomons.
21. de Paarde Poort.
22. de Water Poort.
23. de Fontyn Rogel.
24. 't Graff Esaias.
25. de Pyver Salomons.
26. 't Bad van Siloe.
27. 't Voorhof der Heydenen.
28. de Zaal Israels.
29. de Binnen Zaal.
30. Het Fort Antonia.
31. de Tweede Poort.
32. de Schaeps Put.
33. de Beeste Markt.
34. de Hoek Kamer.
35. de Vee Poort.

het leger van Pompejus

den Bergh Gion

de Hooge Fonteyn Gion

de Waterloop des Konings

't Laage Fonteyn Gion

't Volder Vele

't Asylaets

de Draken Fonteyn

den Berg Calvarien

de Plaets der Doots Beenderen

de Hooge Markt

't Paleis Hero des Agrip.

't Jesus Palatis

de Hooge Markt

de Tempel Salomons

des Konings lust hof

't Duyre Huys

Akeldama

Mijl Schale over een koomende met de Mate des Tempels en met d'Oude en Nieuwe Stadien ook met de halve Italiaensche mylen.
100 200 300 400 500 600 700 800 900 1000

Mate des Tempels
Oude Stadien
Nieuwe Stadien

de halve Italiaensche Mylen.

Jerusalem, c.1716

DANIEL STOOPENDAAL ▪ HAND-COLORED
COPPERPLATE ENGRAVING ▪ NUMEROUS
COPIES EXIST

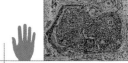

MAP OF JERUSALEM | SCALE

Amsterdam-based Daniel Stoopendaal (1672–1726)
proved a prolific cartographer and printmaker in his
relatively brief career. His map of Jerusalem—viewed,
unusually, from the east—was widely copied, not least
by the popular Dutch printmaker Jan van Jagen in c.1770.
However, the map was itself based on a much earlier
version created in 1604 by the Spanish Jesuit priest,
mathematician, and cartographer Juan Bautista Villalpando
(1552–1608), which is pictured below.

Unlike many plans of Jerusalem that preceeded it,
Stoopendaal's map was not an idealized rendition of the
city. Although he followed Villalpando's exaggerations
(for example, he presents the main Temple as far too
large), Stoopendaal aimed to achieve a plan of the layout
and topography that was as accurate as possible given
its source material. This was in line with the ideals of
the Protestant Reformist movement of the time, which
shunned mysticism for a more literal interpretation of
the Bible. Stoopendaal's map was therefore an important
contribution to Reformation biblical iconography.

▲ **SOURCE MATERIAL** Villalpando's 1604 plan of Jerusalem was the basis for many
later maps of the city. It was first printed in black and white in a commentary on the
Book of Ezekiel from the Old Testament, so Villalpando was eager to show Jerusalem
as it was before the time of Christ. However, he made many incorrect assumptions
about the imposition of Roman architectural tenets on the city at this time.

Bianjing, 12th century

ZHANG ZEDUAN ▪ PAINTING ON SCROLL ▪
PALACE MUSEUM, BEIJING, CHINA

SCALE

ALONG THE RIVER DURING THE QINGMING FESTIVAL

This elaborate riverscape panorama is thought to be of Bianjing (now known as Kaifeng), the capital of the Northern Song Dynasty between 960 and 1127, and it probably captures the city during the bustling time of the annual autumnal Qingming Festival. It was painted by noted painter and calligrapher Zhang Zeduan (1085–1145), and is regarded as one of Chinese art's great masterpieces.

Considerable scholarly controversy surrounds the work, not least around its exact date, although it was probably created shortly before or shortly after the fall of the Northern Song in 1127. Due to the absence of certain identifiable features, it has been debated whether it is truly a representation of Bianjing (then possibly the largest city in the world), or merely an idealized city.

> The watchtowers of the city rise to great
> hcights. The bustling scene is truly impressive.
> It is a chance to explore vestiges of bygone days.

THE QIANLONG EMPEROR, IN A POEM ABOUT THE SCROLL, 1742

However, the topography of the cityscape and other major features, such as the city gates to the left and the central position of the Rainbow Bridge spanning the Huang He (Yellow River), does indeed seem to indicate that the scroll shows Bianjing. It is also not known whether this image depicts the Qingming Festival, or merely daily life. What is clear, however, is that Zhang Zeduan populated his enormous work with as much detail of the activities of the city-dwellers along the banks of the Huang He as possible. The artist illustrates the different lifestyles of all levels of Chinese society. More than 800 human figures (only 20 of which are women), 390 buildings, 28 boats, 60 animals, 28 vehicles, and around 170 trees are vividly depicted.

Visual tour

KEY

▶ CITY STREETS
Traders, entertainers, travelers, visitors, and merchants of all kinds throng the city streets, passing by dwellings that lie just inside the the walls of the city.

1

3

▲ SHIPBUILDING The scroll is one of the few extant documents that presents accurate depictions of Song boats and ships, and even depicts a vessel under construction in a shipyard.

▶ WOODEN RAINBOW BRIDGE The central focus of the painting is the wooden Rainbow Bridge, swarming with travelers and tradesmen. An approaching vessel has failed to lower its masts to pass under the bridge and is in danger of collision. Many on the bridge are shouting warnings and lowering ropes to save the crewmen.

4

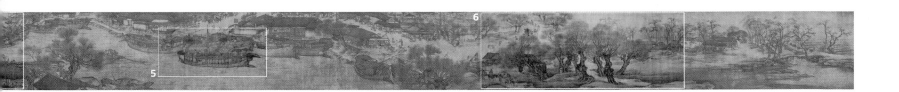

◄ THE GREAT GATE The action inside the city spills out past the unguarded Great Gate, an impressive masonry structure. Many beasts of burden (including camels) and their owners are shown passing through it on their way to or from market.

▼ RIVER LIFE As the Huang He meanders past the city and on into the countryside, the scroll depicts myriad merchant vessels, fishing boats, and ferries plying their trade along the river's course.

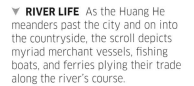

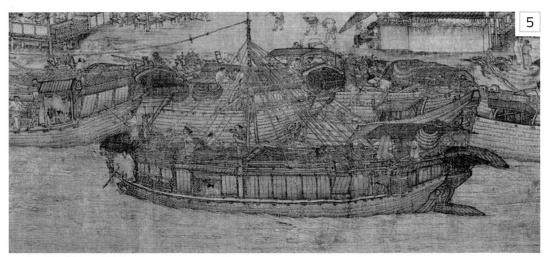

▲ SURROUNDING FARMLAND On the right-hand side of the scroll, rural scenes—showing farmers, fields, market gardens, and willow trees—indicate a more bucolic way of life. Leaving the frenzied activity of the city behind, the artist returns to the countryside with elegant classical Chinese renderings of trees draping the downstream banks of the river.

Constantinople, 1422

CRISTOFORO BUONDELMONTI ■ INK AND WASH ON VELLUM ■ BIBLIOTHÈQUE NATIONALE, PARIS, FRANCE

SCALE

MAP OF CONSTANTINOPLE

This is the earliest surviving map of Constantinople, a city that was first founded with the name Byzantium in the 7th century BCE, and known since 1930 as Istanbul, the most populous metropolis in Turkey. It is perhaps surprising that no earlier maps of the city remain, given Constantinople's importance as a center of Christendom, and as the capital of the Roman Empire and the Eastern Roman Empire from 330 CE to 1453. In fact, the map also happens to be the only extant plan of the city to predate the conquest of Constantinople in 1453 by the Islamic Ottoman Empire, making it a unique representation of the city as a stronghold of medieval Christianity.

The map's creator, the itinerant Italian monk Cristoforo Buondelmonti, captures only the main features of the city at the time: the magnificent Theodosian defensive walls; various outstanding monuments, such as the gigantic basilica of Santa Sophia; and the suburb of Pera, at the top of the map and separated from the rest of the city

by the strait known as the Golden Horn. Despite the lack of building detail on the map, Buondelmonti's carefully delineated street plan is nevertheless a remarkably accurate depiction of the city's layout at the time.

CRISTOFORO **BUONDELMONTI**

1386–c.1430

Buondelmonti was one of several itinerant Italian monks who set out to create authoritative travel guides and maps of areas that were of specific interest to the expansionist medieval Italian states.

Born to a wealthy Florentine family, Buondelmonti probably left home in 1414 and, under the patronage of Cosimo de' Medici, he traveled through the Balkans and the Greek islands in the Aegean, producing two illuminated volumes detailing both the geography and history of the places he visited. *Descriptio insulae Cretae* (*A Description of the Island of Crete*)–unusually written in Italian rather than Latin–was a collaboration with a fellow Florentine, the humanist scholar Niccolò de' Niccoli (1364–1437). *Liber insularum Archipelagi* (*The Book of the Archipelago*) included this map of Constantinople. Both volumes included transcriptions of sailing charts and navigational instructions; various later copies of both manuscripts remain.

Visual tour

KEY

▶ **PERA** The importance of Pera (modern Beyoglu) is vastly overemphasized by the artist. The area was established and walled in the 9th century to provide a northern stronghold and additional harbors. It was dominated by an Italianate piazza and the enormous Galata lookout tower.

1

2

3

◀ **SANTA SOPHIA** In a grand gesture to outdo Rome, Emperor Justinian (ruled 527 to 565) founded the basilica of Santa Sophia, an enormous multistoried domed church with a grand façade fronted by a substantial ceremonial hippodrome. The building is now the Hagia Sofia museum.

◀ **DOCKS** The port facilities of Constantinople were limited for security. The main harbor in the southeast of the city was enclosed by the Theodosian Walls. These comprised an outer shell of walls and towers, an inner moat some 60 ft (18 m) wide and 30 ft (9 m) deep, and a much larger inner wall.

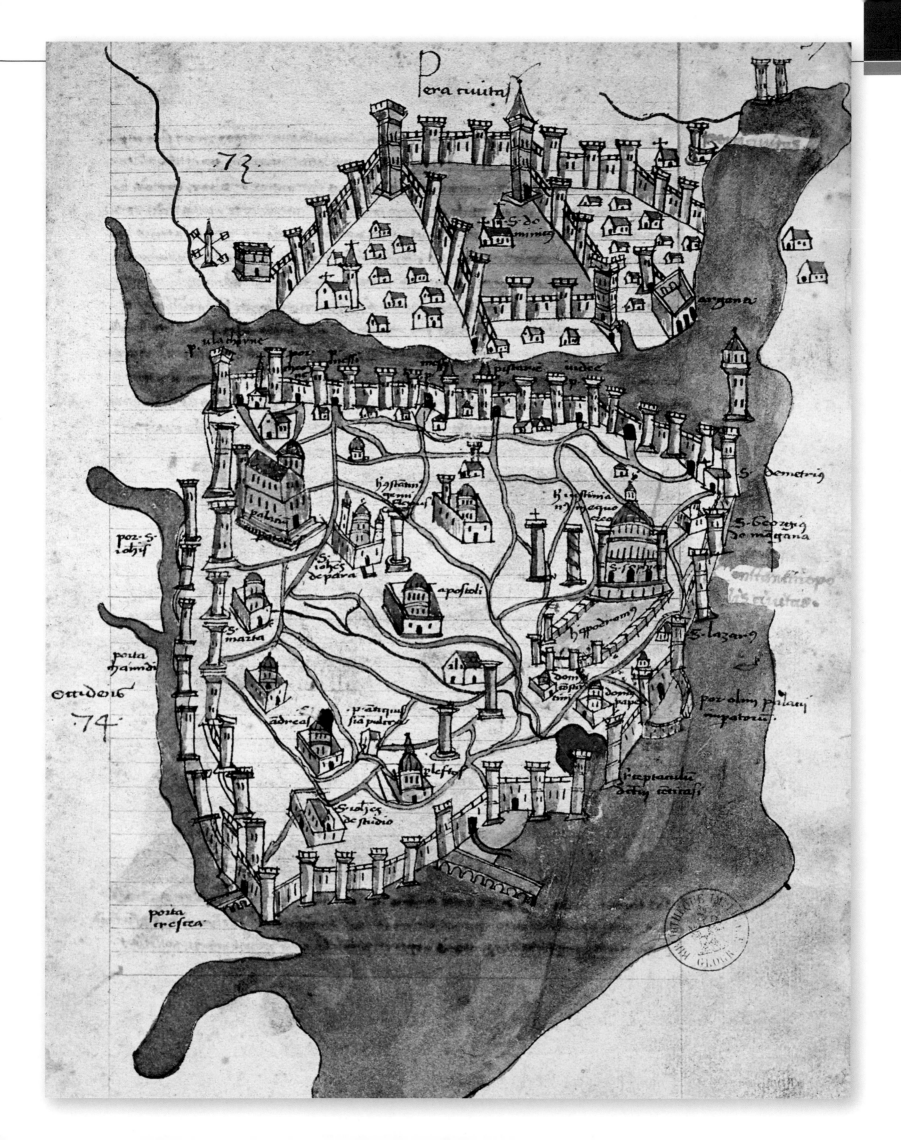

Constantinople, 1521–26

PIRI REIS ■ INK AND PIGMENTS ON PAPER ■
BERLIN STATE LIBRARY, BERLIN, GERMANY

UNKNOWN

MAP OF CONSTANTINOPLE

This map presents a highly accurate portrait of Constantinople (now known as Istanbul) as it was roughly 70 years after its capture by the Islamic Ottoman Empire in 1453. It is one of many maps contained in the *Kitab i-Bahriye*, or *Book of the Sea*, which was compiled in the early 16th century by the Ottoman sailor and cartographer Piri Reis. The mapmaker would have been familiar with the city, having served as a captain in the sultan's fleet, and the orientation Reis used for the map reflected his sailor's view of the world: the top of the map is oriented southward, which is the route out of the city's port to the Marmara Sea, the Mediterranean, and the rest of the world.

An Islamic city

When this map was drawn, the city's population had exploded from around 80,000 at the time of the Ottoman conquest to almost 400,000. This growth is reflected on the map in the crush of red-roofed buildings encirled by the city walls. Already, the city is adorned by numerous grand mosques, with their readily identifiable domes and pencil-like minarets. One of the most prominent of these is the former Santa Sophia cathedral, which was transformed into the supreme imperial mosque. Immediately east of this, the wooded headland has become the site of a new imperial palace, the Topkapi.

PIRI **REIS**

c.1465–1553

It is thought that the man known as Piri Reis ("Captain Piri") was born Ahmed Muhiddin Piri in Gelibolu (Gallipoli) in what is now Turkey. He was a sailor, navigator, and cartographer.

Piri's uncle, Kemal Reis, was a captain, and Piri followed him to sea. As part of the Ottoman fleet, they took part in many naval battles against European powers. Piri spent several years in Gelibolu preparing an ambitious work on navigation. This was the *Kitab i-Bahriye*, a manual for sailors, giving information on routes, distances, and safe harbors around the Mediterranean. It contained more than 200 maps, including nautical charts, coastal plans, and city maps. The number of maps varies as the *Kitab* was formed originally in two different editions (in 1521 and 1526), and copied many times over the next two centuries. More than 30 original manuscript copies survive. Piri went back to sea after completing this work, and later became admiral of the Ottoman fleet in the Indian Ocean; he commanded ships into his 80s. He was eventually beheaded on the order of an irate governor of Basra, who Reis had defied by refusing to lead a fleet against the Portuguese.

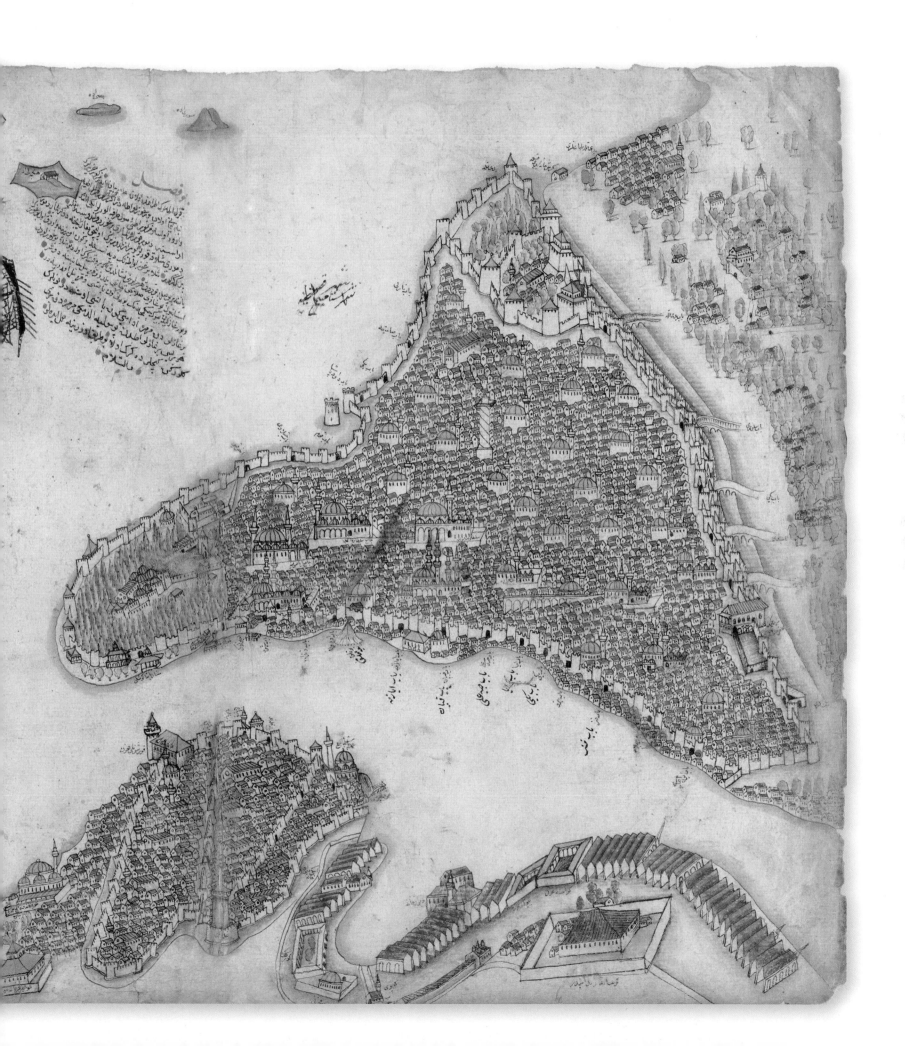

Visual tour

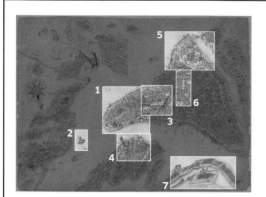

KEY

> **TOPKAPI PALACE**
Overlooking the Bosphorus strait (which runs north to south on the map) and beyond it the Asian shore, this palace was established by Sultan Mehmet II in 1459. Surrounded by sea on three sides and ringed by fortified walls, it had three courts, the last of which contained the sultan's throne room – seat of power of the entire Ottoman Empire.

> **MAIDEN'S TOWER** During the Byzantine era, when Constantinople was the capital of the East Roman Empire, the tower shown here was built on a small rock in the middle of the Bosphorus to protect the city. An iron chain stretched across to the European shore as a defense against attack by ship. In 1453, the Ottoman invaders hauled their galleys overland to bypass the chain. They later used the structure as a watchtower.

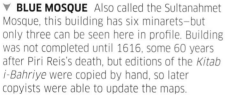

▼ **BLUE MOSQUE** Also called the Sultanahmet Mosque, this building has six minarets—but only three can be seen here in profile. Building was not completed until 1616, some 60 years after Piri Reis's death, but editions of the *Kitab i-Bahriye* were copied by hand, so later copyists were able to update the maps.

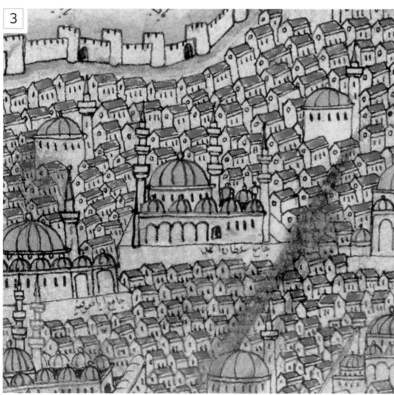

▲ **GALATA** To the north of the imperial center, across the body of water known as the Golden Horn, was the wealthy district of Galata (also known as Pera). Piri's map shows several churches—the area was mainly inhabited by Christians, who were permitted to keep their religion as long as they didn't ring any church bells that would compete with the Muslim call to prayer.

▼ **YEDIKULE FORTRESS** To secure the city that he had taken, Sultan Mehmet II added three towers to the four that were already part of the Theodosian walls, to create the mighty "Fortress of the Seven Towers" (Yedi Kule in Turkish). Later it became a feared prison where the enemies of the ruling sultan—and on occasion the sultan himself—were executed.

▶ **COLUMN OF CONSTANTINE** This map depicts the new capital of the Ottoman Empire, magnifying the grandeur of its mosques and imperial structures. But Piri includes this lone Byzantine monument, a column erected for Constantine the Great in 330 CE to commemorate the declaration of Byzantium as the capital city of the Roman Empire.

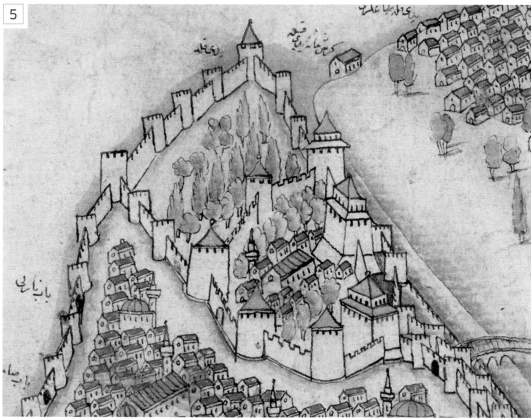

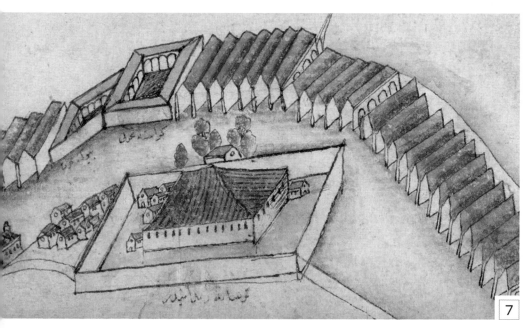

▲ **THE NAVAL YARDS** This mass of red-roofed sheds depicts the imperial dockyards that stretched along the shore of the Golden Horn. One of the largest naval complexes in the world, it was capable of accommodating 200 galleys. The building enclosed within the high wall was the imperial arsenal and gunpowder factory.

IN **CONTEXT**

A key Ottoman map of Constantinople was contained in a book by Matrakçi Nasuh (see p.212) that celebrated the campaigns of Suleyman I. Another comes from *Hünername* (*The Book of Accomplishments*), dated 1580, documenting the lives of the sultans. Along with the *Kitab i-Bahriye*, these maps mix the conventions of Islamic miniature painting with cartographic forms acquired through trade with Europe.

▲ **Matrakçi Nasuh's map** of Constantinople from his account of Suleyman's campaigns *Mecmu-i Menazil* (1537-38)

Constantinople, 1851

KONSTANTINOS KALDIS ■ TINTED ENGRAVING ■
BENAKI MUSEUM, ATHENS, GREECE

SCALE

VIEW OF CONSTANTINOPLE

Konstantinos Kaldis, a Greek Orthodox priest living on the Aegean island of
Lesbos, created this schematic aerial view of mid-19th-century Constantinople,
which was at the time the capital of the immense, though declining, Ottoman
Empire (today the city, now known as Istanbul, lies in modern-day Turkey).
With its explanatory labeling in both Greek and Ottoman Turkish, the view
was probably marketed to the merchants on Lesbos, who plied their wares
in the great metropolis. Although Kaldis made little effort to show the city's
street plan, and a number of its buildings are incorrectly located, the geography
is generally accurate. Above all, the view vividly conveys the exoticism of the
bustling, cosmopolitan city—a meeting point between East and West that had long
attracted traders and other travelers from across Europe and Asia.

The imperial city

The lower half of the view is dominated by the original walled Roman city.
At the tip of the peninsula, two of Constantinople's most iconic buildings can be
seen: the magnificent Hagia Sophia, at this point in time a mosque, and, to its right,
the Topkapi Palace, which until 1856 was the residence of the Ottoman sultan.
To the north—linked to the old city by two bridges built in 1836 and 1845—is
Galata, once a Genoese (Christian) city-state within Muslim Constantinople, with
its 14th-century Galata Tower, topped on the map by a huge red banner. Studding
the network of waterways that define the city—the Sea of Marmara, seen at the
foot of the image; the Bosphorus, the narrow waterway stretching north to the
Black Sea; and the Golden Horn, running west and then north—is a startling array
of shipping. It has been suggested that Kaldis's map was intended to show the
city as it would have appeared to someone arriving by sea; the monuments he
emphasizes are all relatively tall and would have been easy to see from the deck
of a ship entering the harbor.

> These [mosques] with the **towers, ports,
> palaces**… together with the myriads of
> small domes… press an appearance so
> Oriental… as to **defy description.**

ROBERT BURFORD, ENGLISH PAINTER, WHO CREATED HIS OWN PANORAMA
OF CONSTANTINOPLE IN 1846

Θεωρία Κωνσταντινουπόλεως ἰστο
Vue de Constantinople

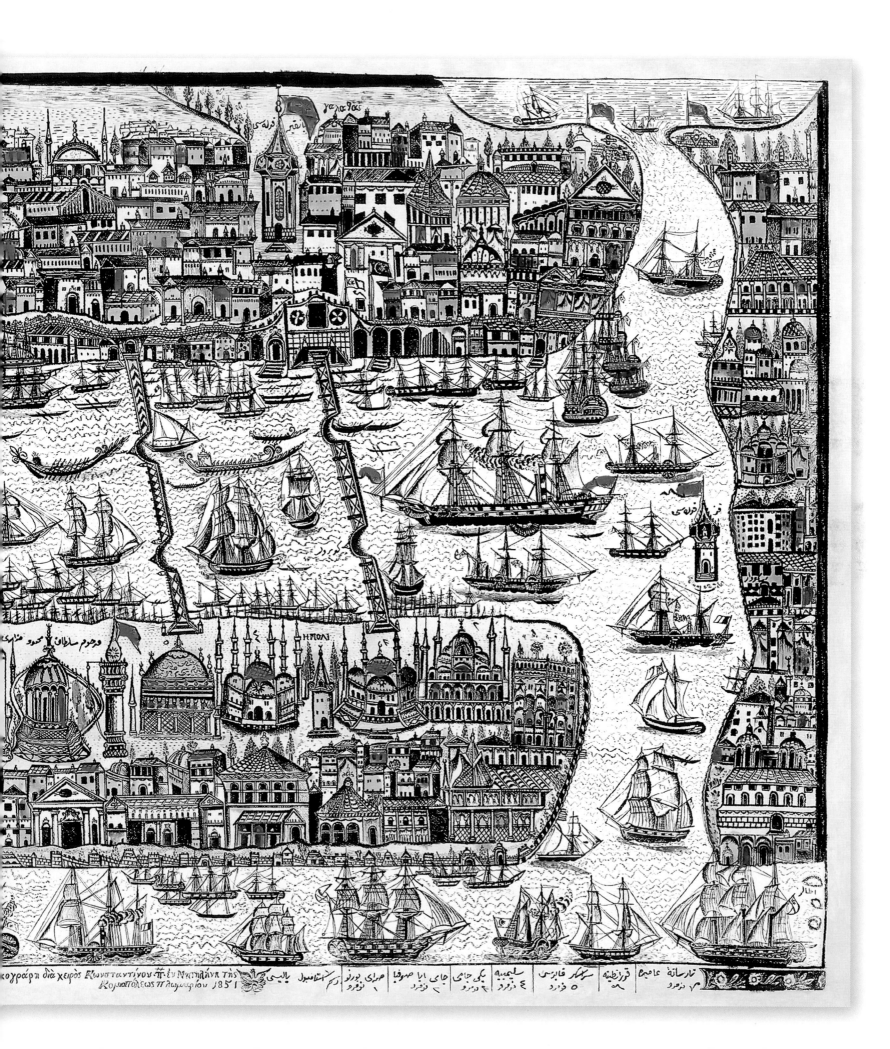

Alexandria, 1575

GEORG BRAUN AND FRANZ HOGENBERG ■
HAND-COLORED WOODCUT ■ NUMEROUS COPIES EXIST

MAP OF ALEXANDRIA

SCALE

Founded in 331 BCE by Alexander the Great as part of his world-spanning empire, Alexandria in Egypt became an important cultural center of the ancient world, and in the 1st century BCE it even challenged the might of Rome through the alliance of its queen Cleopatra with the Roman general Mark Antony. Yet by the 16th century, when this map was produced, the city had been toppled by earthquakes, deluged by tidal waves, and depopulated by plague—Alexandria was no longer the beacon of civilization it had once been. The city's few citizens lived among the ancient ruins. This map, included in the second volume of *Civitates Orbis Terrarum* (*see below*), shows just a handful of clustered quarters within the city walls, surrounded by sandy wastes strewn with collapsed arches and broken columns.

Although the cartographers capture Alexandria's general state of decay, they were less certain in their knowledge of the city's layout. Foreigners were not allowed inside the fortified center, and this led to various errors on the map. The Eastern Harbor (center) is shown as being much larger than the Western Harbor, (right) when the reverse was true; the legendary Pharos is on the wrong side of the entrance to the Eastern Harbor; and what appears to be a great river flowing into the city was actually a canal. What this map does illustrate is how few Europeans had an accurate knowledge of this once famous city, which was by this time a minor port in the backwaters of the Ottoman Empire.

IN CONTEXT

Civitates Orbis Terrarum (*Atlas of Cities of the World*) is the second-oldest printed atlas in the history of world cartography and the first atlas of towns and cities. Its principal creators were editor Georg Braun and engraver Franz Hogenberg. Braun was a Catholic clergyman from Cologne, whose cartographic interest was possibly inspired by *Cosmographia*, a German description of the world, published in 1544. Braun's *Civitates* can be seen as a companion volume to *Theatrum Orbis Terrarum* (*Theater of the World*), a collection of country maps published in Antwerp in 1570, and the first true modern atlas. *Civitates* was published in Cologne in six volumes between 1572 and 1617. The complete edition contained 546 maps. The cities covered are almost all in Europe, with a handful from Asia, Africa, and South America. Such a gathering of information in this period represents an extraordinary achievement, and the work was republished many times.

▲ **Frontispiece** from the original edition of *Civitates Orbis Terrarum*

Lacus Meotis seu Mareotis aquæ dulcis ampliss: et admodu
pisculentus, distans ab vrbe medio miliari italico.

ALEXANDRIA, vetustissimum Ægypti emporium, Amplissima
ciuitas, ab Alexandro Magno condita, muris, turrib. et propugnaculis ea
forma, qua heic depicta videtur, ante Christi aduentum, Annis
CCC.XX. constructa fuit, magnifica olim, et nunc quoque bene
munita conspicitur, sed intra moenia ruinis, et ruderib. plena. Mag-
nitudine Lutetiæ Parisiorum respondet.

Columna Pompei in pro-
à Cæsare erecta, incredibilis
et subtilitudinis ex lapide Th
alij obelisci in ciuitate

ALEXA   NDR   IA.

Porta del peg.

S Catharine

Castelle
noue

MOSQVE

MOSQVE

Domus Alexandri Magni

Genophalo.

ANEVM   MARE

Visual tour

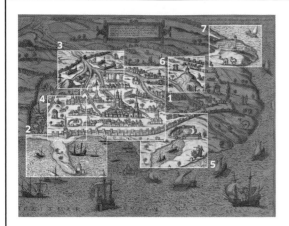

KEY

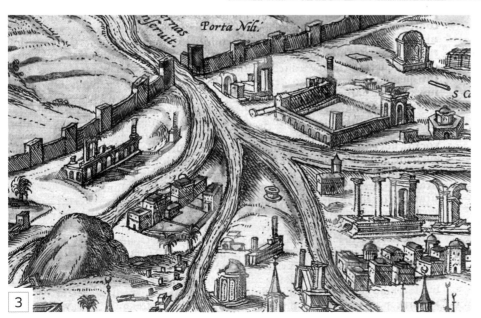

➤ **KOM EL-NADOURA**
Squeezed between a lake and the sea, Alexandria is almost entirely flat. It has just two hills, both of which appear on the map. The hill on the right, topped with what is labelled "New Castle," represents what the Arabs called Kom el-Nadoura, or "Look-out Hill."

➤ **PHAROS LIGHTHOUSE**
Otherwise known as the Lighthouse of Alexandria, the Pharos was one of the Seven Wonders of the Ancient World. It was badly damaged by a series of earthquakes in the 10th to 14th centuries and then quarried for stone for a fortress that was built on the same site in 1480. It is this fortress that is depicted on the map rather than the earlier lighthouse, and it is also shown in the wrong location.

▲ **THE NILE GATE** More properly known as the Bab Rashid, the Nile Gate faced in the direction of Rosetta (in Arabic, Rashid), a town that lay at the mouth of a branch of the Nile some 40 miles (65 km) from Alexandria. The waterway shown running through the gate is actually a canal from the Nile, with channels that fed a network of underground cisterns throughout the city.

▲ **OBELISK** Two obelisks stood in the temple built by Cleopatra (69–30 BCE) to honor her dead lover Julius Caesar. Both monuments survived a tidal wave that submerged the rest of the temple, but one is missing from the map because it was not mentioned in reports.

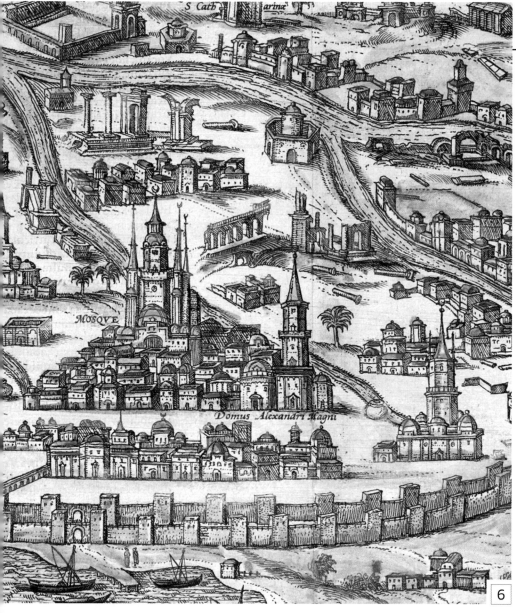

▲ **POMPEY'S PILLAR** One of the few monuments of antiquity still standing in Alexandria, this was a Roman-era triumphal column commemorating the victory of the Emperor Diocletian over an Alexandrian revolt. It was one of the largest of its type constructed outside of the imperial capitals of Constantinople and Rome. It is the only element on this map that still survives intact today.

◄ **THE TOMB OF ALEXANDER** The cartographers were familiar with European cities and their convention of having a central church or cathedral, and this may be why they depicted Alexandria with a grand central mosque—drawn to look like a church—when no such thing existed. A second churchlike building is also imagined, labeled "Domus Alexandri Magni" or the "House of Alexander the Great," which is presumably supposed to be the Greek emperor's tomb.

▲ **WESTERN HARBOR** The more sheltered of the two harbors was reserved for Muslim ships. Access was traditionally controlled by a chain stretched across the harbor mouth, although on this map a gate is shown. In reality a wide peninsula separated the two harbors.

IN **CONTEXT**

In 1798 Napoleon Bonaparte landed a French army at Alexandria that would occupy Egypt until 1801, when it was defeated by British forces. In addition to the soldiers, the French force consisted of some 160 civilian scholars and scientists, whose mission was to record all aspects of the country. They examined, measured, wrote about, and sketched everything from ancient temples to wildlife, and farming implements to the physical characteristics of the locals. All of this information was carried back to France, collated, and eventually published in a series of volumes collectively known as the *Description de l'Égypte*. The first volume appeared in 1809 and the final one appeared in 1829. The work included one whole volume devoted to maps. The map of Alexandria shows a twin perimeter of city walls enclosing little but wasteland. Settlement had shrunk to a small area of ragged and irregular buildings, and mazelike alleys squeezed between the two harbors.

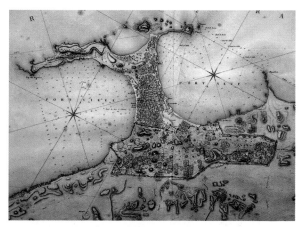

▲ **Napoleon's map** of Alexandria depicts a city even more reduced than the one shown in 1575

Tenochtitlan, 1524

UNKNOWN ARTIST ■ HAND-COLORED WOODCUT ON PAPER ■ NEW YORK PUBLIC LIBRARY, NEW YORK, USA

SCALE

NUREMBERG MAP OF TENOCHTITLAN

When Hernán Cortés's 600-strong force of Spanish soldiers first laid eyes on the Aztec capital city of Tenochtitlan (the site of current-day Mexico City) in November 1519, they were amazed. Although their three-month trek into the interior had shown them that the Aztecs were by no means unsophisticated savages, the city that confronted them, ingeniously constructed across part of a lake surrounded by steep volcanic cones, was unlike any they had seen before.

Cortés, the leader of the expeditionary force of soldiers (known as conquistadores) that would eventually overthrow the Aztecs, sent regular despatches describing the marvels of the city back to Charles I of Spain, including detailed colored woodcut maps, largely drawn up by Aztec artists under the guidance of Spanish friars. This particular map, first published with Cortés's letters in Nuremberg, Germany, in 1524, also features a map of the Gulf Coast to the left of Tenochtitlan. The city plan itself has many inaccuracies, such as the city's relation to Lake Texcoco—in reality it only occupied a small area of the lake system. Nevertheless, the map does include valuable details, such as the layout of the lake-bound center, linked to the mainland by defendable causeways, and the multistoried buildings organized around a huge governmental and ceremonial temple complex.

IN **CONTEXT**

Mesoamerica was home to a rich tradition of mapmaking, much of which was ended by Spanish rule. What remains is characterized by the use of hieroglyphs to depict events and places. These maps saw space connected to time, often blending geography with history. Maps tended to be drawn schematically rather than topographically, as in the map of the Aztec capital to the right, where the foundation myth of the eagle perching on a prickly pear occupies Tenochtitlan's ceremonial center, which is linked to the shoreline by diagonal canals.

▶ **A symbolic representation** of Tenochtitlan from the *Codex Mendoza*, which detailed aspects of daily Aztec life

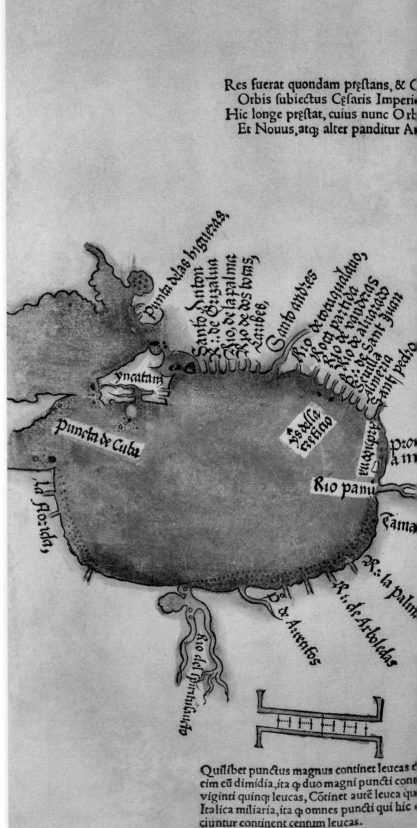

Res fuerat quondam prestans, & C
Orbis subiectus Cesaris Imperi
Hic longe prestat, cuius nunc Orb
Et Nouus, atq; alter panditur A

Quilibet punctus magnus continet leucas e
eim cu dimidia, ita q duo magni puncti cont
viginti quinq; leucas, Cotinet aure leuca qui
Italica miliaria, ita q omnes puncti qui hic
ciuntur continent centum leucas.

There are **four entrances** to the city, all of which are formed of **artificial causeways**… Its streets… are half land and half water, and are **navigated by canoes.**

HERNÁN CORTÉS, SECOND LETTER TO CHARLES I OF SPAIN, 1520

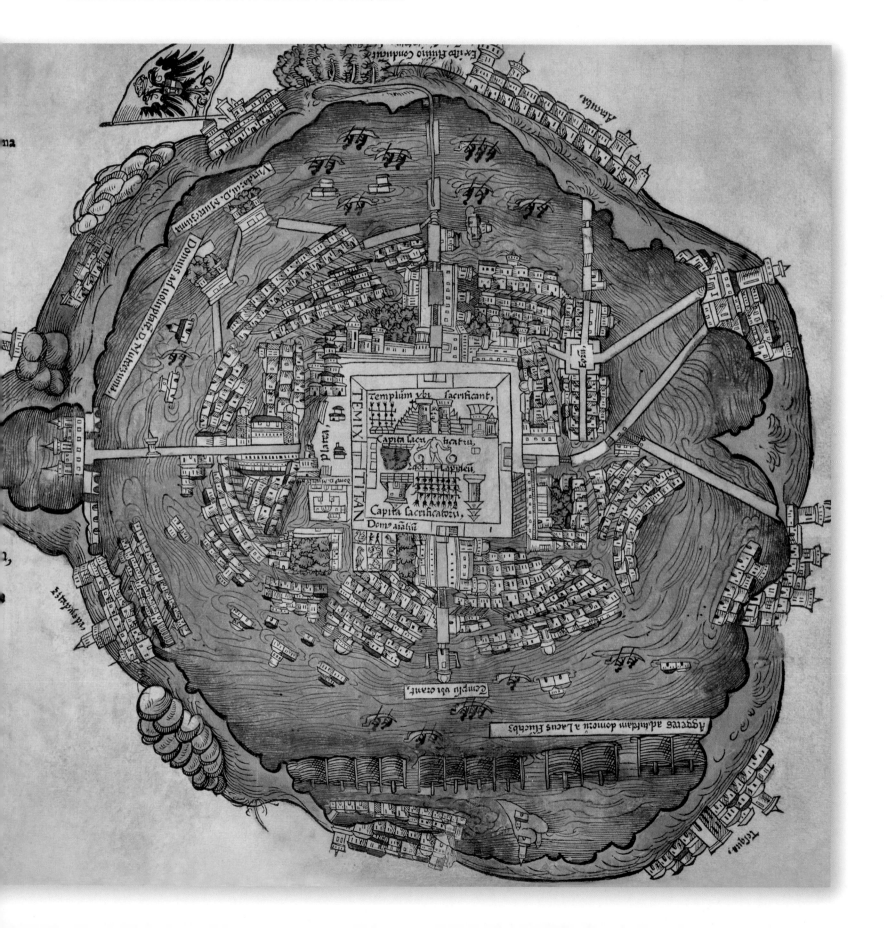

Visual tour

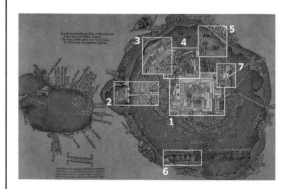

KEY

> **TEMPLE COMPLEX** At the center of the city the sacrificial pyramid precinct bore witness to prolonged, bloody ceremonies to propitiate the Aztec deities, involving the ritual execution of prisoners of war and slaves. These activities fascinated the Spanish invaders; around the time of their conquest, over 20,000 victims were ritually slaughtered in a festival weekend.

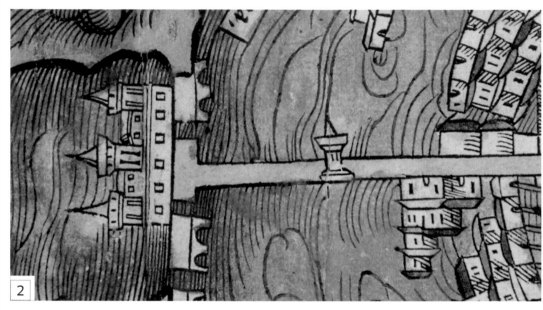

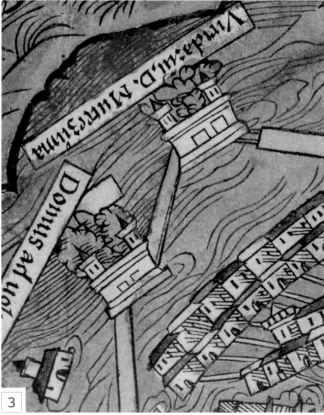

▲ **CAUSEWAYS** Tenochtitlan was linked to the shores of Lake Texcoco by a series of fortified masonry causeways, the number of which was often exaggerated on early maps.

> **FORTIFICATIONS** The warlike Aztecs, often understandably hated by the other Mesoamerican peoples they had subjugated, formidably defended their capital: in addition to the castellated causeways, outlying forts were built in the lake to provide further protection.

▲ **CANALS** The central parts of Tenochtitlan were both linked and divided by navigable canals. The main means of commerce and transport in the city were via water or artificial causeways.

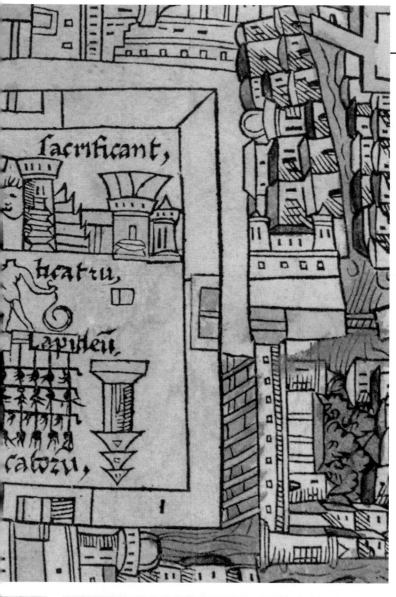

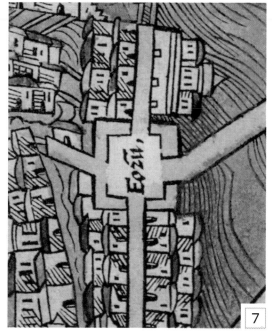

▲ **DYKES** In order to separate the salt and freshwater areas of the lake system, the Aztecs built elaborate filtering barriers of wickerwork, ensuring supplies of potable water for the capital city.

◄ **GATEWAY TO THE CITY** This square sits at the junction of two causeways leading into the city from the edges of the lake.

▲ **FISHING BOATS** The extensive Texcoco lake system encompassed both saltwater and freshwater lagoons. The abundant variety of fish that could be caught in both areas provided a major source of protein for Tenochtitlan's citizens.

IN **CONTEXT**

Tenochtitlan was not the only astonishing architectural achievement that the Spanish conquistadores came across in their New World conquests. The enormous, largely deserted, pyramid temple complex of Teotihuacan just east of Tenochtitlan was breathtaking, and a mere 15 years after the conquest of the Aztecs, Pizarro's troops entered upland Peru to discover exquisite Inca architecture of finely-honed, gigantic dry-stone masonry blocks, notably at Cuzco. Despite being astonished by this sophisticated architecture, the Spaniards either destroyed or built over what they found.

▲ **Teotihuacan**, known today as the site of many of the most architecturally significant Mesoamerican pyramids built in the pre-Columbian Americas

Mexico City, 1737

PEDRO DE ARRIETA ▪ OIL ON CANVAS ▪ NATIONAL MUSEUM OF HISTORY, MEXICO CITY, MEXICO

MAP OF MEXICO CITY

SCALE

> There were **street vendors** invading the **Main Plaza** and all the plazas, there were **channels from Xochimilco** and on the **bridges** they were **selling food** and other products

LUIS ORTIZ MACEDO, *PLANO DE LA CIUDAD DE MEXICO DE PEDRO DE ARRIETA, 1737* (2008)

The conquest of Mexico by Spanish explorers in 1519–21 led to the overthrow of the Aztec Empire and, in a calculated act of imperial dominance, the destruction of its chief center, Tenochtitlan (*see pp.54–57*), the largest city in pre-Columbian America. On top of its ruins, the Spanish built what was intended as an enduring symbol of their power—a European-style metropolis. A building boom in the 1670s and '80s saw Mexico City grow dramatically, yet, aside from a few idealized map-views commissioned from artists and architects—most notably, a 1628 painting that was part of a project to protect the city from flooding—the authorities made little effort to create an accurate ground plan of the capital, in turn making its efficient administration a matter of guesswork rather than precise direction.

Center of the grid

To address this shortcoming, in 1737 architect Pedro de Arrieta (1691–1738) was tasked with producing "an original and perfect map of the entire city." The result is as much a decorative aerial view as a map; there is no scale, and it is oriented with east at the top. However, beneath the proliferation of terra-cotta-tiled roofs, the city's grid plan is clearly visible. The map is centered precisely on the grand central plaza, the Zócalo, site of the immense Baroque Metropolitan Cathedral and the imposing Viceroy Palace.

IN **CONTEXT**

Colonial-era Mexico City had pretensions to imperial grandeur. It served as the capital of the Vice Royalty of New Spain—a region that stretched from Wyoming in the US to Panama, and included all of present-day Texas. It was the seat of the Viceroy of Spain, the direct representative of the Spanish monarch, and of the leading archbishop of New Spain.

It was also the commercial heart of this enormous colonial edifice, yet it soon acquired an air of frontier-town shabbiness. Contemporary accounts of the city consistently highlight its disorder and chaos, describing dilapidated buildings, corrupt officials, and streets thronged with beggars. Order was only imposed with the appointment of Güemes Pacheco (1740–99) as Viceroy in 1789. However, in 1821, after a decade of war and upheaval, Mexico asserted its independence from Spain, and the country returned to a state of economic and political chaos.

▲ **A 1695 painting of the Zócalo**, depicting the damaged Viceroy Palace (top right), burned by a mob in 1692

Mexico City, 1932

EMILY EDWARDS ▪ LITHOGRAPH ▪ NUMEROUS COPIES EXIST

SCALE

PICTORIAL MAP OF THE CITY OF MEXICO AND SURROUNDINGS YESTERDAY AND TODAY

This vibrant pictorial map of Mexico City, produced 400 years after the Spanish founded a colonial city on the remains of Tenochtitlan, the conquered Aztec capital, offers a unique past-present view that simultaneously celebrates the city's pre-Hispanic origins, its colonial-era expansion, and its early 20th-century, post-independence modernity. The map was commissioned as a promotional tool by the Mexican Light & Power Company and the Mexican Tramways Company from American artist and historian Emily Edwards, and was distributed widely.

A Mexican artistic mentor

From the mid-1920s, Edwards spent 10 years in Mexico, where she became a close friend of the leading Mexican Modernist painter and muralist Diego Rivera (1886–1957) and his young wife Frida Kahlo. During her studies with him, Edwards learned the art of combining cultural and historical themes with Modernism's graphic style—Rivera's large-scale murals of daily life in Mexico were realistic interpretations with symbolic allusions, and packed with references to both contemporary media (including cinema) and the art of Mexico's pre-Columbian civilizations.

Many of these stylistic ideas are employed in Edwards' visionary map of Mexico City, in which the symbols of an industralized, modern metropolis—communication links, railroad lines, power plants, streams of electicity towers—are juxtaposed with evocations of the city's tumultuous past, including the coats of arms of Spanish conquistadores and Aztec iconography. The main road routes through the city, linking its key centers, are highlighted in a bright orange, while the other main streets are yellow. Edwards' ingenious incorporation within the street plan of an Aztec priest wearing an eagle headdress is startling, forcing the viewer to decide whether this motif is part of the plan or part of an imaginary plan of an imagined city.

By the 1930s, almost all traces of the Aztec capital had been built over during Mexico City's commercial and economic development (*see box p.61*). Edwards' creative map, meanwhile, paid tribute to the city's indigenous past while at the same time functioning as a symbol of its modernity—a product created for mass consumption.

EMILY **EDWARDS**

1888–1980

Born in Texas, where she lived for much of her life, Edwards showed a talent for art, and an enthusiasm for social activism, from a young age.

Edwards trained in her hometown of San Antonio under the Italian-born sculptor Pompeo Coppini. From 1905 she attended the Art Institute of Chicago where, in addition to becoming familiar with its huge collection of contemporary European and American fine art, and Asian, Islamic, and indigenous decorative arts, she also taught classes. In 1917, she returned to San Antonio to teach art, although she took on various other jobs too, spending time working as a stage designer in New York, and as a puppeteer.

In 1924, Edwards and a female friend, concerned that San Antonio's growth was threatening its historic sites, established the San Antonio Conservation Society. From 1925, Edwards spent time in Mexico, drawing and undertaking research for a book on Mexican murals. In the 1930s, as well as producing her map of Mexico City, she exhibited watercolors and prints of Mexican subjects.

> Mexico is an ancient thing that will still go on forever telling its own story … Tenochtitlan is still here beneath our shoes and history was always just like today ”

BARBARA KINGSOLVER, *THE LACUNA*, 2009

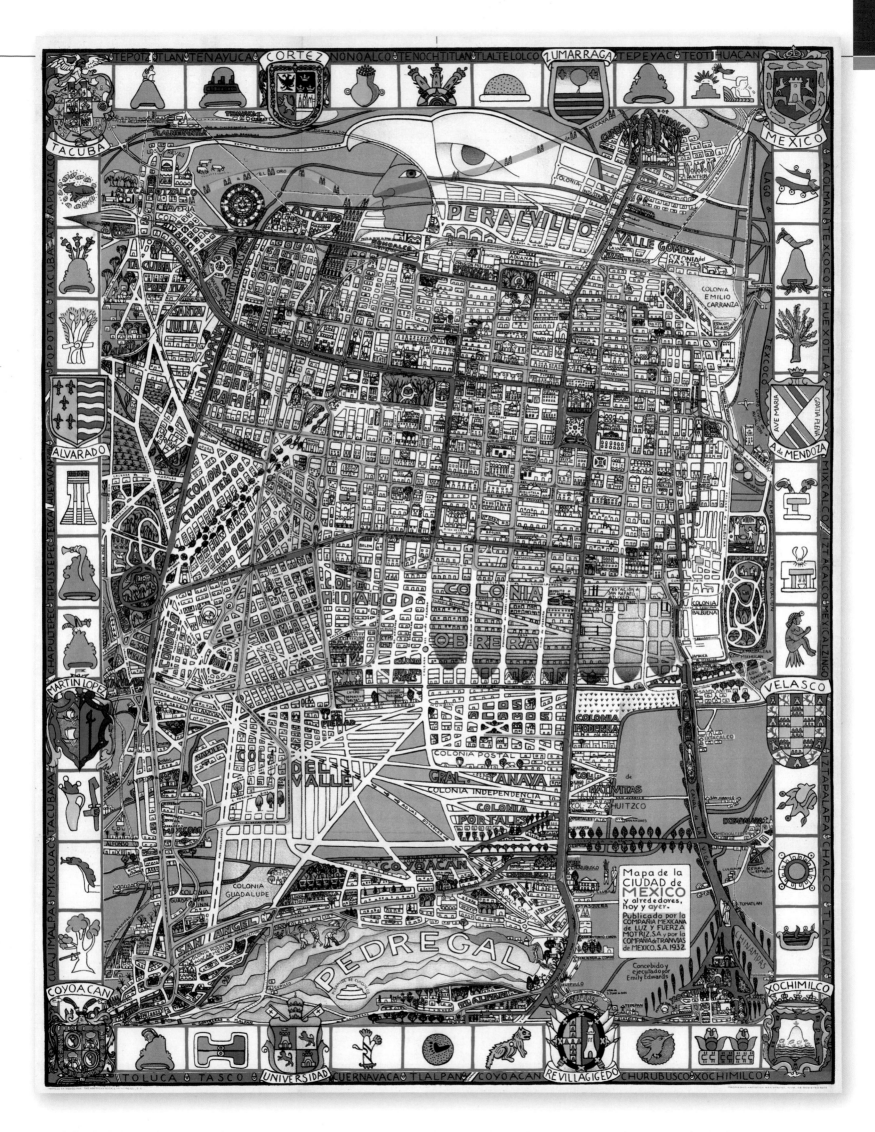

Mapa de la CIUDAD de MEXICO y alrededores, hoy y ayer.

Publicado por la COMPAÑIA MEXICANA de LUZ Y FUERZA MOTRIZ, S.A. y por la COMPAÑIA de TRANVIAS de MEXICO, S.A. 1932

Concebido y ejecutado por Emily Edwards

Visual tour

KEY

1

▶ **OUR LADY OF GUADALUPE** Lying to the north of the main city, on the hill of Tepeyac (site of an Aztec "earth mother" temple), this basilica rapidly became the most important Catholic pilgrimage shrine in Mexico after five apparitions of the Virgin Mary were reported there in 1531.

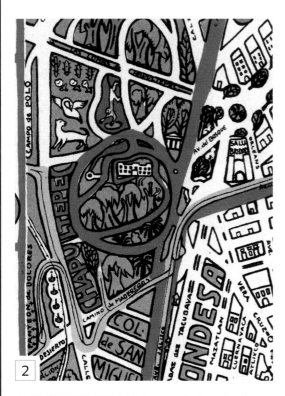

2

▲ **CHAPULTEPEC** Originally a rural retreat for the Aztec court, this huge park, which covers around 1,695 acres (686 hectares), was incorporated into the modern development of the city as a public recreation ground. As the city expanded further, it was retained as a "green lung," in the manner of New York's Central Park. Today, the park includes woodland areas, lakes, the colonial Chapultepec Castle, museums, and a zoo.

▶ **PERALVILLO** This area to the northwest of the city center had been run down since colonial times: a hive of slums that, although colorful, could not shake off its criminal associations, despite attempts at urban reform. It is no accident, therefore, that Edwards drew a positive image of a man in an eagle headdress in this part of her map, looking back to the Aztec past, and forward to a potentially ideal future.

3

4

IN **CONTEXT**

The wars for Mexican independence (1810–21) left the country devastated, impoverished, and politically unstable, although the appearance of Mexico City itself was largely unaltered. In 1847, the capital was captured by US forces during the Mexican–American War, and from 1863–67, it was under French military occupation; during this time, a grand avenue, now the Paseo de la Reforma, was built and lined with mansions.

During the dictatorship of Porfirio Díaz, which began in 1876, the city was modernized along the lines of Paris. Great improvements were made to services, utilities, and transportation, and Díaz built both grand middle-class districts and affordable housing developments that reflected his ambitions to create an internationally significant nation. The population grew in the 1910s, as people fled the countryside during the Mexican Revolution.

▲ **ZÓCALO** The city's main public square, the Plaza de la Constitución (commonly known as the Zócalo), was paved in the 1520s with stones taken from the ruins of the main temple complex in Aztec Tenochtitlan, which was sited nearby. Throughout its history, the square, which is one of the world's largest, has hosted civic, religious, and cultural celebrations and events throughout the year.

▲ **The Postal Palace**, which exemplifies the modern architecture constructed in the city under Díaz

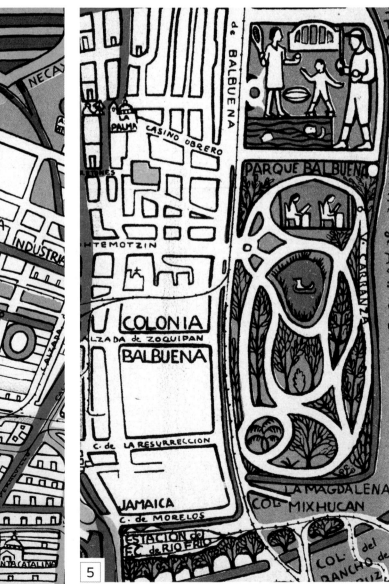

5

6

▲ **BALBUENA PARK** Designed by the innovative city planner Miguel Angel de Quevedo in 1910, this was the first public space specifically created to meet the needs of Mexico's working-class population. It included tennis courts, baseball fields, playgrounds, and forested parkland. Nearby Colonia Balbuena was a modern housing complex for workers that replaced earlier tenements.

▲ **PYRAMID OF CUICUILCO** Probably the city's oldest pre-Columbian temple (c.600 BCE), this unusual circular structure sits to the south of the city, on a lava field on what was once the southern shore of Lake Texcoco. The difficulty of excavating the basaltic lava meant the area was not built up into the wealthy residential district of Pedregal until the mid-20th century, although construction workers are seen here.

MEDIEVAL TRADING CENTERS

CHAPTER 2

Medieval Trading Centers

Trade played by no means a minor part in the ancient world, with amber, spice, incense, and silk routes evolving in the first millennium BCE. These gradually developed into an intricate network, binding together disparate transcontinental regions via increasingly wealthy urban trading cities across the world. However, the fragmentation of the Roman Empire by around 450 CE broke many established trading bonds, although the wave of Mongol conquests from central Asia to the Mediterranean in the 13th century temporarily revived trans-Asian trade.

These events paved the way for the emergence of a new and highly entrepreneurial trading lifeblood, largely emanating from European centers such as Venice and Genoa. Whereas, in the ancient world, much trade was conducted overland, by the late medieval period an ever-increasing amount of goods was borne by sea—often across vast distances. The great wealth generated fueled the growth of a network of urban trading cities around the globe, but particularly in Europe.

It was at precisely this point that European cartography emerged as a significant new science. Accurate charts of trading routes were required, as were plans of the towns and cities that merchants were dealing with. The tradition of mapmaking was at this time a distinctly European phenomenon—the wealthy empires of Asia felt little need to illustrate how their economies worked.

Maritime trading centers

As the maritime trading nations—especially those of west and northwest Europe, such as Portugal, Spain, France, Britain, and the Netherlands—prospered, their mastery of navigation allowed them to expand their activities even further. City maps of maritime ports, such as Amsterdam (*see pp.86–87*), Marseille (*see pp.94–95*), Lisbon (*see pp.104–05*), and Venice (*see pp.112–115*) highlighted the importance of maritime trade by filling moorages or coastal harbors with a variety of shipping as an indication of their global outreach and influence.

▲ **FLORENCE, 1490** Lorenzo Rosselli's stunning aerial view of Florence is not only an early masterpiece of perspective, it also highlights the impressive buildings that were constructed with the assistance of the Medici, the city's wealthy patrons.

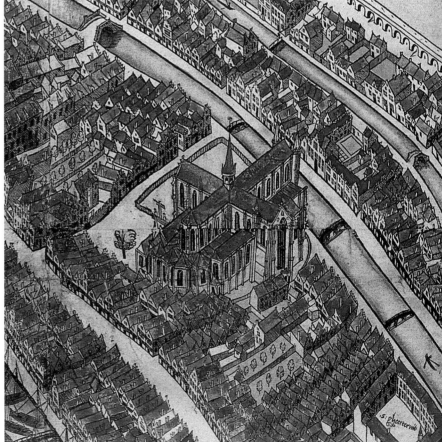

▲ **AMSTERDAM, 1544** Commissioned by Amsterdam's city council, this map by Cornelis Anthonisz. shows off the city as a hub of 16th-century trade, focusing on the canals and waterways that brought its mercantile bounty.

It is no coincidence that some of the busiest port cities also became notable centers of cartography, in particular Amsterdam, which led the field in the 17th century.

Yet it was not only maritime ports that became major trading centers—farther upstream, along rivers such as the Rhine, the Danube, and the Elbe, inland European cities such as Delft and Frankfurt also flourished.

Mapping the commercial world

It was also at this time that the first European atlases—as well as compendiums of city plans and views—were published, drawing on knowledge acquired through trade. Such atlases were not confined to far-off lands but also depicted places closer to home. One of these atlases, the *Civitates Orbis Terrarum* (*Atlas of Cities of the World*), was the first atlas of city maps (*see box p.48*). It contained 546 city views, including the first printed map of London (*see pp.68–71*), as well as plans of Venice (*see pp.112–115*), Frankfurt (*see pp.98–99*), and Wrocław (*see pp.100–03*).

> Famed amongst many people for its commerce… Goods from all over the world are brought hither on the Thames.

GEORG BRAUN ON LONDON, *CIVITATES ORBIS TERRARUM*, 1572

Toward the end of the medieval period, the huge wealth brought by trade also inspired city leaders to promote their city's success and prosperity, both as a matter of civic pride and to show off its potential as a place to do business. The earliest known map of Ghent shows the city at the height of its commercial power (*see pp.90–93*); in a similar fashion, Lorenzo Rosselli's 15th-century map of Florence (*see pp.116–117*) shows off its architecture to underline the city's cultural and economic power.

▲ **VENICE, 1575** This map of Venice from *Civitates Orbis Terrarum* concentrates on portraying the bustling maritime and naval shipping that was the source of the city's wealth and power from the late medieval period.

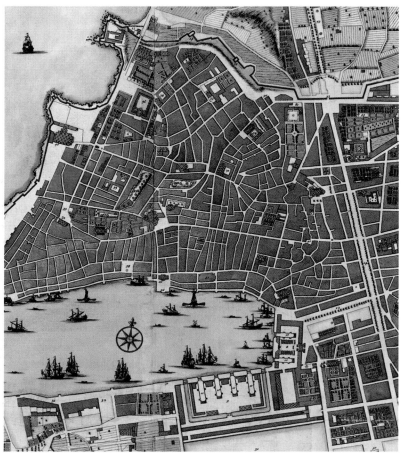

▲ **MARSEILLE, 1754** Marseille's status as France's principal Mediterranean trading port is made clear in this early 18th-century map, which places the harbor and its many ships at the heart of its depiction of the city.

Stockholm, 1805

CARL FREDRIK AKRELL ▪ ENGRAVING ▪ STOCKHOLM CITY MUSEUM

UNKNOWN

MAP OF STOCKHOLM

This beautiful and unusual oval map, engraved by Carl Fredrik Akrell and published in 1805, places the island of Gamla Stan at its center. The position of the island reflects its status as the birthplace of Stockholm— it is where a first mighty fortress was constructed in 1252 to guard the gateway from the Baltic Sea to the trade routes of Lake Mälaren. In the following centuries, the capital city of Sweden expanded north across the Norrström waterway to create the district of Norrmalm and south across the Söderström to create Södermalm. During the reign of King Gustav II Adolf (ruled 1611-32) these areas eventually developed along the rectilinear street plan that is highlighted in red on this map.

The city grew little over the next two centuries, as it was ravaged by fire and disease, including a plague in 1710 that killed about a third of the population. Sweden was defeated in several wars—ceding territories to Prussia and, in particular, Russia—and the country was no longer the great northern European power it had been.

However, at the dawn of the 19th century when this map was created, Stockholm was emerging from its state of stagnation. Already, a few notable developments had been sponsored by King Gustav III Adolf (1771-92), who had created Gustav Adolf Square and inaugurated a Royal Opera there in 1782, both on this map. The advent of industrialization would more than quadruple Stockholm's population in the coming century, making this 1805 map a snapshot of a city on the cusp of inexorable change.

CARL FREDRIK **AKRELL**

1779-1868

While still in his teens, Akrell placed his skills as a mapmaker at the service of the Swedish military. He most probably owed his prodigious cartographic talent to his father, who was also an engraver.

Akrell's map of Stockholm was drawn in the years 1802-03, when he was barely in his 20s, and this version was published in 1805. Working as an army surveyor and cartographer, Akrell eventually reached the rank of Lieutenant General, and also became the first director of the Swedish Topographical Corps. He made a fascinating and historically valuable set of engravings based on sketches taken by a Swedish naval officer, Axel Leonhard Klinkowström, on a tour of the United States in 1818-20. Akrell also produced many more maps and charts, although perhaps none as notable as his early work on Stockholm.

The island of Kungsholmen

The freshwater Lake Mälaren

The Royal Swedish Opera, next to Gustav Adolf Square

The island of Gamla Stan ("Old Town")

The Baltic Sea bay of Saltsjön

The district of Södermalm

London, 1572

GEORG BRAUN AND FRANZ HOGENBERG ▪ HAND-COLORED WOOCUT ▪ NUMEROUS COPIES EXIST

SCALE

LONDON, FERTILE ENGLAND'S CAPITAL CITY

Thought to be the first printed map of London, this view of the city is taken from *Civitates Orbis Terrarum* (*see p.48*). Aside from the reduced extent of the city when compared with today, its most obvious feature is the solitary nature of London Bridge—when this map was produced, it was the only crossing over the Thames River in London. Ever since pre-Roman times, London had been identified as the last practical opportunity to cross the river, since farther downstream tidal waters flooded in from the North Sea. London Bridge therefore proved a crucial link between southern and eastern Britain, straddling a broad but relatively sheltered estuary that allowed London to develop enormously as a port in the medieval era.

The map also makes clear that as London had grown, a dense and compact urban complex—the City of London—had developed on the north side of the bridge, in preference to the marshy south bank of Southwark. Along with the precipitous buildings that can be seen on the bridge itself, much of this medieval older city was comprised of timber dwellings that increasingly arched out over the streets as the city expanded upward. These tightly packed wooden buildings proved perfect kindling for the Great Fire of London, which was to ignite in a baker's shop in Pudding Lane in 1666.

> Sweet Thames, run softly, till I end my song "

EDMUND SPENSER, "PROTHALAMION," 1596

Hæc est regia illa totius Angliæ ciuitas LONDINVM, ad fluuium Thamesim sita. Cæsari, ut plures existimât, Trinobantum nuncupata, multarum gentium comertio nobilitata, exculta domib. ornata templis, excelsa arcibus, claris ingenijs, viris omnium artium doctrinarumq genere præstantibus, percelebris. Deniq, omnium rerum copia, atque opum excellêtia mirabilis. Inuehit in eam totius orbis opes ipse Thamasis, onerarijs nauibus per sexaginta millia passuum, ad vrbem præalto alueo nauigabilis

LONDINVM FERACISSIMI ANGLIAE REGNI METROPOLIS

Clarkenwell

The Spitel fields

Smythe Fyeld

S. Gyle

Moor Gate

Y Goouref ewuders P

S. Iames

The Barne

Wyrt

Black fryers

Bernard Castle

Brydewell

Quene Hyue

Thre Crane

Stiliard

Styliyarde

Bilinsgate

Towr hyll

Pultern Gate

Beere howse

Rillini Gate

THE TOWRE

Beere howst

Parys Garden

Wynchester Pl.

S. Mary Ouery.

S. Towlles

The Bowll bay tyng

The Beare bay ting

South warke

STILLIARDS) Hansa, Gothica dictio, conuentum, vel congregationem sonans, multarum ciuitatum est confoederata Societas, tum, ob praesita Regibus, ac Ducib. benefi-
cia: tum, ob securam terra, marique, mercaturae tractationem, tum denique, ad tran-
quillam Rerumpub. pacem, & ad modestam adolescentum institutionem conseruan-
dam, instituta: plurimor Regum, ac Principum, maxime Angliae, Galliae, Daniae, ac
Magnae Moscouiae, nec non Flandriae, ac Brabantiae Ducum priuilegijs, ac immuni-
tatib. exornata fuit. Habet ea quatuor Emporia, Cuntores quidam vocant, in quibus
ciuitatum negotiatores resident, suosque mercatus exercent. Hor, alterum heic Londi-
ni, domestica oeconomia nitet, habens domum Gildehalla Teutonica, qua vulgo Stiliard, nucupat

Visual tour

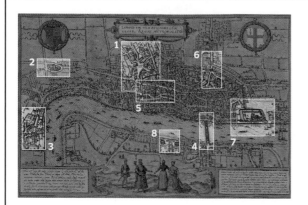

KEY

1

> **SMITHFIELD** This important market on the edge of the city wall is where drovers brought in thousands of head of cattle, sheep, poultry, and pigs to feed the city on a daily basis. This is reflected in the number of substantial roads that can be seen converging on the market site.

> **ST. GILES IN THE FIELDS**
A remnant chapel of a medieval monastery that had been dissolved under Henry VIII, St. Giles survived ostensibly as a leper house and hospital far outside the city. The church became known as the last stop for condemned prisoners on their way to execution at the village of Tyburn.

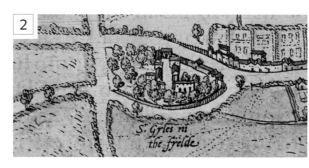

2

3

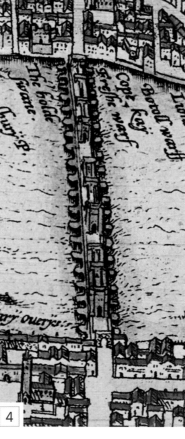

4

5

▲ **WESTMINSTER** The palace of Westminster became the principal London royal residence and center of government in the 13th century. Located upriver, it was far from the overcrowding and stench of the City. The palace attracted other important governmental buildings into the area, which remained geographically distinct from the City well into the 16th century.

▲ **OLD LONDON BRIDGE** By the 16th century, this masonry bridge was overpopulated with towering buildings, and the narrow waterways between its piers had become extremely hazardous. The bridge was irrevocably damaged during the fire of 1666.

▲ **OLD ST. PAUL'S CATHEDRAL** A huge monument, Old St. Paul's was constructed from 1087. By the time of its initial completion in the mid-14th century, it had survived several fires and was the largest and highest cathedral in Europe. It underwent successive design changes over the next two centuries, including the addition of a Palladian façade by Inigo Jones in 1621. The old cathedral's wooden roof proved its downfall in the Great Fire of 1666.

▼ **BISHOPSGATE** One of the eight major fortified gates piercing the Roman city wall, Bishopsgate straddled the principal route from the north and east into the City. The gate was used to collect taxes imposed on merchants entering the City, and also displayed the severed heads of miscreants.

▼ **THE TOWER OF LONDON** Dominated by the Norman citadel of the White Tower, this was an important royal residence, which explains the moat and double wall that can be seen on the map. Markets, churches, and legal institutions grew up around its western perimeters and toward London Bridge, giving birth to the modern City of London.

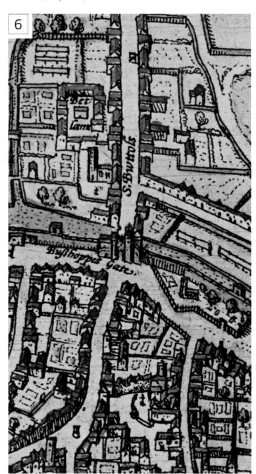

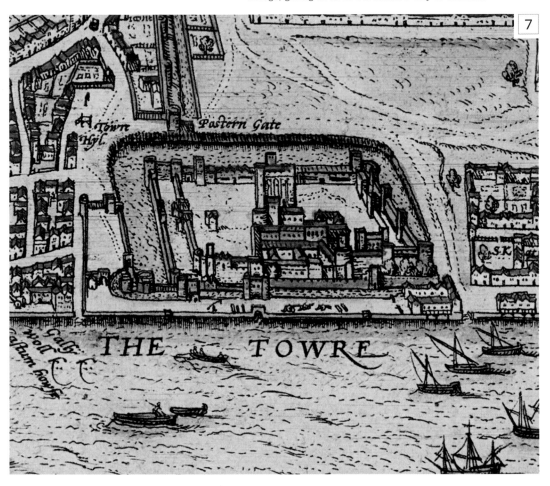

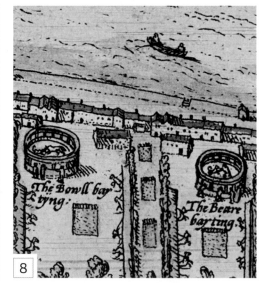

IN **CONTEXT**

Between 1550 and 1700, the population of the City of London quadrupled from 120,000 to almost 500,000, resulting in an increased density of building. The City by the mid-Tudor period became an enormous district and included very few squares or open spaces, and only a few major thoroughfares. Most buildings were timber-framed and divided or linked by narrow lanes or alleyways, most of them darkened by the addition of new overhanging stories to existing buildings. The City's landscape was punctuated by only a handful of major buildings such as the Tower and St. Paul's.

▲ **SOUTHWARK** Many of the more scurrilous places of entertainment, such as bear- and bull-baiting pits, lay south of the river in and around Southwark, adjacent to London Bridge, as this area was outside of the City's authority. Within a few years, the famous Swan, Hope, Rose, and Globe theaters would be established in the district.

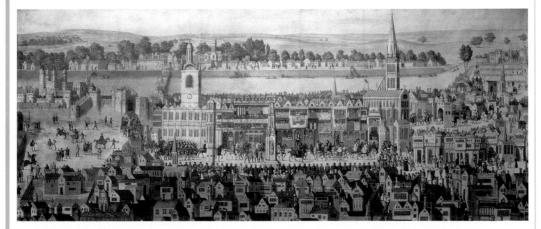

▲ **The coronation procession of Edward VI** from the Tower to the palace of Whitehall via the City and St. Paul's

London, 1682

WILLIAM MORGAN ▪ ENGRAVING ▪ LIBRARY OF CONGRESS, WASHINGTON D.C., USA

SCALE

LONDON ACTUALLY SURVEY'D

Morgan's remarkably detailed and ornate map is notable for a number of reasons: first, it is the earliest record of how rapidly the topography of modern London emerged from the ashes of the devastating Great Fire of 1666; second, it uses a consistent scale and projection, without emphasizing major landmarks or sites, as was traditional in cartography at the time; and third, it is based on accurate surveying techniques such as triangulation and precise measurement. It remains a triumphant early street map of a complex city, celebrating the remergence of a hugely damaged capital.

Morgan's map also reflects three enlargements of the city itself: rapid extension westward over the previous two centuries; its expansion east up the Thames to better moorings below the "Pool" of London (the area of the river from London Bridge to Limehouse); and its encroachment on the south bank of the Thames in Southwark.

The many annotated details and listings arrayed around the main map, the decorative cartouches, and the panorama of London that sits below the map make this an important and unprecedented approach to representing a city. It also slides back and forth in time, displaying the old, the present, and the future (Wren's new St. Paul's, pictured in the top right corner, would not be completed until 1708). As a vital document of a city in flux, recovery, and expansion, it is unsurpassed.

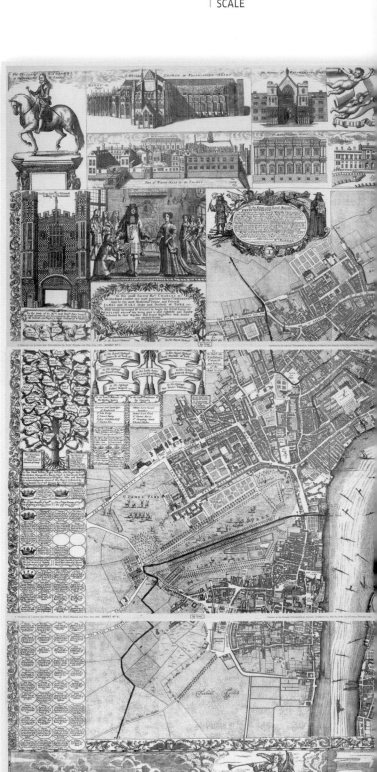

IN **CONTEXT**

The Great Fire of London started at a bakery on Pudding Lane on Sunday, September 2, 1666. It ravaged London for four days, devastating the medieval city and reducing it to ashes— with more than 13,000 buildings destroyed. To avoid another cataclysm, Charles II ordered that a new city be built of "brick or stone," and many notable humanists and architects (all members of the recently convened Royal Society) put forward proposals. These included John Evelyn's delicate Italianate plans based around convenient piazzas, Robert Hooke's more practical grid plans, and Christopher Wren's Parisian vision of diagonal boulevards. None proved practicable, although Wren's designs, based on replacing churches as key points around London, essentially won the day. Many gifted architects, such as Nicholas Hawksmoor and James Gibbs, assisted in the rebuilding of the city.

▲ **The Great Fire** seen engulfing buildings from London Bridge on the left and the Tower of London on the right, with St. Paul's Cathedral in the distance surrounded by the tallest flames

> [I] saw all the town burned, and a miserable sight of Paul's Church, withal the roof fallen, and the body of the quire fallen...

SAMUEL PEPYS, FROM HIS DIARY, SEPTEMBER 1666

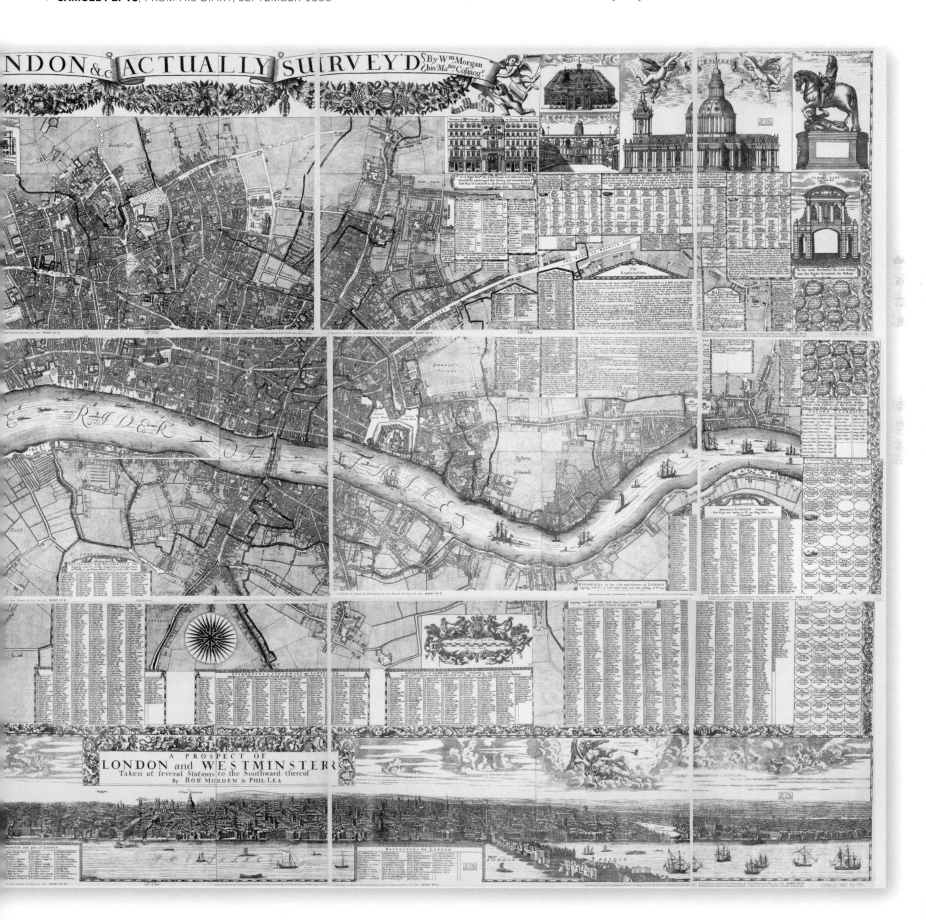

Visual tour

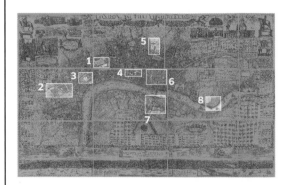

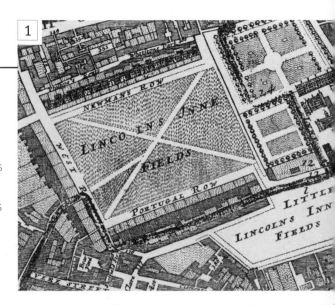

➤ **LINCOLN'S INN FIELDS** From the 1630s, sponsored by the developer William Newton, Lincoln's Inn Fields became a very upmarket residential area. The famous British architect Inigo Jones was one of the those responsible for the development of the area. Lincoln's Inn was unaffected by the Great Fire, and its proximity to the law courts at Chancery Lane attracted many legal firms to establish their offices there. It remains the largest public square in London.

➤ **ST. JAMES'S** The area west of Haymarket and south of Piccadilly was given over to development by Charles II in 1662, and granted freehold rights in 1665. It rapidly became a fashionable area to live in, near to both St. James's Palace and the Palace of Whitehall. St. James's Square was always central to the layout of the district.

▼ **COVENT GARDEN** Originally the site of the Saxon town of Ludenwic, and then a market garden owned by Westminster Abbey, this area was granted to the earls of Bedford in 1552. It was developed into an Italianate piazza by Inigo Jones during Charles I's reign, flanked by St. Paul's Church and grand residential buildings. It escaped the Great Fire, but by the early 18th century had become a flower and vegetable market, and an area that was notorious for brothels and prostitution.

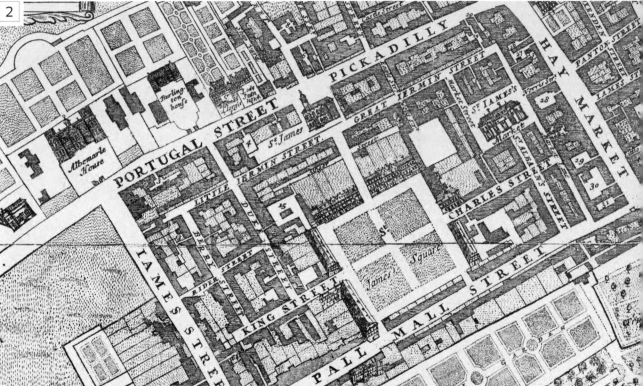

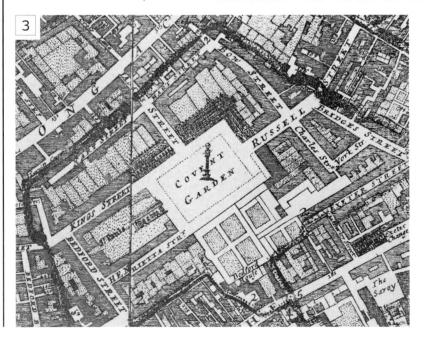

▲ **ST. PAUL'S CATHEDRAL** The St. Paul's Cathedral that Morgan shows never existed. He based his image on Wren's first plan for the church's reconstruction following the Great Fire, an attempt to combine the Gothic qualities of the original cathedral with the Palladian façade Inigo Jones had added in the 1630s. However, this vision was never realized. By the time of the basilica's completion in 1710, it had evolved into the domed Roman Baroque edifice we see today.

▼ **ARTILLERY GROUND** Lying to the north of the city walls, bounded by Chiswell Street and Bunhill Fields (or City) Cemetery in what is now Finsbury, this was a parcel of land reserved for practising archery and shooting from 1498.

▼ **THE CITY** The area most devastated by the Great Fire was soon to be revived, although the imposition of a new structure on the City was hampered by the pattern of existing arteries—Bishopsgate, Cornhill, Leadenhall, Gracechurch Street, and Fenchurch. In some ways, this made reconstruction simpler and faster, with many buildings replaced essentially on their existing ground plans.

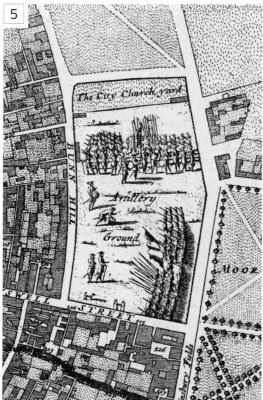

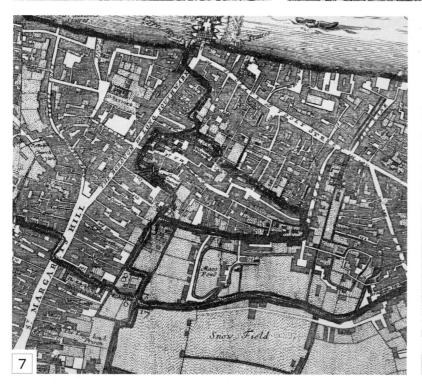

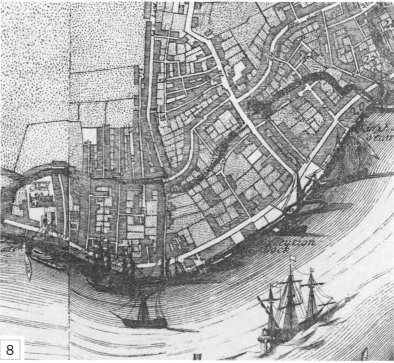

▲ **SOUTHWARK** At the time of this map, the area south of London Bridge lay outside the administration of the City in the county of Surrey. Southwark had expanded considerably during the early 17th century, especially as a place for entertainment, in spite of its marshy ground. Unaffected by the Great Fire, the rickety, largely wooden buildings of the area had fallen victim to their own fire 10 years later, in 1676.

▲ **WAPPING** The area immediately east of the Tower of London, along the north bank of the Pool of London and bounded to the north by marshland, had developed into a maritime trading district, studded with many jetties. It was populated by tradesmen who catered to seafarers—shipyards, inns, victuallers, sailmakers, and chandlers. Its constricted area, basically one north-south street, was described by the historian John Stow as "a filthy strait passage".

London, 1827

CHRISTOPHER AND JOHN GREENWOOD ▪ COLORED STEEL ENGRAVING ▪ NUMEROUS COPIES EXIST

SCALE

MAP OF LONDON FROM AN ACTUAL SURVEY

Although the familiar snakelike shape of the Thames River flowing through the city dominates this beautiful image of London, the Greenwoods' map also reveals the astonishing number of changes that had occurred since the 17th century. First, the urban area had become much larger, extending in every direction beyond the confines of the original city, outlined here in red. Second, the City of London had been extended along the north bank of the Thames, linking Whitehall, Westminster, and St. James's Palace. Third, the shortage of anchorages in Wapping and the Pool of London—the stretch of river situated between London Bridge and Limehouse—had been met by the creation of docks dug out of marshes north of the Isle of Dogs. Last, various major parks in and around the city had been laid out and upmarket houses had been built around communal gardens, squares, and green spaces to the west of the expanding urban area. Similar residential developments would begin in Paris, Washington, D.C., and New York but not until almost half a century later.

The impact of Nash

The man behind this replanning was the Prince Regent's favored architect, the visionary John Nash (1752–1835). Nash fully embraced Neoclassicism in the creation of Regent's Park, incorporating the ideals of simplicity and symmetry found in Classical Greek and Roman architecture into the magnificient suburban villas that skirted around the park's edge. Nash also designed individual dwellings, churches, and theaters for the revamped London, even working on plans for expanding "The Queen's House," which would go on to become, over the next century, Buckingham Palace.

This city now doth, like a garment, wear / The beauty of the morning; silent, bare, / Ships, towers, domes, theatres, and temples lie / Open unto the fields, and to the sky. "

WILLIAM WORDSWORTH, "COMPOSED UPON WESTMINSTER BRIDGE," 1802

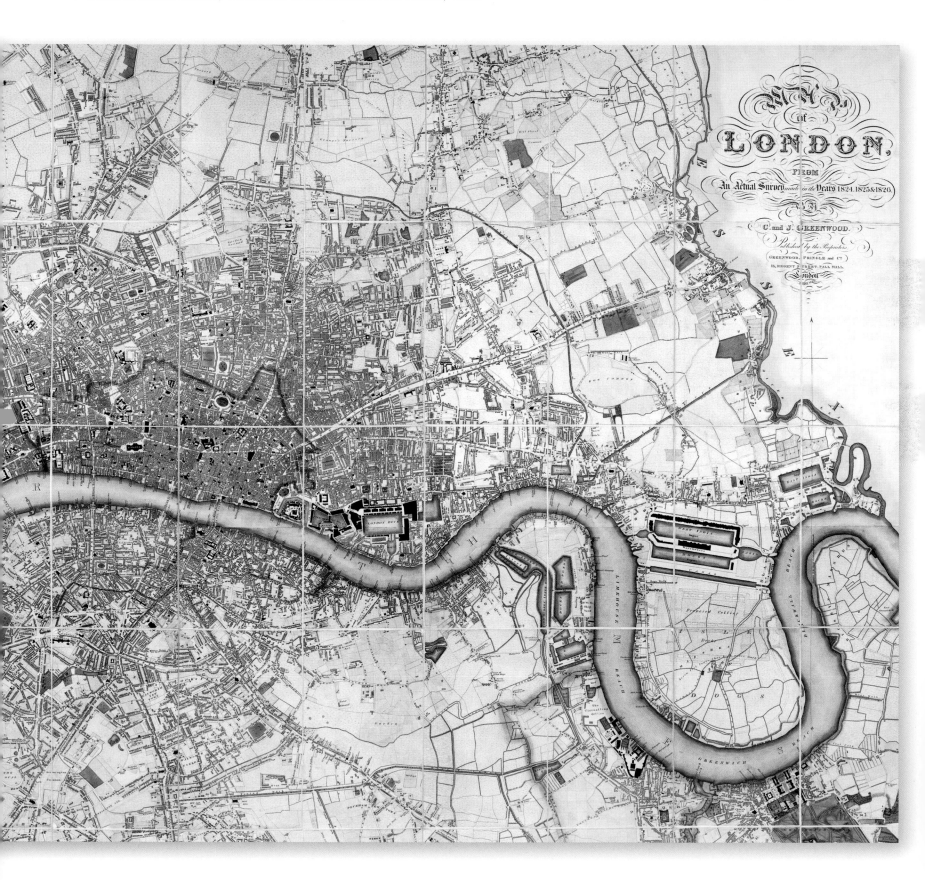

Visual tour

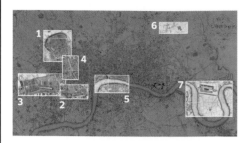

KEY

▶ **REGENT'S PARK** The jewel in the crown of Nash's designs for west London was the creation of the enormous public facility and recreation area known as Regent's Park. Ornamented by walkways and a landscaped lake, the park is framed to the north by a canal, and surrounded by luxurious villas. The zoological gardens in the north of the park were opened in 1828.

▼ **ST. JAMES'S PARK AND GREEN PARK** As the city became increasingly built up, the need to retain some designated green spaces became clear. The old leper grounds of St. James the Less had been acquired by the Crown in 1532 to become parkland north of St. James's Palace. Green Park was an extension of this, flanking the creation of the processional route of Pall Mall toward Buckingham Palace, which became an official royal home in 1837.

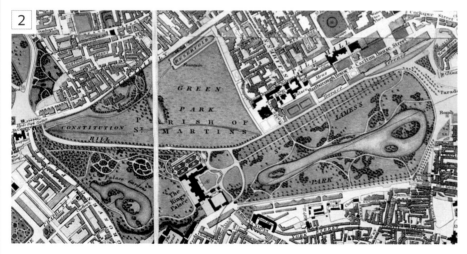

▲ **HYDE PARK** By far the largest of the four London royal parks, Hyde Park, with its ornate Serpentine lake, linked Kensington Palace and its gardens with the West End. Originally a private royal hunting ground for Henry VIII, from the 17th century it became a space open to all, and was chosen to host the Great Exhibition of 1851.

▼ **THE WEST END** Nash's vision included planning two avenues leading into the heart of what would become the West End, Portland Place and Regent Street, in an extended, curved, grand arcade that would intersect with Oxford Street at Oxford Circus. Nash also designed two theaters in the area: the Theatre Royal, and Her Majesty's Theatre (originally the King's Opera House).

IN **CONTEXT**

The Pool of London was the stretch of the Thames downstream from the barrier created by London Bridge. By the 18th century it was becoming increasingly clogged with shipping. London Dock at Wapping was created in 1801, but more capacity was still needed. The West India Docks were dug out of the Isle of Dogs in 1805, the East India Docks opened the same year, while on the South Bank, the Surrey Commercial Docks were opened in 1807. These developments, accommodating more than 1,200 oceangoing vessels, plus more than 2,000 coastal freighters, barges, and lighters per annum, are shown on the Greenwood map.

▲ **The Rhinebeck Panorama (1820)**, illustrating the congestion on the river in the Pool of London near London Bridge

▼ **HACKNEY** Where building was feasible, the marshes around the Lea River to the northeast of the city had, by the beginning of the 19th century, become another area of suburban expansion.

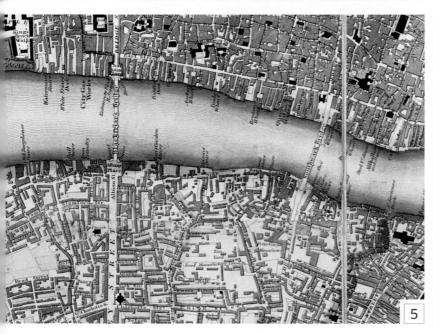

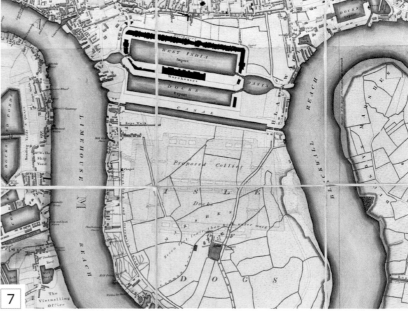

▲ **THE SOUTH BANK** The suburban sprawl of London began to encroach south of the river into Southwark, and into Lambeth to the west. With more bridges being built across the Thames, these areas became more accessible, making them both convenient and popular places to live.

▲ **THE ISLE OF DOGS** By the early 19th century, the docks had been excavated at the northern neck of the Isle of Dogs, and merchant ships could enter from the east and exit to the west. They deposited their cargoes in what would become one of the busiest ports in the western hemisphere.

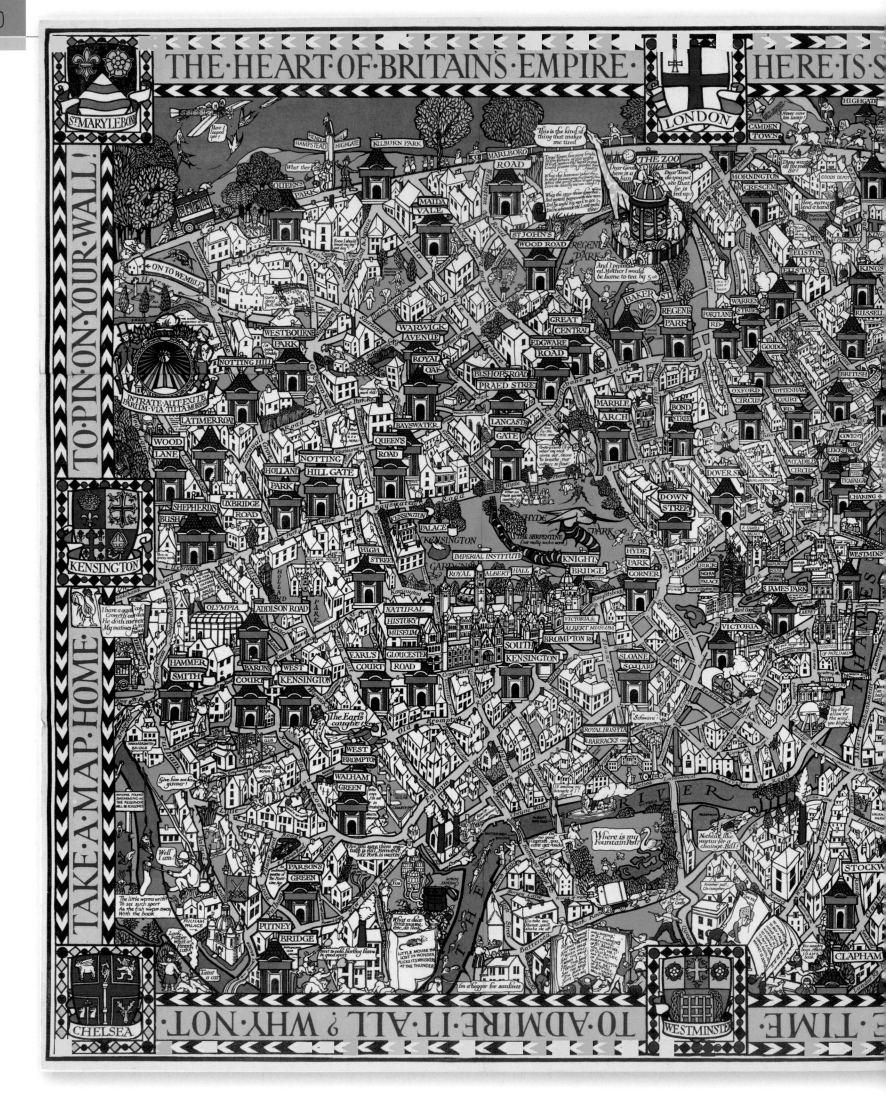

London, 1914

LESLIE MACDONALD GILL ▪ CHROMOLITHOGRAPHIC
POSTER ▪ NUMEROUS COPIES EXIST

SCALE

THE WONDERGROUND MAP OF LONDON TOWN

Commissioned shortly before the outbreak of World War I
by Frank Pick, the commercial director of the Underground
Electric Railway Company (now London Underground), and
displayed in Tube stations across the metropolis, this is an
eye-catching, charming, and comical poster map of London
and its attractions. Its creator, architect and graphic designer
Leslie MacDonald "Max" Gill (1884–1947)–brother of the
famous sculptor and typographer Eric Gill–was highly regarded
for his pictorial and decorative maps.

A fairy-tale London
Gill's technicolor, bird's-eye-view poster was intended to amuse,
entertain, and distract passengers as they stood waiting for the
unpunctual, dirty, and overcrowded trains of the time, and did
not attempt to offer directional information. It proved a brilliant
marketing tool for the beleaguered Electric Railway Company.
Gill set out his (or Pick's) vision for the map in the decorative
typographic border that surrounds the cityscape–the message
encouraging customers to "take a map home" worked extremely
well: thousands of folded copies of the poster were sold.
  In addition to the rich menu of witty observations and
cartoonlike visual jokes embedded within it, the map has some
topographical accuracy: it shows the main roads through
London (in yellow)–therefore also identifying the major bus
routes–and is dotted with templelike symbols representing
most of the Underground stations: a stylistic innovation almost
two decades ahead of Harry Beck's influential schematic
London Underground plan of 1933 (see p.240).

I get a **funny feeling** inside of me,
Just walking up and down,
Maybe it's because **I'm a Londoner,**
That **I love London** town. **"**

HUBERT GREGG, "MAYBE IT'S BECAUSE I'M A LONDONER," 1947

Dublin, 1756

JOHN ROCQUE ▪ HAND-COLORED ENGRAVING ▪
DUBLIN CITY LIBRARY, REPUBLIC OF IRELAND

SCALE

AN EXACT SURVEY OF THE CITY AND SUBURBS OF DUBLIN

John Rocque's spectacular map of Dublin, the capital city of Ireland, is remarkable in many ways. It is, most obviously, incredibly detailed: the map's exceptionally large scale of 1 in to 200 ft (2.5 cm to 60 m) allows Rocque to show and name not only every street but also each individual building. Although it is not possible to know just how much license Rocque allowed himself in this painstaking detail, his determination to produce as precise a map as possible is reflected in his use of different shadings—cross-hatching, stippling, diagonals—for various types of buildings, as detailed in the key in the lower-left corner. The denominations of the city's churches are indicated as well. The visual impact of the map is underlined in the title at top center, which is contained within an elaborately illustrated frame, featuring a series of figures in an imagined landscape.

The map is also important because it depicts Dublin at a time when it was being transformed from a modest, medieval tangle of streets into one of the most spacious and handsome cities in Europe. Along with the city of Edinburgh in Scotland (*see pp.206–07*), 18th-century Dublin was at the forefront of a revolution in urban planning. This was a reflection not just of the city's growing commercial prosperity but of its burgeoning sense of civic worth.

JOHN **ROCQUE**

c.1705–62

John Rocque was the most important British cartographer of the first half of the 18th century. He was born in France to Protestant, or Huguenot, parents, and his family was driven by religious persecution to settle in England when Rocque was still a child.

Rocque worked as an engraver and landscape gardener before making a career in cartography, a field in which he achieved rapid and lasting success; in 1751, he was made cartographer to the Prince of Wales. His "Large Survey of London in 24 Sheets," published in 1746, was the most detailed, authoritative, and influential map of the city at the time. It remains a vital reference for historians of 18th-century London. Between 1754 and 1760, Rocque was in Ireland, employed chiefly by Ireland's leading nobleman, the Earl of Kildare, for whom he produced a huge number of maps of his estates. In addition to his "Exact Survey of the City and Suburbs of Dublin," he produced maps of other leading Irish towns—Cork and Kilkenny among them—as well as a series of maps of Irish counties, and a map of Ireland itself. He similarly oversaw the production of maps of Paris, Rome, and Berlin.

Dublin is one of the finest and largest Cities of Europe

JOHN ROCQUE, IN THE NOTES ACCOMPANYING A REVISION TO THIS MAP, 1757

Visual tour

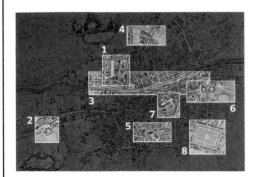

KEY

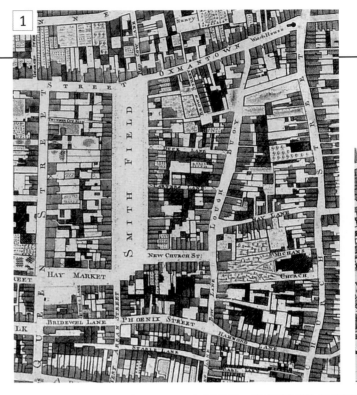

> **SMITHFIELD** On the north bank of the Liffey River, Smithfield, was Dublin's main market, a large open space that still exists today. It was laid out in the 17th century and surrounded by urban farmyards. Its agricultural origins are highlighted here by streets such as Hay Market to its south and Duck Lane and Carter's Lane to its east.

▽ **CITY WORKHOUSE** Dublin's workhouse on the south bank of the Liffey was established in 1703 for the city's poor and indigents: "sturdy beggars" and "disorderly women." From 1730, it was a foundling hospital for Dublin's armies of orphans. As such, it emerged as a place of enduring horror with alarmingly high death rates.

▽ **LIFFEY RIVER** The Liffey was the reason Dublin existed. In Gaelic, the "Dubh Linn," or "black pool," refers to its waters, which drew the Vikings to settle here in the 9th century. By the 1700s, the city was a major river port. Rocque's map vividly shows the shipping that crowded the Liffey.

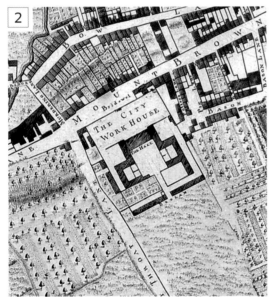

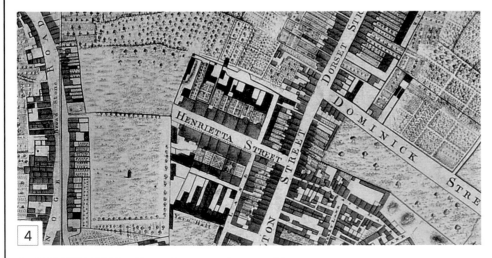

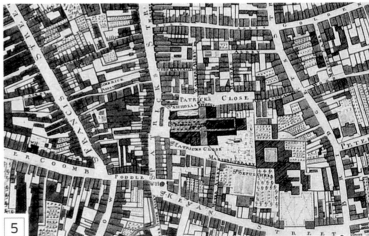

▲ **HENRIETTA STREET** The modest street shown on this map was developed from the 1720s. It consisted of no more than a handful of sober Georgian townhouses, though far grander examples followed. Henrietta Street established the model for the exacting urban planning that underlined the city, which emerged later in the century.

▲ **ST. PATRICK'S CATHEDRAL** Medieval Ireland was a crucible of Christian teaching and this map shows St. Patrick's Cathedral at the medieval heart of Dublin. Built from 1191, it remained a symbol of an enduring Christian faith despite being recast as a Protestant church in the 16th-century. It was restored in the 19th century.

▼ **TRINITY COLLEGE** The glories of 18th-century Dublin are epitomized by its university, Trinity College. The map shows this stately structure at the heart of a complex of buildings clustered around College Green. To the east is Parliament House, begun in 1728, the first specially built parliament building in Europe.

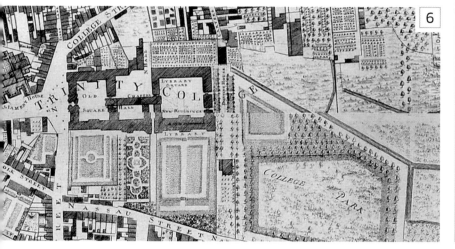

6

IN **CONTEXT**

The growth of 18th-century Dublin was far from haphazard. In the 17th century, the Lord Lieutenant of Ireland, the Earl of Ormonde, had ordered that all buildings overlooking the Liffey must face rather than back onto the river. This transformed the city, instilling a sense of structure and civic good order. By the time of Rocque's map, a number of similar initiatives had been launched. They were followed in 1757 with the creation of the Wide Streets Commission, charged with overseeing the creation of a new, more logically ordered city. The majority of Dublin's major streets, many of its bridges, and most of its stately public spaces and buildings owe their existence to its forward-looking work.

▲ **View over Essex Bridge** (now Grattan Bridge) from Capel Street in 1800

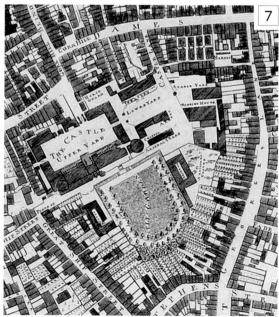

7

◄ **DUBLIN CASTLE** Medieval Dublin was dominated by the forbidding fortification the Normans imposed as a mark of conquest in the 12th century. At the time of this map, Dublin Castle was the official residence of the British-appointed Lord Lieutenant of Ireland, and a more subtle symbol of Irish subjection. It long remained an indication of Anglo-Irish supremacy.

► **ST. STEPHEN'S GREEN** The harmonious expanses of St. Stephen's Green, the earliest of Dublin's 18th-century residential squares, highlight how the social and political hub of Dublin shifted in the 18th century from the north to the south bank of the Liffey. By the time of Rocque's map, it had emerged as a key focus of the new city.

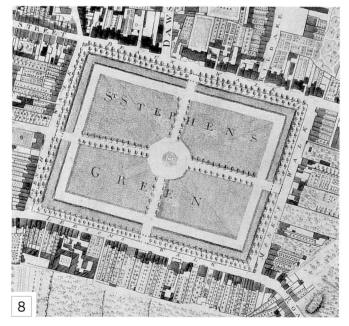

8

Amsterdam, 1544

CORNELIS ANTHONISZ. ▪ HAND-COLORED WOODCUT ▪
RIJKSMUSEUM, AMSTERDAM, THE NETHERLANDS

SCALE

MAP OF AMSTERDAM

This aerial view of Amsterdam by Cornelis Anthonisz. is the second image of the city produced by the Dutch engraver and painter. The first, a painting commissioned by Amsterdam council and completed in 1538, is the earliest known map of the city and the basis for this later woodcut. Anthonisz. was working at a critical moment in the city's history, when it was poised to emerge as a major maritime and financial powerhouse. The city would also go on to become the most important mapmaking center in Europe, and the work of Anthonisz. influenced maps of Amsterdam until well into the 17th century. The profusion of shipping shown on the map, as well as the presence of Neptune in the upper right-hand corner, illustrates the role played by seaborne trade in the city's rise to power. Although the canal network was soon to be extended dramatically, the waterways at the heart of the map remain fundamentally the same today.

Visual tour

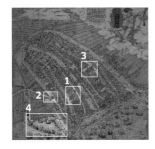

KEY

▶ **OUDE KIRK** A striking statement not only of religious piety but also of burgeoning civic pride, the 13th-century Oude Kirk (Old Church) had been substantially remodeled in the 15th century.

1

▼ **ST. ANTHONY'S GATE** Originally part of the city walls, St. Anthony's Gate is Amsterdam's oldest non-ecclesiastical building. Retained when the walls were demolished from 1603, it became a weighing house known as the Waag.

2

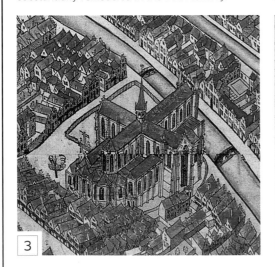

3

▲ **NIEUWE KIRK** The Nieuwe Kirk, or New Church, was constructed from 1408 to accommodate the spiritual needs of Amsterdam's swelling population. It was almost entirely rebuilt after a fire in 1645.

4

▲ **SHIPYARD** Located at the confluence of the river IJ and the huge inland body of water stretching north from Amsterdam–known as the IJmeer–Amsterdam's shipyard was among the busiest in Europe at this time.

Amsterdam, 1770

JAN MOL AND COMPANY ▪ HAND-COLORED ENGRAVING ▪
UNIVERSITY OF AMSTERDAM, THE NETHERLANDS

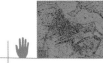

SCALE

NEW MAP OF AMSTERDAM AND ITS ENVIRONS

Although this map is an exact image of late-18th-century Amsterdam, and a precise example of the scientific cartography developing in Europe at the time, it effectively shows the city that had emerged almost a hundred years earlier. Throughout the previous century, Amsterdam was the most dynamic—and the richest—city in Europe. The hub of a growing global trading network, it reaped the benefits of a revolution in finance and banking, including the world's first stock market. It also pioneered land reclamation programs that would transform its otherwise unpromising, marshy location and in turn make an agricultural revolution possible. Many of the same technological means were pressed into service to allow the expansion of the city, here seen within city walls that had been extended to accommodate the needs of Amsterdam's swelling population, which had increased from 40,000 in 1550 to 240,000 in 1770.

Visual tour

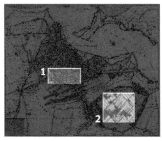

KEY

1

2

▲ **THE CANAL RING** The 17th-century expansion of Amsterdam was focused on the Canal Ring or Grachtengordel. Shown encircling the medieval city at the heart of the map, this concentric network of four canals had a length of 8½ miles (14 km) and was crossed by 80 bridges. Development took place in two bursts, the first beginning in 1610 and the second in 1660.

◀ **RECLAIMED DIEMER LAKE** The Diemer Lake or Diemermeer, here shown as agricultural land south of the city, is a classic polder—reclaimed land lying at or below sea level. It was drained over two years after 1627. Water levels were controlled by a network of canals laid out on a grid plan. Today it is entirely urban.

Ghent, 1534

UNKNOWN ARTIST ■ OIL ON CANVAS ■ BIJLOKEMUSEUM, GHENT, BELGIUM

SCALE

GHENT, LARGEST CITY OF GALLIA BELGICA

There are few more compelling images of any late medieval north European city than this lavish 1534 view of Ghent, the earliest existing plan of the city. The map details Ghent precisely—its major buildings in particular—along with the city's surroundings and the elaborate network of rivers that cut through it. As an imagined aerial view of one of the most significant of Europe's 15th-century powerhouses of trade, this image stands as a potent expression of the emerging civic pride that such material successes produced.

Ghent, today in Belgium but in 1534 an important city in the County of Flanders, grew rich as part of a medieval trading network that extended across northwest Europe and into northern Italy. However, when this painting was produced, wider conflicts were poised to tear apart the certainties that had allowed the city to prosper. After the Revolt of Ghent in 1539 (*see below*), the city went into a slow decline.

IN **CONTEXT**

The Ghent-born Holy Roman Emperor Charles V (reigned 1519–56) was the most powerful ruler in Europe, and the Low Countries were among his many scattered territories. His determination to tax them heavily to fund his endless wars provoked resentment. In defense of its ancient "liberties," in 1539—just five years after this map was produced—Ghent rose up against Charles. His revenge was absolute. When the revolt was suppressed, the city's leading figures were humiliatingly ordered to parade before the emperor wearing only undergarments and with nooses around their necks. All of Ghent's ancient rights, including those of its once all-powerful guilds, were revoked, and as a further mark of subjection, in addition to demolishing the ancient abbey of St. Bavo, eight of the city gates, symbols of Ghent's self-reliance, were destroyed.

▲ **The Guild of Noose Bearers** commemorating the revolt by parading through the streets dressed as the humilliated town leaders

City full of all types of joy, / with festively bedecked streets and houses, / with theater figures, many youngsters about, / and bonfires on the street.

LIEVEN BAUTKIN, POET AND RHETORICIAN, ON FESTIVITIES FOR CHARLES V'S BIRTH IN GHENT, 1500

Visual tour

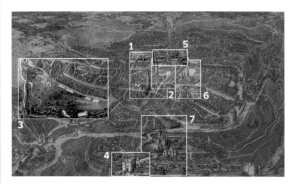

KEY

▶ **CENTRAL TOWERS**
Three huge towers loomed over medieval Ghent. They are, from top to bottom, the church of St. Nicholas, the beffoi or belfry, and the church of St. Bavo. Each alone was impressive, but as symbols of the economic strength required to construct them, together they highlight the power of this trading city.

▶ **STADTHUIS** In the center of the image stands the Stadthuis, or town hall, a potent symbol of Ghent's medieval civic virtues. Built from 1482, it was a temple to trade–as lavish as any church– and reflected the riches merchants brought into the city.

▲ **MARSHLAND** Low-lying Ghent sits where two major rivers, the Scheldt and the Leie, meet. Both rivers are shown here with their many tributaries, surrounding a marshy landscape. This land produced rich salt grasslands–*meersen*–on which sheep thrived. The wool from these sheep drove the trade that underpinned Ghent's wealth.

▲ **CITY GATE** Though the rivers surrounding Ghent acted as natural defenses, the city had a number of fortified gates. The one pictured here, astride a major point of entry to the river island, was effectively a small fortress. Charles V destroyed the city's gates following the Revolt of Ghent in 1539.

▼ **KORENLEI AND GRASLEI** The quays that flanked the Leie River—to the west, the Korenlei or Wheat Quay, and to the east the Graslei or Grass Quay—formed Ghent's most important port. The elaborate merchants' buildings lining the quays show the importance of trade to the city.

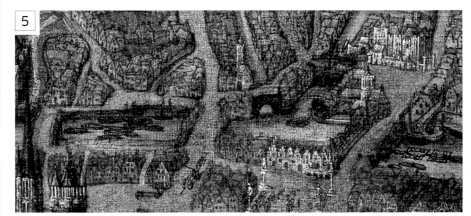

5

6

▲ **ST. JACOB'S CHURCH** The map shows Ghent's many imposing places of worship in an attempt to reflect its piety. The church of St. Jacob is among the oldest. Its 12th-century origins are seen in the two plain towers at the main entrance. A tall, 14th-century spire rises above the body of the building.

IN **CONTEXT**

Ghent became an important producer of wool cloth in the 11th and 12th centuries. The production of cloth for export to other cities began to be the driver of Ghent's economy, and the source of its political significance. The clothmaking industry became so huge that eventually the wool needed to create cloth had to be imported from England and Scotland, as demand exceeded what could be sourced locally. However, by the late 15th century, the cloth trade had begun to wane, and the city shifted its economy into the shipping that passed along the Leie and Scheldt rivers.

▲ **18th-century Flemish tapestry** of the *Triumph of Pallas*, by the weaver Urbanus Leyniers (died 1747)

7

▲ **ST. BAVO'S ABBEY** St. Bavo, patron saint of Ghent, founded an abbey on the island to the south of the city in the 7th century. It was later extensively rebuilt. Five years after this map was produced, Charles V had the abbey destroyed after the Ghent Revolt. A fortress, the Spanjaardenkasteel (Spanish Castle) was built in its place.

Marseille, 1754

JOSEPH RAZAUD ▪ HAND-COLORED ENGRAVING ▪ NATIONAL LIBRARY OF FRANCE, PARIS

SCALE

GEOMETRICAL MAP OF THE CITY, CITADELS, HARBOR, AND ARSENALS OF MARSEILLE

Military engineer Joseph Razaud (1685–1754) produced this map of France's second-largest city, and its largest Mediterranean port, from systematic surveys. It was a reflection of the growing trend toward the use of scientific mapping methods in mid-18th-century Europe: any forward-looking state needed precise data to exploit its resources efficiently. In France, this modernizing process was begun by Louis XIV who, in 1679, had the Royal Academy of Sciences draw up a map of his domain using the latest technologies for measuring terrestrial space.

Razaud's 1754 map—with the city's long, narrow harbor studded with shipping at its heart—shows the fortifications and other architectural additions made by Louis in the 1660s as part of his redevelopment of Marseille. This was a bid to exert greater control over the notoriously rebellious inhabitants, while also reinforcing the city's role as a center of Mediterranean commerce. The jumble of tiny streets to the north of the harbor is clear, as is the more ordered layout of the later districts to the east and south. All of the major buildings are identifed in the key. Yet, despite the rational spirit behind the map, its title still features a traditional flourish: a female sea deity flanked by mermen.

IN CONTEXT

▲ **Detail from French artist** Claude-Joseph Vernet's idealized view of Marseille's harbor, painted the same year this map was produced

With its 2,000-year history of trading in the Mediterranean, Marseille was France's most important port. During the 18th century, France attempted to cast itself as the heir to ancient Rome, with Marseille at the center of maritime commercial operations. Business in the city boomed, and by 1765, Marseille had established trade links as far afield as the New World.

France was also determined to challenge the growing naval dominance of Britain, and after the improvement of its coastal defenses, Marseille became the country's main naval port. By the end of the 18th century, Marseille had lost its naval preeminence in France to neighboring Toulon, which also had a large natural harbor, but commerce continued to grow and the port city came to serve a different role: as the key link between France and its most important colony, Algeria.

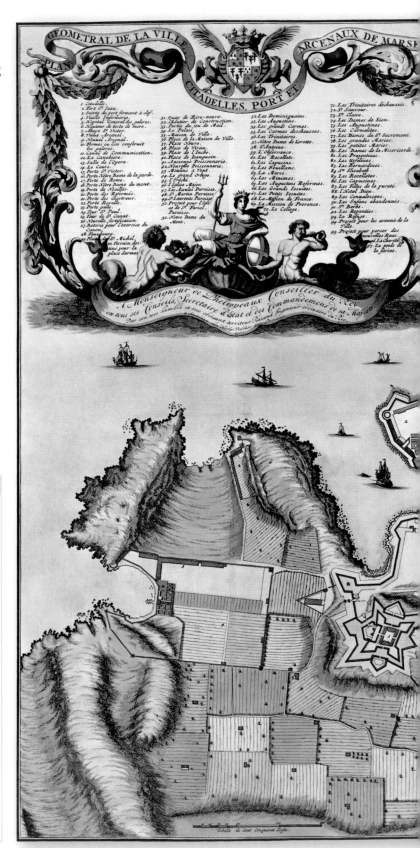

We noticed that the **inhabitants of Marseille** were extremely appreciative of **attractive fortresses.** We wanted to have our own at **the entrance** to this **great port.**

LOUIS XIV, ON BUILDING THE FORTS OF ST-JEAN AND ST-NICOLAS, 1660

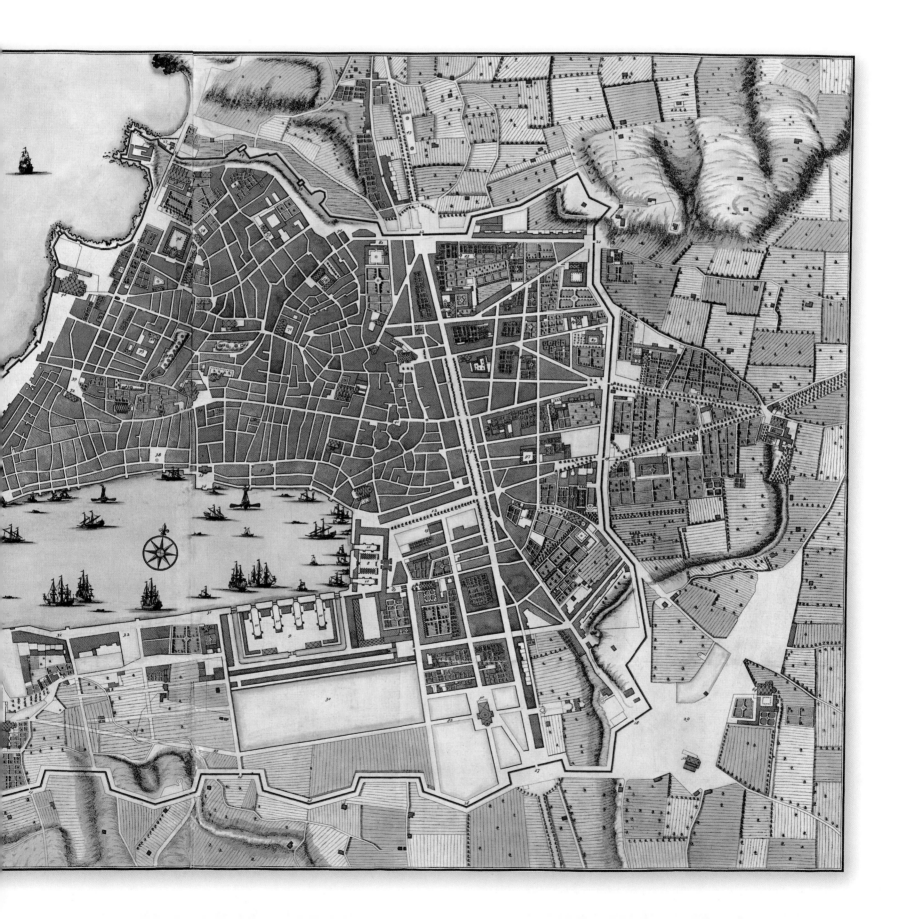

Visual tour

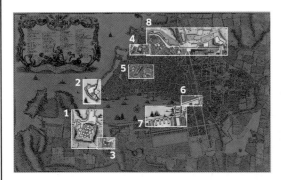

KEY

▶ **FORT ST-NICOLAS** In 1660, King Louis XIV's determination to strengthen Marseille's defensive capabilities was given concrete form by the construction of two formidable fortresses at the mouth of the city's harbor. The one guarding the southern entrance, Fort St-Nicolas, was an entirely new building, a substantial, star-shaped fortification also intended to underline the prowess of the Sun King himself.

▶ **FORT ST-JEAN** Looming over the northern entrance to the harbor, Fort St-Jean was built over a fortification founded in the 13th century by a religious military order, the Knights Hospitaller of St. John of Jerusalem, some elements of which were incorporated into Louis's new building. The purpose of both the St-Jean and St-Nicolas forts was not so much to protect the city from invaders as to deter its unruly inhabitants from rising up against the Crown.

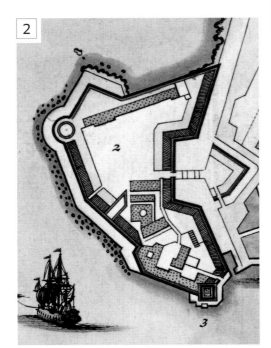

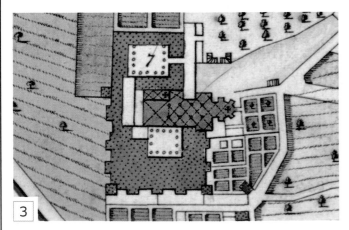

▲ **ST-VICTOR ABBEY** Named for a 4th-century Roman martyr, this fortresslike abbey is one of France's oldest Christian sites. Founded by the Romans in the 5th century, it was rebuilt in the 10th and 11th centuries as a Benedictine monastery. From 1739–51, the abbey was secularized, and later stripped of its treasures. It was returned to religious use in the 20th century.

▲ **LA VIEILLE CHARITÉ** A key example of Marseille's growing civic identity is provided by the substantial complex of La Vieille Charité, an almshouse (begun in 1671 and completed in 1749) to house the city's hordes of beggars. It is a deliberately imposing structure, with a substantial courtyard overlooking a monumental chapel. When Razaud completed his map, the building already housed more than 1,000 of the city's destitute citizens.

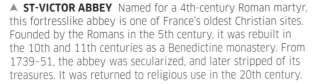

▼ **WINDMILLS** Razaud's map faithfully portrays a series of precisely aligned *moulins* (windmills) located in the highest areas of Marseille. These formed part of the city's defenses: in the event of a siege they could provide the Marseillais with flour to produce bread—the staple food of almost all French citizens at the time. The windmills are commemorated today by the Place des Moulins.

▼ **LA CANEBIÈRE** Louis XIV's 1666 expansion of Marseille included the laying out of a majestic tree-lined boulevard heading just over half a mile (1 km) northeast from the port. Its name, La Canebière, is a corruption of the Provençal word *canebe*, which means hemp— a reference to Marseille's thriving medieval trade in nautical rope, woven from hemp plants cultivated in the city's fields.

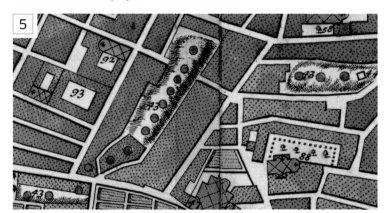

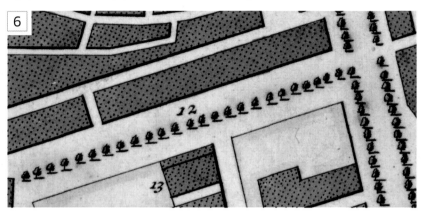

◄ **ARSENAL DES GALÈRES** This naval shipyard at the head of the harbor was founded in the second half of the 17th century to build and accommodate the royal fleet of *galères* (galleys), whose crew was made up of professional sailors, convicted criminals, and slaves. The shipyard was progressively abandoned from the end of the 18th century as the galleys were replaced by more modern military vessels.

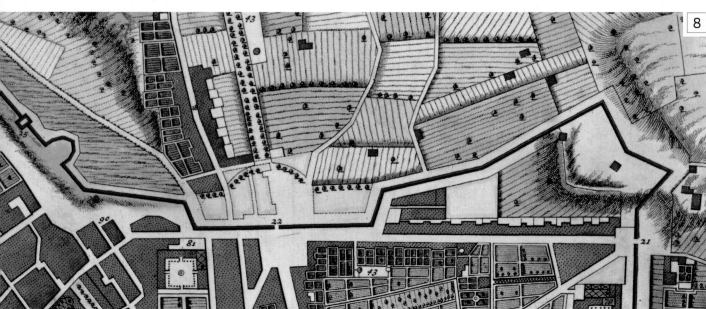

◄ **CITY WALLS** The strategic importance of Marseille to Louis XIV's aggressively assertive France was further emphasized by the construction of new defensive walls around the entire city. They were an unmistakable statement of bristling military intent.

Frankfurt, 1572

GEORG BRAUN AND FRANZ HOGENBURG ▪ HAND-COLORED WOODCUT ▪ NUMEROUS COPIES EXIST

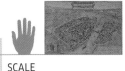

SCALE

THE CITY OF FRANKFURT AM MAIN

This view of Frankfurt, one of Europe's great trading cities, is taken from Braun and Hogenberg's *Civitates Orbis Terrarum* (*see p.48*). By the time the map was produced, Frankfurt was already established as an international mercantile center and commercial hub. It had two great trade fairs, one in the fall, which was established in the 12th century, and another in the spring that began in the 14th century. Both attracted merchants from across the entire continent. The huge variety of currencies circulating in the city in the late 16th century meant that official rates of exchange were soon established, a move that led directly to the city's first stock exchange.

Twin cities

The view shown here is oriented with northeast at the top and the Main River flowing from top to bottom. Across the river, on the south side, sits Frankfurt's smaller twin, Sachsenhausen. The two cities are linked by a single, multivaulted bridge. Both communities are shown behind extensive, moated city walls, the Main diverted around each to provide additional defenses. The most prominent feature in Frankfurt is the Cathedral of St. Bartholomew, its highly elaborate late-Gothic spire dominating the city. It was here from 1356 that the Holy Roman Emperor was elected by the empire's seven Electors— three archbishops and four lay rulers of the empire's kingdoms and realms. Farther to the left are the Römer and Goldener Schwan houses, which were used as the town hall. Over the river, the most prominent building in Sachsenhausen lies at the heart of the settlement—the mid-14th-century Church of the Magi. In 1525 it became the city's first Protestant cathedral.

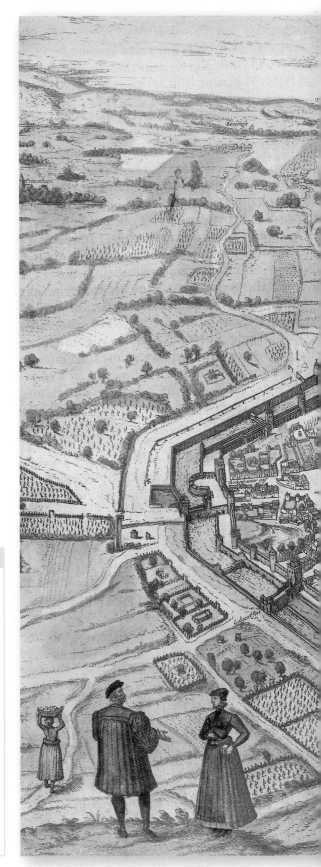

IN **CONTEXT**

▲ **The coronation procession of Maximillan II** in 1612, showing the future emperor parading toward the Cathedral of St. Bartholemew

The 18th-century French writer and wit Voltaire remarked that the Holy Roman Empire was neither holy, nor Roman, nor an empire. Yet for 850 years from 962, it managed to dominate much of Europe. Never a single coherent entity, the empire was a patchwork of states, large and small, over many of which the Holy Roman Emperor exercised only nominal authority. Frankfurt played a key role not merely as the site of the emperor's election, but from 1372, as an Imperial Free City under direct rule of the emperor himself, and from 1562, as the site of the emperor's coronation. The empire was eventually dissolved by Napoleon in 1806.

The **most famous trade city** in all Germany, very
well known amongst all the peoples of Europe;
the **Roman Emperor** is elected here…

99

GEORG BRAUN, FROM THE INSCRIPTION AT THE BOTTOM RIGHT OF THE MAP

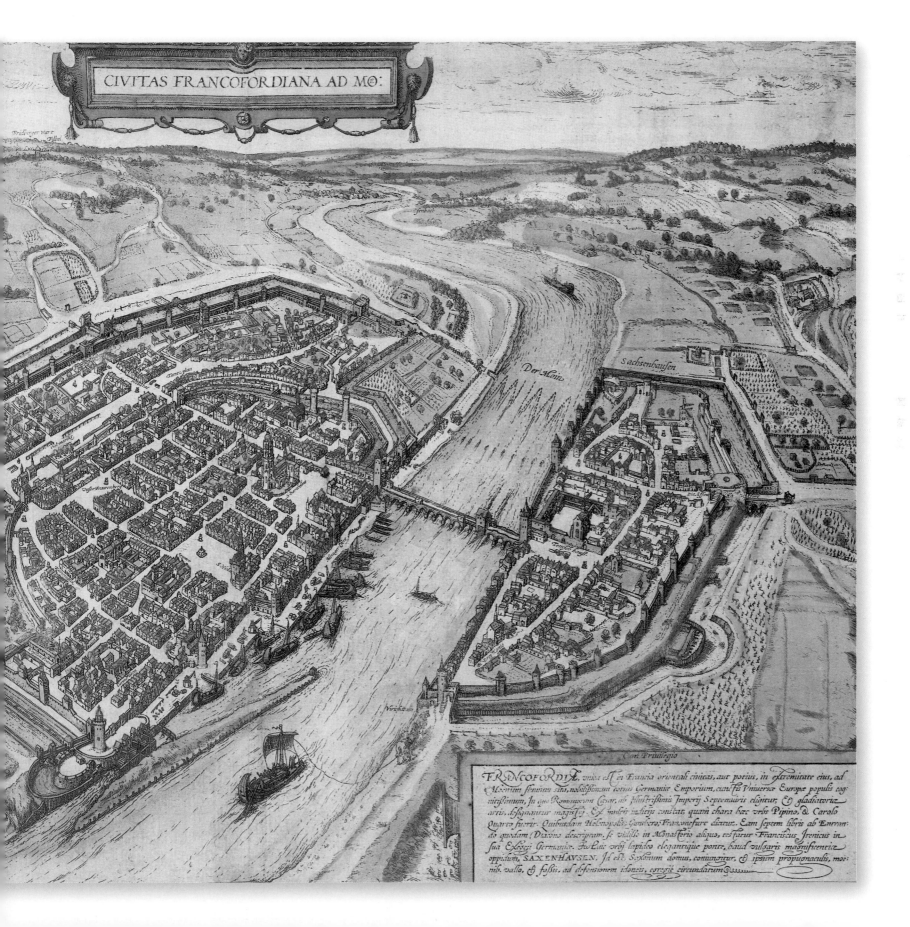

Wrocław, 1588

GEORG BRAUN AND FRANZ HOGENBERG ▪
HAND-COLORED COPPER ENGRAVING ▪
NUMEROUS COPIES EXIST

MAP OF WROCŁAW

SCALE

Built at the crossroads of two trade routes in the Silesian Lowlands of central Europe, the strategically important city of Wrocław (now in southwestern Poland) had been coveted by competing regional powers since its founding in the 10th century. At the time this bird's-eye view was made for the fourth volume of *Civitates Orbis Terrarum* (*see p.48*), the city of Wrocław was under Austrian Habsburg rule (before that it had been part of Bohemia and the Kingdom of Poland). Despite these frequent regime changes, by the late medieval period it was a prosperous economic and cultural center.

The map shows a large double-walled city set on islands in branches of the Oder River, upon which clearly differentiated districts had developed. Commercial activity was centered on the Market Square, or Rynek, in the heart of the city; political power was held in the immediate environs of the castle; and religious life was focused on Ostrów Tumski, or Cathedral Island—seen on the far right—which was the site of the original Slavic settlement. The keys in the lower corners of the map list 91 buildings and sites of interest in the city.

IN **CONTEXT**

Wrocław benefited economically from its close proximity to the Oder, one of central Europe's great waterways, and its favorable location at the intersection of two of the major overland trade routes in medieval Europe—the north-south Amber Road (along which amber from the Baltic and the North Sea had been transferred to the Mediterranean since pre-Roman times), and the east-west Via Regia (Royal Highway), which connected Santiago de Compostela in Spain to Moscow. In Wrocław's bustling Market Square, or Rynek, merchants from across Poland, Lithuania, and Russia traded their wares and forged business deals.

▲ **The Rynek, second oldest market square** in Poland after Kraków

1. Niclas thor
2. Reuſche gaſſe
3. Nicolaus gaſſe
4. S. Barbara
5. Burgvelt
6. Zeughaus
7. New ſpital
8. Kinder ſpital
9. Muhlpfort
10. S. Elizabeth
11. Oder thor
12. Oder gaſſe
13. Der rinck
14. Rathhaus
15. Kaufhaus
16. Wage
17. Fiſchmarckt
18. Saltz ringk
19. Saltz bauden
20. Roſmarckt
21. Muhle beim rade
22. S. Dorothea
23. S. Hieronimus
24. Creutzhoff
25. H. Leichnam
26. Schweidnitzthor
27. H. Dreifältigkeit
28. Schweidnitzegaſs
29. Schmiedebrugke
30. Kayſerliche brog
31. Kayſers thor
32. Newe Poſtey
33. New thor
34. Fiſcher pfort
35. Gerber pfort
36. S. Matthis muhl
37. Waſſerhaus
38. S. Matthis
39. S. Agnes
40. S. Clara
41. S. Vincentius
42. S. Marien thor
43. Zeughaus
44. Zum H. Geiſt
45. S. Clemens
46. Newſtat
47. Liggelthor
48. S. Bernhardin
49. Einſlus der Ole
50. Ketzelmuhle

WRATISLAVIA.

ODER

FLVV.

51	S. Albricht	72	Elbing
52	Albrichts gasse	73	Eilf 1000 bngfrau
53	S. Catharina.	74	S. Claren muhle
54	Newmarckt	75	H. Leichnams muhl
55	Heringbauden	76	S. Marien muhle
56	S. Maria Magdalē	78	S. Anna
57	Olische thor	79	der Sant
58	Olische gasse	80	der Thum
59	S. Christophorus	81	S. Petri vnd Paulj
60	Taschenthor	82	S. Martinus
61	Vor der muhlen	83	die Burgk
62	Wasserhaus	84	H. Creutz
63	Mittelmuhle	85	S. Ioannes
64	Maltzmuhle	86	Bischofs hoff
65	Schleiff muhle	87	Ziegelscheune
66	Brettmuhle	88	vor S. Mauritio
67	Hinter muhle	89	New begrebnus
68	Papyr muhle	90	Meuseteich
69	Burger werder	91	Saltzhaus
70	Schieswerder	77	S. Maria
71	Walckmuhle		

Visual tour

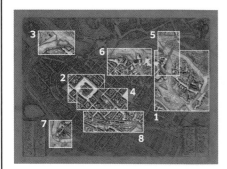

KEY

▶ **CATHEDRAL ISLAND** The Bishopric of Wrocław was established here in 1000 CE by the Polish king Boleslas the Brave, and subsequently the district's history was closely tied to Catholicism. Among the cluster of religious buildings is the Cathedral of St. John the Baptist (center right), its two great towers topped by tapering green spires.

▼ **THE RYNEK** The Market Square (Rynek) and much of the urban grid around it was laid out by city planners in the 1240s. It is dominated by one of the most sumptuous edifices of any central European medieval city: the Town Hall, or Rathaus, built over almost two centuries in a style known as Brick Gothic, in which red brick was pressed into service in the absence of local stone.

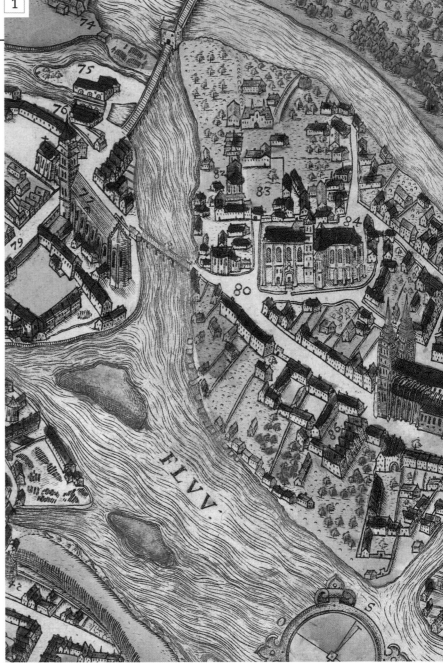

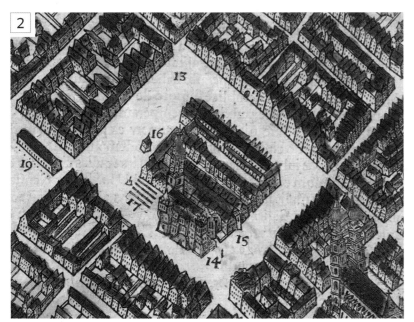

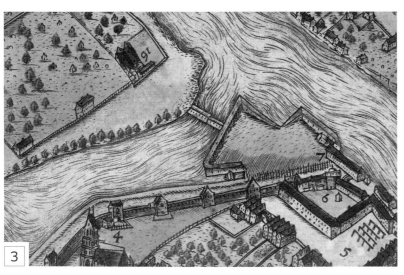

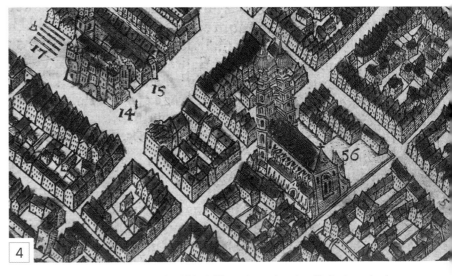

▲ **FORTIFICATIONS** Wrocław may have owed its existence to the natural defenses provided by the Oder River, but it remained vulnerable to incursions by hostile neighbours and defense was therefore a key priority. As with all medieval cities, it was surrounded by substantial defensive walls, shown here fronting the river.

▲ **ST MARY MAGDALENE CHURCH** This 14th-century church with its two sturdy square towers switched hands during the Reformation – the religious revolution that tore apart the Christian Church in the 16th century. It was taken over by Protestants, who returned it to the Catholic Church only after World War II.

▼ **THE AMBER ROAD** In Wrocław, two major trade routes, the Amber Road, pictured below, and the Via Regia (Royal Highway), crossed the turbulent Oder River, a formidable barrier that would not become fully navigable until the 19th century.

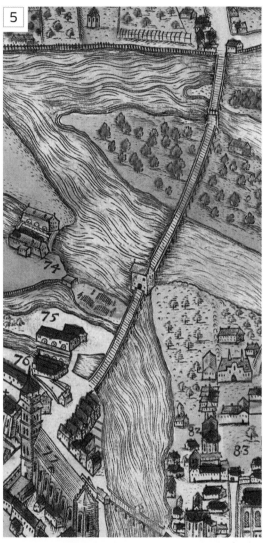

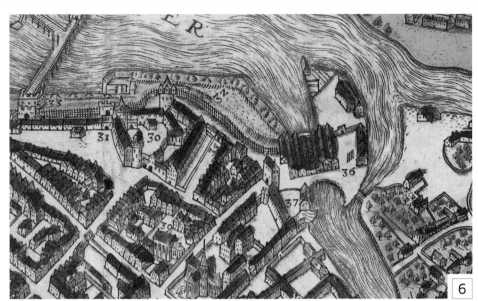

▲ **CASTLE** The construction in the late 12th century of a fortress overlooking the Oder River reinforced the creation of distinct districts within Wrocław: the one set around the castle was concerned as much with administrative and legislative affairs as with the security and defense of the city.

◄ **CHURCH OF CORPUS CHRISTI AND ST. JOHN'S HOSPITAL** These were constructed in the 13th and 14th centuries respectively by the crusading order the Knights of St. John, which was established in Poland in 1166. The church's façade, rebuilt in the 1400s, features a soaring, slender window under a gabled, high-pitched roof.

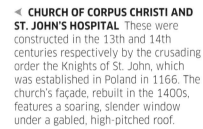

▲ **THE CITY MOAT** The Fosa Miejska, built in the early 16th century, was an integral part of Wrocław's defenses. The result of a deliberate diversion of the Oder to form a canal—in effect a moat—around the south of the city, its purpose was to enclose the city within a more readily defended core.

Lisbon, c.1740

MATTHÄUS SEUTTER ■ HAND-COLORED ENGRAVING ■ NUMEROUS COPIES EXIST

MAP OF LISBON

SCALE

There are earlier maps of Lisbon, but what gives this engraving by the important German mapmaker Matthäus Seutter of Augsburg particular resonance is that it was published shortly before the great earthquake that destroyed the city in 1755. Lisbon, one of the most prosperous and cosmopolitan centers of Europe at the time, had recently been further enriched by the exploitation of its colony in Brazil. Many opulent buildings had been commissioned in the Portuguese capital, as well as additions to the already magnificent royal Ribeira Palace, which can be seen on the waterfront.

The map views the city from a vantage point high above the Tagus River and illustrates the importance of Lisbon as an international trading center by including a number of merchant ships. The text in the lower panel—written in German— is a history of the city; this would soon need to be rewritten after the catastrophic earthquake.

IN **CONTEXT**

On All Saints' Day, November 1, 1755, one of the most powerful earthquakes in recorded history hit Lisbon. The first shock struck at 9:40 a.m., a second 20 minutes later, and a third at noon. It ripped wide fissures in the earth, and the shaking was felt as far away as North Africa. A devastating tsunami followed, together with raging fires that rampaged for six days. The city was almost totally destroyed, with thousands of buildings, including the Ribeira Palace and many churches, reduced to rubble. Of the city's 180,000 inhabitants at the time, it is estimated that between 30,000 and 60,000 died.

▲ **A huge tidal wave** drowned many of the city's population who were trying to escape the collapsing buildings beside the Tagus River

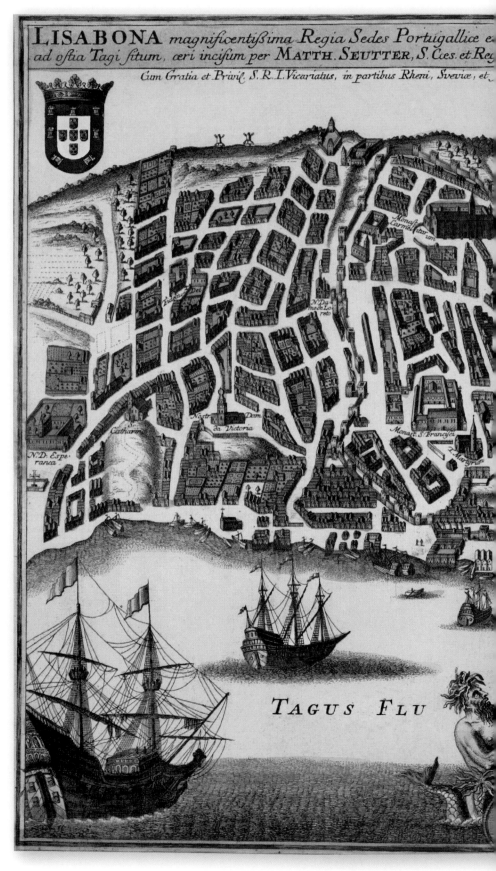

LISABONA *magnificentißima Regia Sedes Portugalliæ ad ostia Tagi situm, æri incisum per* MATTH. SEUTTER, *S. Cæs. et Reg.*

Cum Gratia et Privil. S. R. I. Vicariatus, in partibus Rheni, Sveviæ, et

TAGUS FLU

Did fallen Lisbon deeper drink of vice Than London, Paris, or sunlit Madrid? 99

VOLTAIRE, *POEM ON THE LISBON DISASTER*

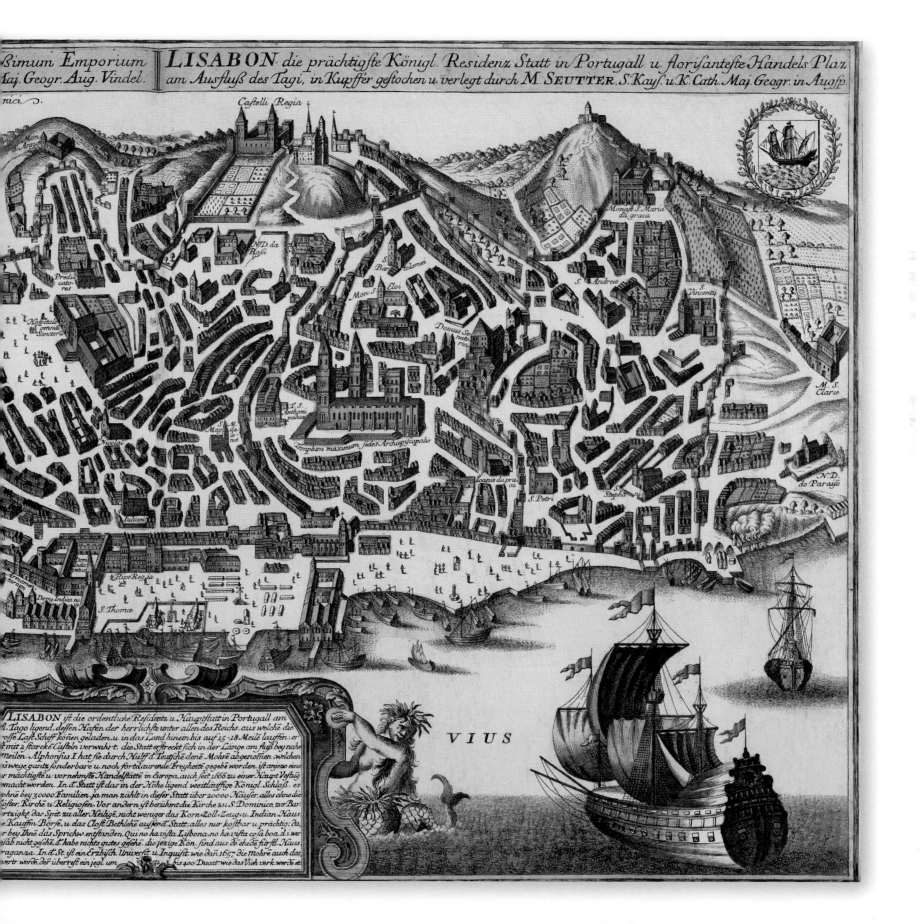

Lisbon, 1844

UNKNOWN ARTIST ▪ HAND-COLORED ENGRAVING ▪
NUMEROUS COPIES EXIST

SCALE

MAP OF LISBON

A former failed businessman, Charles Joseph Meyer (1796–1856) finally made his fortune when he founded what would become one of the most important German publishing houses of the 19th century, the Bibliographisches Institut. Meyer's output of books included his various "Hand Atlases," which were some of the most respected atlases of the time. Within these volumes, in addition to country maps, were dozens of city plans, such as this map of Lisbon. Meyer's atlases combined highly accurate cartography, rendered in exquisite detail, with etched panoramas on the lower half of the sheets.

   Meyer's map of Lisbon shows the city in its rebuilt form in the wake of the devastating earthquake of November 1, 1755. The most notable redevelopment is in the Baixa, the city center, just inland of what had been the Ribeira Palace. This was the area hit hardest by the earthquake and it was completely rebuilt, its formerly narrow twisting streets replaced by the grid of wide avenues and connecting streets depicted on the map. Curiously, the panorama beneath shows none of this new development as it is drawn from a point well inland, looking south over the city rooftops to the Tagus River. No information is given on the artist of the map, as Meyer typically compiled his maps from published sources.

Visual tour

KEY

▶ **PRAÇA DO ROCIO**
The long, wide avenues of the redesigned Baixa connected the Praça do Comércio with the city's other grand square, the Praça do Rocio. Here, the large All-Saints Royal Hospital, which had been destroyed in the earthquake, was replaced by fine civic buildings.

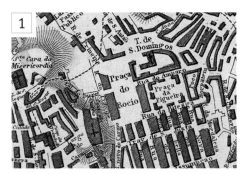

▲ **PRAÇA DO COMÉRCIO** The former Palace Square on the waterfront was redesigned as a new commercial center, flanked by large warehouses and commercial buildings. By the time of this map, the buildings were occupied by a naval yard, a stock exchange, and the customs building ("Alfandega").

▲ **CASTELO DE SÃO JORGE** This old medieval fortification, originally built by the Moors, was dedicated to St. George in the 14th century. Badly damaged in the 1755 earthquake, today it is one of Lisbon's main tourist attractions.

LISSABON
(LISBOA)
1844

MAASSTAEBE

LISSABON von der Quinta da Torrinha Val de Fereir

Barcelona, 1706

UNKNOWN ARTIST ■ HAND-COLORED ETCHING
ON PAPER ■ RIJKSMUSEUM, AMSTERDAM,
THE NETHERLANDS

SCALE

PLAN OF BARCELONA AND THE CASTLE OF MONTJUÏC

This anonymous French plan of Barcelona and the neighboring fortress of Montjuïc is as much an account of the unsuccessful French–Spanish attempt to seize the city in April 1706 as it is a map of the area. During the War of the Spanish Succession (1701–14)–a Europe-wide conflict waged by Britain, Austria, and the Netherlands to prevent French domination of the continent–Barcelona, a highly valued prize, had been seized by Britain and its allies the year before. The focus of the map is squarely on the military campaign that followed.

Although its walls are shown with precision, the city itself is represented largely schematically, with no attempt to depict even its most significant buildings. By contrast, the positions of the attacking French forces are shown in great detail, as is the fall of the French cannon and mortar shells. The panel in the upper right records, in French, the course of the campaign with equal attention, charting changing positions, marked by letters on the map, day by day. The arrival of the substantial British fleet is similarly shown. As is appropriate for a campaign map, the scale is given precisely, in the archaic measure known as *pas géométriques* meaning "geometric paces," each of which is equivalent to around 4 ft (1.6 m).

IN **CONTEXT**

▲ **British commanders watch** as Barcelona is bombarded during the siege of 1705

The unsuccessful siege of Barcelona between April 3 and 27, 1706, was in fact the second of three the city endured in the War of the Spanish Succession. For Britain and its allies, who took the city in the first siege of October 1705, Barcelona was a natural target. The city was valued not only as a thriving port, but also because its strong Catalan identity made it resentful of rule from Madrid. When Barcelona fell, the whole region of Catalonia fell with it. For France and Spain, its recapture was critical. That the French-Spanish force failed in 1706 was due to Britain's unchallenged naval dominance in the Mediterranean. But in the final siege of 1914, Barcelona fell to Franco-Spanish forces; Catalonia became part of the kingdom of Spain.

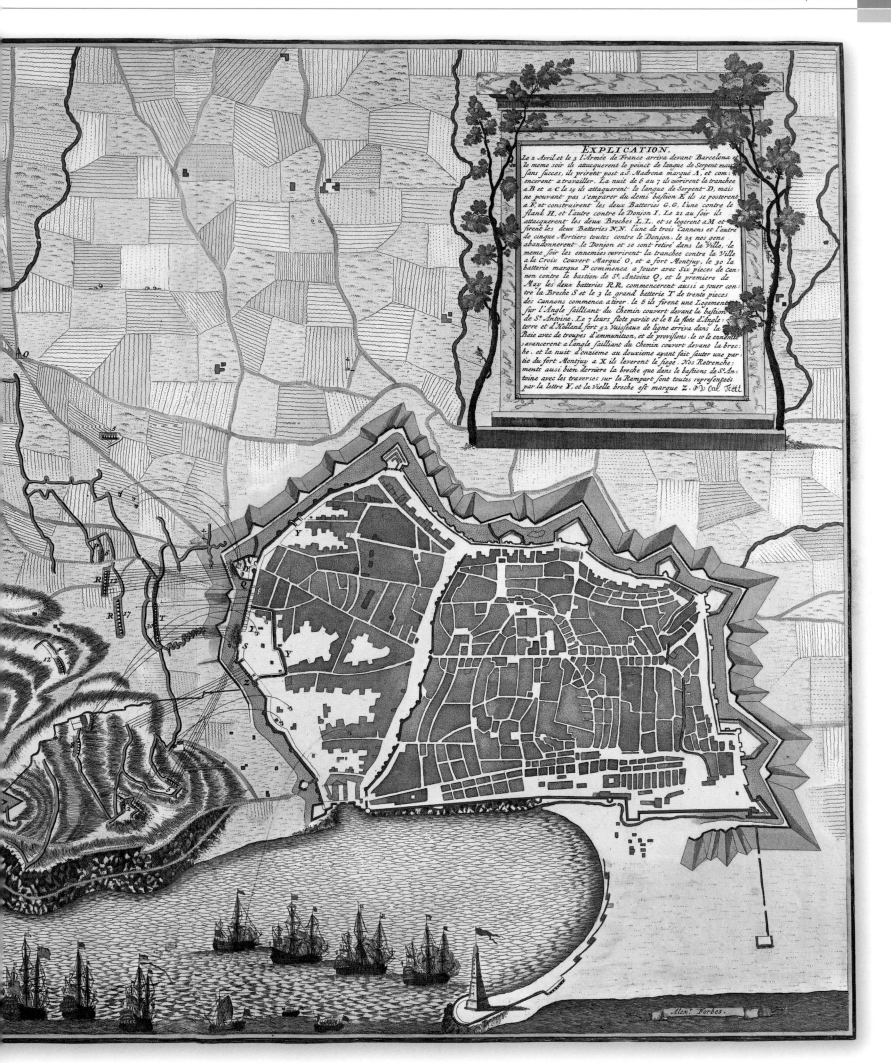

EXPLICATION.

Le 2 Avril et le 3 l'Armée de France arriva devant Barcelona et le meme soir ils attaquerent le poinct de langue de Serpent mais sans succes, ils prirent post a S. Madrona marqué A, et commencerent a travailler. La nuit de 6 au 7, ils ouvrirent la tranchee a B et a C le 15 ils attaquerent le langue de Serpent D, mais ne pouvant pas s'emparer du demi bastion E ils se posterent a F, et construirent les deux Batteries G, G, l'une contre le flank H, et l'autre contre le Donjon I, Le 21 au soir ils attaquerent les deux Breches L, L, et se logerent a M et firent les deux Batteries N, N, l'une de trois Cannons et l'autre de cinque Mortiers toutes contre le Donjon. le 25 nos gens abandonnerent le Donjon et se sont retire dans la Ville, le meme soir les ennemies ouvrirent la tranchee contre la Ville a la Croix Couvert Marqué O, et a fort Montjuy, le 30 la batterie marque P commenca a jouer avec Six pieces de cannen contre le bastion de St. Antoine Q, et le premiere de May les deux batteries R, R, commencerent aussi a jouer contre la Breche S et le 3 la grand batterie T de trente pieces des Cannons commenca a tirer. le 6 ils firent une Logement sur l'Angle saillant du Chemin couvert devant le bastion de St. Antoine. Le 7 leurs flote partit et le 8 la flote d'Angleterre et d'Holland fort 52 vaisseaux de ligne arriva dans la Baie avec de troupes d'ammunition, et de provisions. le 10 le ennemis s'avancerent a l'angle saillant du Chemin couvert devant la breche. et la nuit d'onzieme au douzieme ayant fait sauter une partie du fort Montjuy a X ils leverent le siege. Nos Retrenchements ausi bien derriere la breche que dans le bastions de St. Antoine avec les traverses sur la Rampart, sont toutes representés par la lettre Y, et la vielle breche est marque Z. D. V. Col. Hetl.

Alexr. Forbes.

Barcelona, 1910

F. NORIEGA ▪ HAND-COLORED ENGRAVING ▪ HARVARD
COLLEGE LIBRARY, CAMBRIDGE, MASSACHUSETTS, USA

UNKNOWN

GUIDE MAP OF BARCELONA

In the 1850s, the old medieval walls that surrounded Barcelona, the capital of Catalonia in northeast Spain, were torn down. The decision to remove them was based on the need to facilitate the growth of the city beyond its medieval area. From 1897, Barcelona expanded substantially, absorbing the town of Gracia and other outlying villages. This map, which color codes each of the districts of the newly expanded city, was produced just over a decade later.

While the original medieval core of the city with its tangle of tiny streets is plainly visible at the foot of the map—picked out in blue and brown—what is immediately obvious is the exact grid plan of the new city to the left, the top, and the right. Still known today as the Eixample ("expansion"), it was the most radical and ambitious example of late 19th-century urban planning in the world. Even if the original vision of its creator, Ildefons Cerdà (1815–76), would never be fully realized (*see box below*), it nonetheless led to an entirely new, ideal city. This updated Barcelona was rational, efficient, and logical—a fitting symbol of the most advanced industrial region of Spain. Although they are not shown on this map, the city benefited, too, from a series of exceptional buildings, products of a uniquely Catalan contribution to art nouveau architecture known as *modernisme*.

IN **CONTEXT**

In putting forward his plan for the new Barcelona, Ildefons Cerdà, a civil engineer rather than an architect, brought practical solutions to the problems of urban planning in an industrial age. He sought to create a model, modern city from scratch. A grid plan, orderly and regular, had obvious logical advantages, but Cerdà was no less concerned with quality of life. This meant more than proper sanitation and the two substantial diagonal streets he proposed to ease traffic flow—of which only one was eventually built. Cerdà was also concerned with adequate natural lighting and ventilation. He proposed that the corners of city blocks be angled to form a series of public spaces. Here his plan was followed, as can be seen on the map and in the shape of the city today (short-stay parking spots now frequently fill the triangular spaces formed by these angles). He also intended that each city block would only be built on three sides, leaving the fourth side open; and that the interior of each block would have gardens that spilled out onto this open side. However, these plans were never realized, as the commercial realities of the city's property market trumped the idealism of Cerdà's communal green spaces.

▲ **Ildefons Cerdà's vision** of octagonal city blocks, as seen in a modern-day aerial photograph of the Eixample

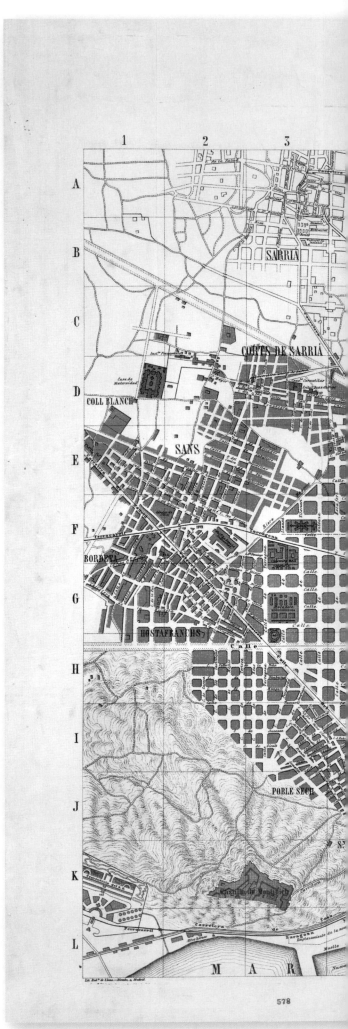

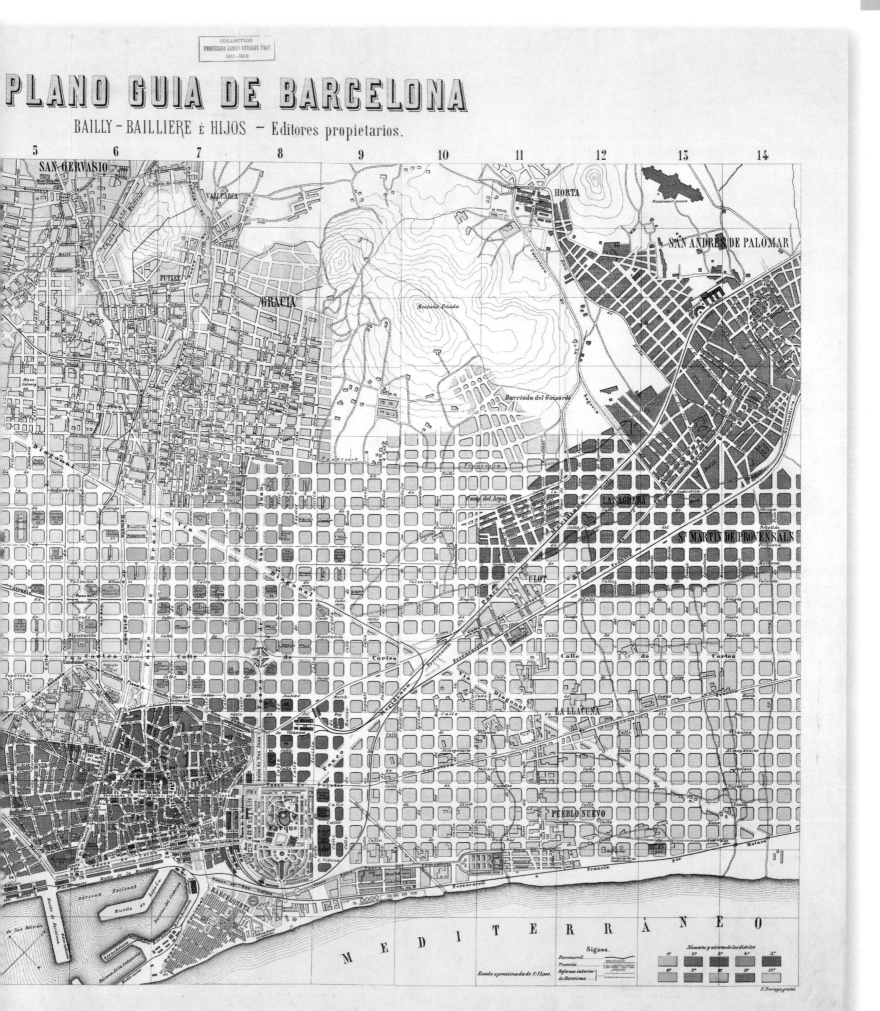

PLANO GUIA DE BARCELONA

BAILLY - BAILLIERE é HIJOS — Editores propietarios.

SAN GERVASIO

VALLCARCA

PUTXET

GRACIA

HORTA

SAN ANDRES DE PALOMAR

Montaña Pelada

Barriada del Guinardó

Camp del Arpa

LA SAGRERA

S.t MARTIN DE PROVENSALS

CLOT

LA LLACUNA

PUEBLO NUEVO

BARCELONETA

Parque

MEDITERRÁNEO

Signos.

Escala aproximada de 1:11.000

Número y colorado los distritos

Venice, 1575

GEORG BRAUN AND FRANZ HOGENBERG ▪ HAND-COLORED COPPER ENGRAVING ▪ NUMEROUS COPIES EXIST

SCALE

MAP OF VENICE

This view of Venice, the Serene Republic, published in 1575 in the second volume of Braun and Hogenberg's *Civitates Orbis Terrarum* (*see p.48*) depicts the city when it was perhaps just past the peak of its commercial and naval power. Venice was still, as it would remain for the next two centuries, a formidable force, yet its domination of trade in the Adriatic and West Asia, which had made it the richest city in Christendom and the most powerful republic in Italy, was already waning.

The map instantly highlights Venice's close relationship with the sea. The city was built on marshy islands in what was once a swampy lagoon; an unpromising terrain that actually made it easier to defend. From the 12th century, Venice prospered as the most important center of the trade in luxury goods between Europe and the Far East—silks and spices in particular. Over the centuries, the city saw the construction of increasingly opulent buildings on its many intertwined waterways and tiny backstreets, and the resulting fusion of architectural influences produced a series of fantastic structures. Yet all this is lost on the map—although all the principal buildings are shown, and are numbered and listed in its extensive key, the portrayal of them is formulaic. The exuberance of the part Arabic, part Gothic Doge's Palace, for example, is scarcely hinted at. In the same way, there is almost no attempt to show distances accurately. Nonetheless, the self-conscious majesty of the city is underlined by the illustration in the key below the map, which shows the doge (*see box below*), surrounded by officials, processing through St. Mark's Square.

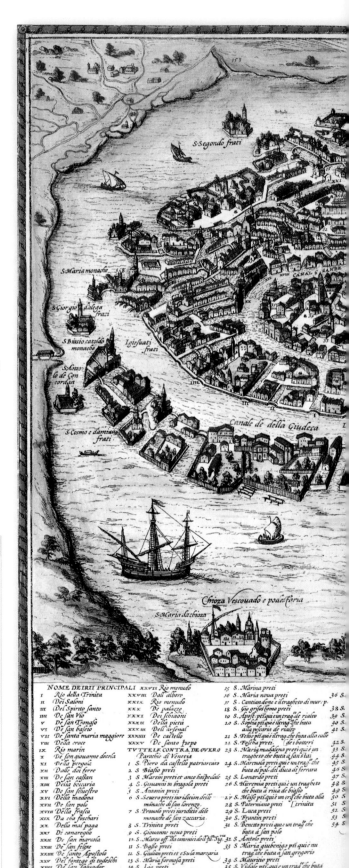

IN **CONTEXT**

▶ **The Doge and his council**, with scribes working below, in a detail of an illustration from a 15th-century French manuscript

The systems that formed the heart of Venetian government were in place as early as the 8th century. At its head was the doge, or duke. This was an elected position rather than hereditary office. Though the process through which the doge was chosen inevitably evolved over time, the goal was always to prevent the government from falling under the control of a single clique or family. By doing this, the Venetians strived to "defend the freedom and right of the people." In fact, from the 14th century the city was administered by a Council of Ten, elected by the nobility. This proved to be a remarkably stable system, enduring until the end of the republic's end in 1797, when Napoleon conquered the city.

Michelangelo. This is the city celebrated by the engraver and cartographer Francesco di Lorenzo Rosselli (1447–1513), who produced the *Pianta della Catena*, or "Chain Map" (so-called because of a decorative chain device that formed a border around the image).

The painting shown here is a faithful reproduction of Rosselli's original woodcut. Like other medieval maps before it, the *Pianta della Catena* celebrates the grandeur of architectural creation. What was different, however, was Rosselli's innovative use of the new drawing method of perspective. The artist also shows the city complete with all its buildings, streets, and squares, and this is the earliest detailed cartographic view of its kind known of any city. However, some buildings have still been exaggerated, notably the monumental "Duomo" cathedral and the rusticated Palazzo Vecchio, the city's major symbols of religious and civic power, respectively. These buildings were the source of lucrative commissions for freelance artists—and are therefore accorded due respect by the cartographer.

Visual tour

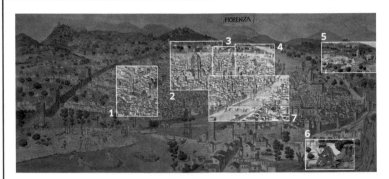

KEY

▼ **CATHEDRAL OF SANTA MARIA DEL FIORE** More commonly known as the "Duomo," the city's most famous building was begun in 1296 and consecrated in 1436 on the completion of its grand dome. Engineered by Brunelleschi, this audacious dome was higher and wider than any previously built.

▲ **BASILICA OF SANTA MARIA NOVELLA** One of the oldest Florentine churches, the basilica was begun in the mid-13th century, but not completed until 1470. It contained a wealth of artistic masterpieces, including Masaccio's *Trinity* (1424–25), one of the earliest paintings to demonstrate perspective.

▶ **PALAZZO VECCHIO** Part fortress, part palace, the Palazzo Vecchio was the seat of power in Florence from the early 14th century. The severe architecture concealed sumptuous halls within, notably the magnificent Salone dei Cinquecento, which was under construction at around the same time this map was drawn.

◄ **BASILICA OF SANTA CROCE** When construction began in the late 13th century, this church lay in marshy fields outside the city walls, but by the time of the *Pianta della Catena* it had been subsumed by the city. The basilica was patronized by some of the richest Florentine families, and its numerous chapels contained many magnificent frescoes.

4

IN **CONTEXT**

Painting styles before the advent of the Renaissance produced beautiful works of art, but these were all composed on a single plane, and there was little effort to create the illusion of three-dimensional space. Early Italian masters made some attempts at using shadowing to create depth, but the first known picture to properly use perspective was created around 1413 by the Florentine architect Filippo Brunelleschi (1377–1446). He painted the outline of Florence's Baptistery, the octagonal building in front of the cathedral onto a mirror, using "vanishing points," on which all the lines converged at eye level on the horizon. Soon afterward the concept of perspective caught on, and it became a common tool of Renaissance mapmakers, and indeed the basis for most representative art in Western culture.

▲ **The original woodcut** of the *Pianta della Catena*, which used perspective to highlight architecture

5

◄ **ABBEY OF SAN MINIATO AL MONTE** This Romanesque church was dedicated to the Christian martyr St. Minius, who is said, after his death, to have walked out of the city, across the river, and up the hillside, with his head tucked under his arm.

6

▲ **PORTRAIT OF THE ARTIST** The mapmaker included himself in the image, drawing from a high vantage point to the southwest of the city.

◄ **THE BRIDGES OF FLORENCE** Four bridges are shown on the map and named, from front to back, as the Ponte alla Carraia, Ponte Santa Trinita, Ponte Vecchio, and Ponte alla Grazie. All had been rebuilt several times over by the time this map was first produced, most notably following floods in 1333.

7

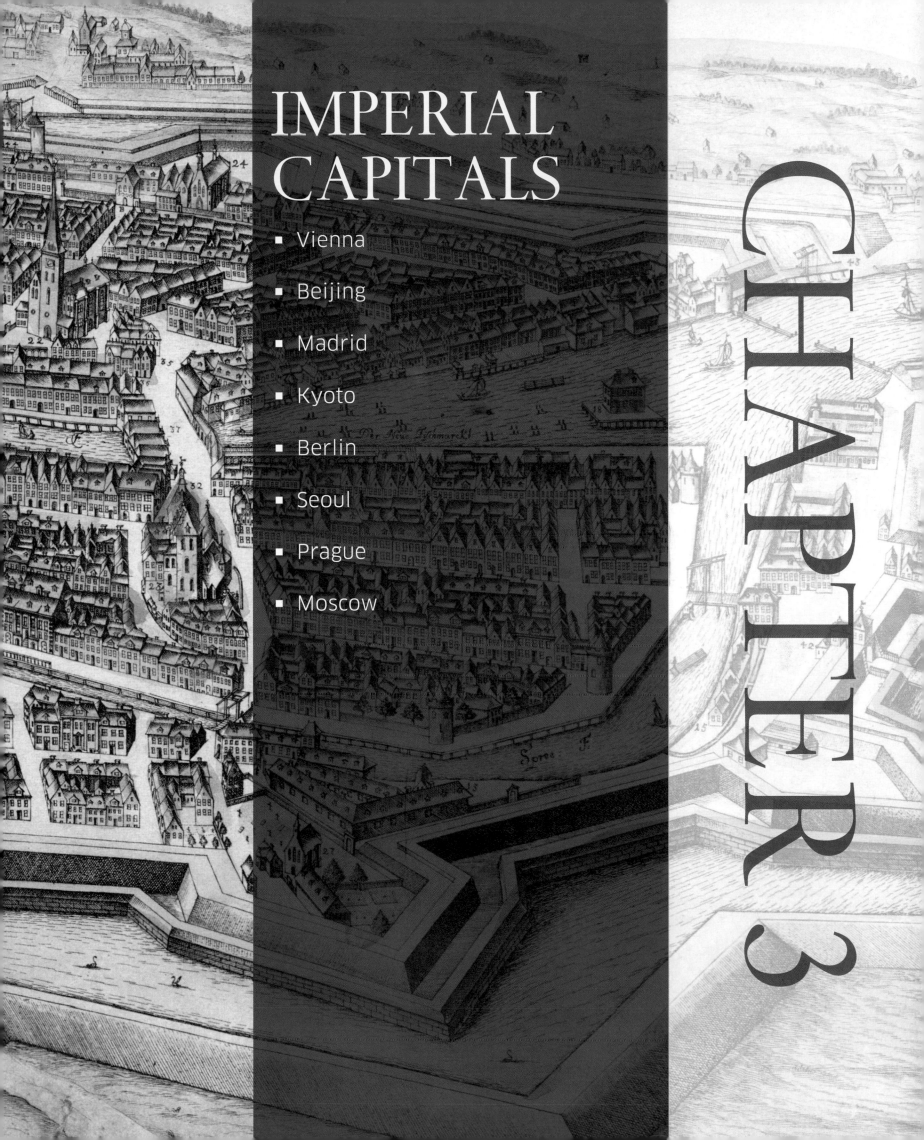

IMPERIAL CAPITALS

CHAPTER 3

Imperial Capitals

The founding, or redevelopment, of cities that embodied "empire" through the planning and design of their royal and public buildings, street names, and fortifications, was largely a European preoccupation. While the great imperial cities of Asia, such as Beijing in China and Kyoto in Japan, had evolved organically to meet the shifting needs of their rulers over time, many of those in Europe were built rapidly, with the specific goal of making it clear—both to their citizens and their overseas subjects—who was in control.

The first modern European imperial capital was Madrid, which was redeveloped into an architectural wonder by Philip II and his successors in the 16th and 17th centuries. Its glories, funded by the silver and gold extracted from Spain's colonies in the New World, were captured in a monumental map created by Pedro Teixeira Albernaz in 1656 (*see pp.136-39*), which was intended to exalt the kings of Spain and their capital. In the 17th century, Berlin, not yet at the heart of an empire, was redesigned by Frederick William, ruler of Brandenburg-Prussia, who

had lofty ambitions for the city. The map produced in the final year of his reign (*see pp.146-49*) is crowned by an oversized imperial black eagle—a symbol of the growing prestige of this impressively fortified royal seat.

While Berlin and Madrid both contained royal residences whose locations were dictated by the city's topography, China's capital, Beijing, revolved entirely around the vast imperial palace complex at its center—the Forbidden City, home of the emperors. In fact, Beijing had come into being only as a function of the Forbidden City—a relationship that maps of the city (*see pp.130-31*) made explicit.

A revolution in mapping

The preparation of reliable and accurate maps of these hubs of imperial power required the skillful interaction of surveyors and cartographers working hand in hand. During the 18th century, modern techniques and scientific instruments began to be used for surveying, especially in Britain and France. A growing demand for detailed military survey maps, naval charts, and topographic

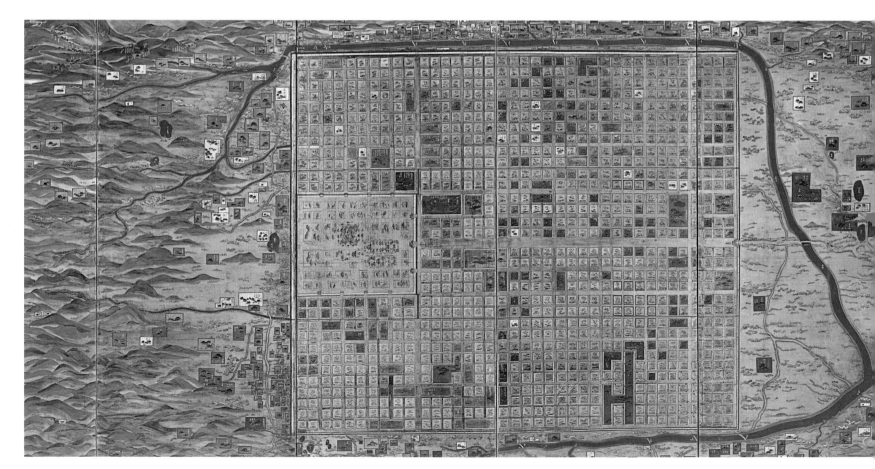

▲ **KYOTO, c.900-1100** The capital of Japan for more than 1,000 years (from 794 to 1868), Kyoto was modeled on the Tang Chinese capital of Chang'an (Xi'an) and conformed to the principles of feng shui. Over the centuries, the city's growth was carefully regulated using a strict grid plan, as can be seen in this 17th-century view.

surveys of new imperial territories (such as Britain's Great Trigonometrical Survey of India, which lasted from 1800 to 1913 and measured the entire subcontinent), enabled a greater degree of accuracy in the mapping of cities. These were increasingly rendered in a "bird's-eye" perspective, although Teixeira Albernaz and Italy's Giambattista Nolli had, much earlier, managed to create remarkably accurate overhead maps of Madrid and Rome (*see pp.22-25*).

The advent of scientific mapping

These technical advances are best seen in the maps of the imperial capitals Prague and Vienna (*see pp.128-29*) produced by Austrian military man Joseph Daniel Huber in the 1760s and '70s. Based on accurate surveys, they were executed in precise isometric projection (a drawing technique that distorts shapes to keep all upright lines vertical). Previously, most city maps had offered painterly impressions of their subjects, albeit often very good and convincing ones, but Huber's maps appeared to render the cities in exquisite miniature–at this time, even the

> ## Give me a map, then let me see how much / Is left for me to conquer all the world.
>
> **CHRISTOPHER MARLOWE,** *TAMBURLAINE,* 1587-88

largest cities were still small enough to be mapped in their entirety. The French cartographer Louis Bretez had used a similar technique to create his equally stunningly detailed map of Paris 30 years earlier (*see pp.198-201*).

Court cartographers also proved especially important in producing detailed city maps that promulgated the goals and ambitions of their royal patrons. These were often commissioned when Europe's imperial capitals were at the height of their power and influence. On a more pragmatic level they provided accurate street plans of not only new, but rapidly expanding, urban environments–maps that were of use to both royal and municipal administrators.

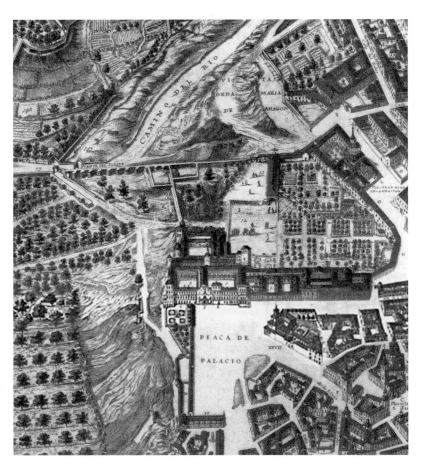

▲ **MOSCOW, 1617** An interesting example of a hybrid "bird's-eye" street plan and a medieval "view," this map from the *Civitates Orbis Terrarum* (*see box p.48*) shows the concentric growth of the Russian capital and its riverine defenses.

▲ **MADRID, 1656** The map produced by court cosmographer Pedro Teixeira Albernaz was created to be seen and interpreted: it was hung on a wall in the Royal Palace of Madrid, where it helped to convey a powerful message of empire.

Vienna, 1529

NIKLAS MELDEMANN ▪ COLORED WOODBLOCK PRINT ▪
VIENNA MUSEUM, VIENNA, AUSTRIA

SCALE

MAP OF VIENNA

As much a piece of reportage as a piece of cartography, this striking, circular map depicts Vienna under siege from an Ottoman army led by Suleyman the Magnificent. In late September 1529, the invading army was encamped outside the city, ready to attack, and Niklas Meldemann, a German printer and publisher, was eager to depict the story of the siege. At the center of the map is the city's major site of Christian worship, St. Stephen's Cathedral, which is shown in elevation. The original drawing on which the map is based is believed to have been made from the vantage point of the cathedral tower: the surrounding city and its hinterland are spread out from this central point. The area around the cathedral is left empty of buildings and filled with the pike-carrying ranks of the city's defenders.

Depicting the siege

Events from the whole month-long siege are combined into this one single image so that everything is happening at once: the map teems with people fighting, running, and manning the defenses. Landmarks and topographical details are roughly in the right places, but the cartographer's main goal seems to have been to convey the reality of the siege rather than the accuracy of the terrain. The projection, which approximates a view from on top of the cathedral, allows the viewer to see the inside face of the city ramparts, the walls pockmarked by cannon shot, and the gates barricaded with earth to keep out the attackers. To the northwest of the cathedral, a section of the wall has been reinforced with tree trunks. Brown earthen burrows represent the tunneling that had been undertaken by the Ottoman army in its attempt to circumvent the walls. Beyond the city fortifications, the suburbs are shown largely in ruins. Further in the distance are burning villages, razed by the Ottomans.

IN CONTEXT

▲ **Ottoman artillery unsuccessfully bombards Vienna** in a painting by the Flemish war scene painter Peeter Snayers (1592-1667)

The 1529 siege of Vienna lasted almost exactly a month. The Ottomans lacked the heavy artillery needed to breach the city walls; their attacks and mining operations were repeatedly thwarted; and the Austrians made successful counterattacks. When it did seem that the city might finally fall, the torrential rains that had been hampering the Turkish forces turned to snow. Unequipped for such conditions, the Ottoman army began a hurried retreat through deepening snowdrifts.

The German mercenary who led Vienna's defenders in the siege, Nicholas Graf von Salm, had been injured in the Ottoman's final attack and died soon after. Austrian emperor Ferdinand I commissioned a monument in his honor. Ferdinand's son, Maximillian II, later built the summer palace of Neugebäude on the spot where Suleyman pitched his tent.

Visual tour

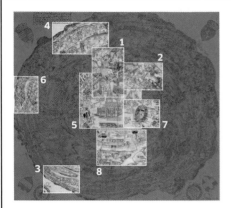

KEY

KEY

> **CARINTHIAN GATE**
Of the city's four main entrances, the Carinthian Gate (*Kärntnertor*) was the main focus of the Ottoman assaults. They attempted to blow it up with gunpowder placed in tunnels they had dug. In retaliation, the defenders put buckets of water and dried peas on the walls, so that when the walls shook, they would act as an alarm. Counter-miners would then start digging to intercept the Ottoman tunnelers.

▼ **THE HOFBURG** The red-roofed building with the three towers is the Hofburg, the imperial palace from which Austrian royalty had ruled as emperors of the Holy Roman Empire since 1452. Beside it is the Burgtor (Castle Gate), its defenses strengthened with makeshift mounds of earth and a hastily erected stockade.

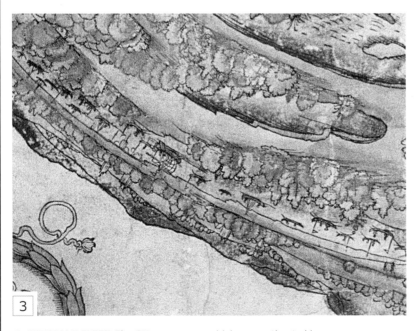

▲ **OTTOMAN FLEET** The Ottoman army, which was estimated by contemporary chroniclers to number anywhere between 120,000 and 300,000 men, was supported by a fleet of over 600 supply ships stationed on the Danube River.

▲ **TURKISH ATTROCITIES** Meldemann's map contained scenes of Turkish brutality, such as the gallows on the horizon and the men impaled on spikes and tied to wheels that can be seen to the lower left of center. The intention was to remind viewers of the map not to be complacent about the threat from the East.

5

◀ **ST. STEPHEN'S CATHEDRAL** Built in the mid-14th century on the remains of two earlier churches, the cathedral, which was the city's highest building, was also the headquarters of those defending the city. A building crane is shown on the unfinished North Tower.

▼ **SULEYMAN'S HEADQUARTERS** At the center of an Ottoman encampment on the far left of the map is a tent that is visibly far larger than all the rest: the headquarters of Suleyman himself. The tents of his chief minister—the Grand Vizier—and of his most senior military commanders, would have been close to the sultan's pavilion. The entire complex is surrounded by a hung screen for privacy.

6

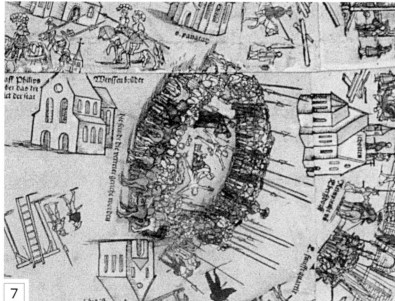

7

8

▲ **INTERROGATION** This detail appears to show the interrogation of two prisoners. They lie, stripped, at the center of a circle of pike-wielding soldiers, and are being attended to by a man with a knife and two cross-wielding clerics. A gibbet with two waiting ropes stands nearby.

▲ **CITY WALLS** Vienna's medieval city walls proved inefficient during the siege. As early as 1530, work was undertaken to build modern fortifications and bastions, including the provision of a wide strip of land around the city to be kept clear of construction.

Vienna, 1769–73

JOSEPH DANIEL HUBER ▪ PEN-AND-INK DRAWING ▪
ALBERTINA MUSEUM, VIENNA, AUSTRIA

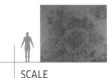

SCALE

BIRD'S-EYE MAP OF THE CITY OF VIENNA WITH ITS SUBURBS

Maps are drawn for a variety of purposes: to catalog territorial acquisitions, aid military strategy, support plans for urban regeneration, or to promote towns and cities, for example. This map of Vienna was commissioned by Maria Theresa, the Habsburg Holy Roman Empress and Archduchess of Austria (reigned 1740–80), probably to facilitate city planning. Although Vienna's massive fortified walls had played a crucial defensive role in the past, by the late 18th century they were hindering the city's development by obstructing traffic between the inner and outer districts. The empress needed a detailed map to examine how to resolve the problem.

A royal commission

By chance, a major in the Austrian army, Joseph Daniel Huber (1730–88), presented Maria Theresa with a fine bird's-eye map of Prague he had drawn, and she was sufficiently impressed to ask him to create a similar map of the imperial capital. Huber began work in May 1769. Four years later, he presented the completed pen-and-ink drawing to the empress. It covered 24 sheets and showed not only the city center but also the surrounding suburbs. Huber sought permission to publish the map, which was eventually granted, and the work appeared in commercial form in 1778. However, it was not a financial success, and Huber lived out his last years in poverty; he pawned the copper plates used to print his map and they were sold for scrap after his death. His original line drawings survive in Vienna's Albertina museum.

IN **CONTEXT**

▲ **A colored detail** of Huber's map revealing his basic method of depicting 3-D objects in two dimensions

Huber's map is drawn in "military perspective," a variation of a simple method of technical drawing known as "oblique projection." The objects are not in perspective—they do not diminish in size as they get farther away, and sight lines do not converge on a single point. Instead, lines are drawn at a consistent angle to represent depth. Military perspective takes a ground plan as its base, but adds vertical lines to represent height. The vertical lines are to scale, so the map shows the true relative heights of the buildings.

In China, mapmakers were employing the oblique projection technique as early as the 1st and 2nd centuries CE to depict rectilinear objects such as houses and temples. French military artists adopted their own version of the technique in the 18th century, which became known as the "cavalier projection."

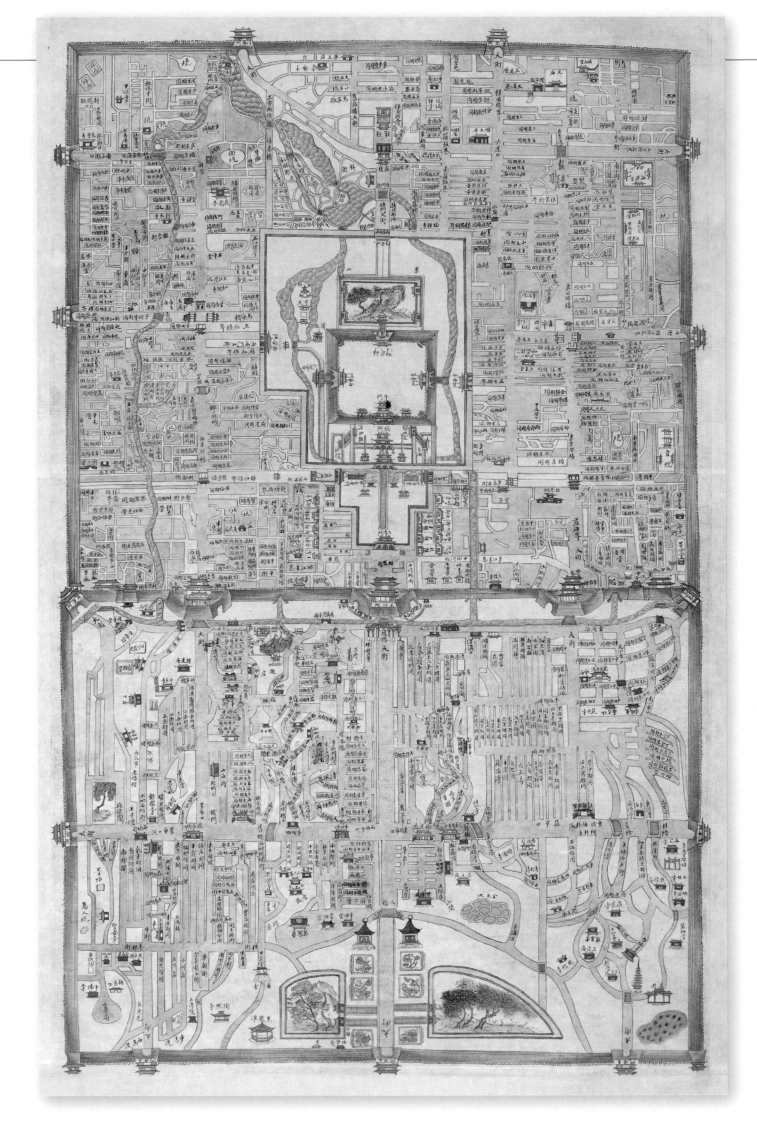

Beijing, c.1800

UNKNOWN ARTIST ▪ PEN AND INK ON PAPER ▪ THE BRITISH LIBRARY, LONDON, UK

MAP OF BEIJING

This manuscript map of Beijing (also known as Peking or Peiping) was based on a survey conducted during the 18th century during the reign of the Qing Dynasty emperor Qianlong (reigned 1735–96). This was a time that marked the height of imperial power in China, when the empire was extended to its farthest reaches and Beijing was one of the most powerful cities in the world. The map is somewhat confusing: in some sections builtup areas are shaded with the roads left uncolored, while in other sections this colouring is reversed. However, what the map does show clearly is the system of grids and symmetrical walled compounds on which the city was planned, which was based on strict cosmological principles.

Located right at the heart of Beijing is the palatial compound of the Forbidden City, ringed by the walls of the Imperial City beyond. Surrounding these walls is the Inner City, which is in turn enclosed by a further set of almost perfectly square walls.

South of the Inner City is the Outer City, which is laid out in a similarly symmetrical fashion along a prominent north-south axis that runs through the center of the Forbidden City. The precise planning was designed to reinforce the might of the emperor and his government, who were placed at the nucleus of the city. In its simple grid design, the city itself provided the template for the ordering of the imperial capital's social structure.

Visual tour

KEY

▶ **FORBIDDEN CITY** At the heart of the map is the imperial palace, clearly structured as a diagram of court hierarchy. Its series of courtyards and halls become increasingly more private. The emperor—who was accorded the title "Son of Heaven"—sat at the very center of this model.

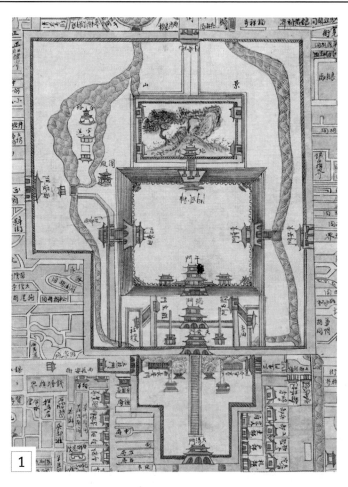

1

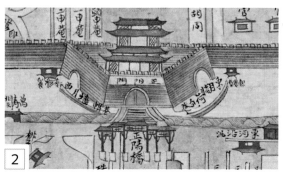

2

▲ **QIANMEN** Drawn in delicate detail, this great central gate was set in the huge, 30ft- (10m-) thick southern wall of the Inner City and flanked by two other great gates. The idea of a trio of gates was intended to represent the elements of the universe: heaven, earth, and man.

3

▲ **YONGDINGMEN** Each gate had a function, according to the traffic that was allowed to enter through it. The gate of Yongdingmen detailed here, at the middle of the Outer City's southern wall, was primarily for traders, with many street markets between here and Qianmen.

Beijing, 1936

FRANK DORN ▪ **FOLDOUT PICTORIAL MAP** ▪ **NUMEROUS COPIES EXIST**

SCALE

A MAP AND HISTORY OF PEIPING

Frank Dorn's pictorial map of Beijing (a city also known historically as both Peiping and Peking) may play fast and loose with scale and lack geographical accuracy, but it is nevertheless a highly educational map. His purpose in producing it was likely to instruct his fellow Americans in China on the history and culture of the imperial capital.

The map was sold inserted inside a 22-page booklet bearing the same title, and has a border that summarizes the basic chronology of the city's history in a series of playful annotated images. From the center top to the top right of the map, the initial sequence of images is a picture of a delivery stork (labeled "Birth of original Chou city..."), followed by a boy kicking over a pile of building blocks ("which was destroyed many times..."), followed by another boy carefully piling them up again ("but which was always rebuilt...").

Inside and outside the city walls

The map shows the whole of the city enclosed within its ancient fortified walls, which at this time were still largely intact. The area inside the walls, if not quite to scale, places the roads, parks, lakes, and monuments in roughly the correct locations. The artist covers the map with a dense array of amusing pictorial vignettes illustrating both the main sites and the local populace of Beijing engaged in all manner of employment; from depictions of rickshaw haulers and beggars to traffic policemen and even an executioner.

The map also doubles as a practical guide for the foreign visitor, with small labels in white boxes indicating essential businesses such as hotels, clubs, souvenir and

curio sellers, and a money exchange. Particular attention is also given to amenities of interest to more long-term resident Westerners, such as the race course, two golf courses, and the duck-shooting opportunities situated just to the west of the city walls.

It is here, outside the city, that the artist abandons all notions of scale and accuracy. Dorn places the Summer Palace close to one of the city gates, when in reality it is some miles from the city. Into the top left corner he squeezes the Great Wall and the Ming Tombs, both of which are much more distant than they are shown, although, as indicated, they do lie to the northwest. Signposts placed around the edges of the map point to further areas that may be of interest to the foreign visitor and resident alike.

FRANK **DORN**

1901–81

Born in San Francisco, Dorn spent three years studying at the city's Art Institute before attending the US Military Academy at West Point, New York.

As a US Army officer, Dorn spent the greater part of his career in Asia. After a spell in the Philippines he was moved to Beijing in 1934, where he served as an army attaché gathering intelligence on Japanese aggression against China. His drafting talents found a ready subject in this new posting, where he created this pictorial map. Dorn's plan of the city owes an obvious conceptual and visual debt to the cartoon-cartographic style of the remarkable Uruguayan painter, muralist, and cowboy Jo Mora (1876–1947), who resided in California in the US from 1907, and who produced several illustrated maps. Dorn left China in 1938, and during World War II he served in Burma (now Myanmar). He retired from the military in 1953, and returned to San Francisco, where he devoted the remainder of his life to painting and writing; he authored several novels and cookbooks, as well as a history of Beijing's Forbidden City.

> The **first result** of my researches was a **pictorial map** of Peking, after which I was **completely hooked** on the whole fascinating subject.

FRANK DORN, *THE FORBIDDEN CITY: THE BIOGRAPHY OF A PALACE*, 1970

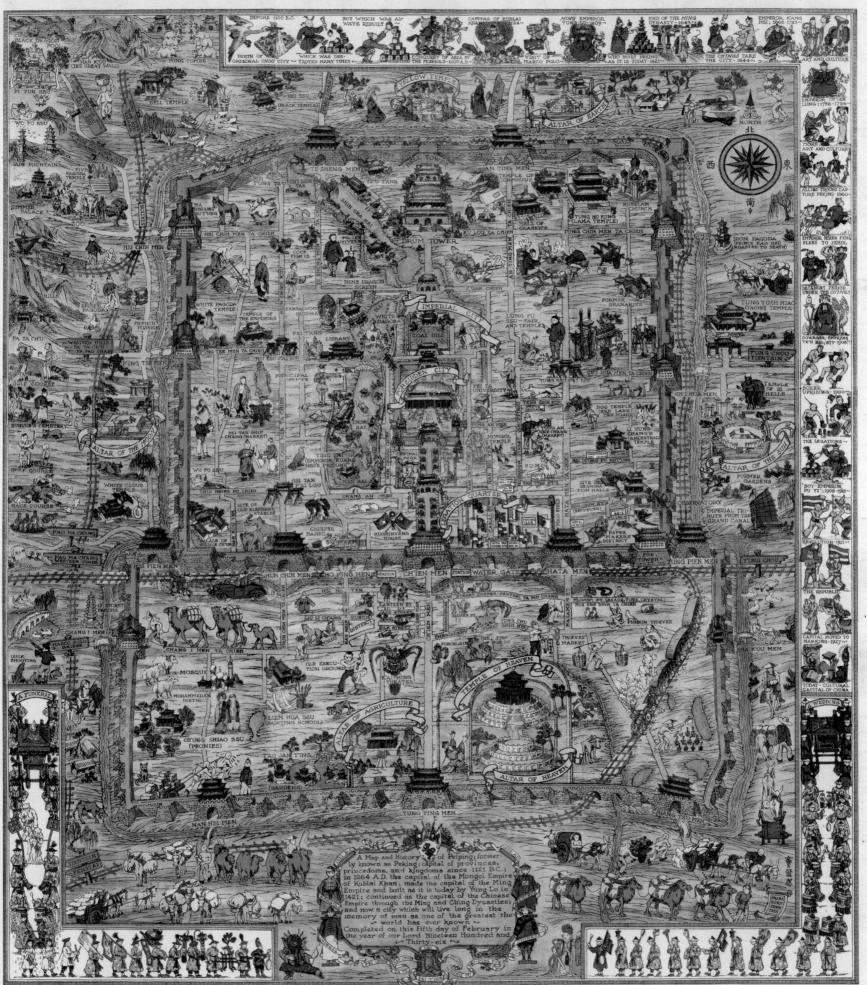

PEIYANG PRESS. LTD. TIENTSIN-PEIPING.

Visual tour

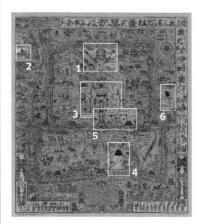

KEY

▶ **BELL AND DRUM TOWERS** In Dorn's drawing the two separate towers almost appear as one. The two-story Drum Tower is in front, capped by a straw-colored roof, with the two pink stories of the Bell Tower behind it. The pair are beside a popular leisure lake—the chopsticks and tea represent the many cafes in the area.

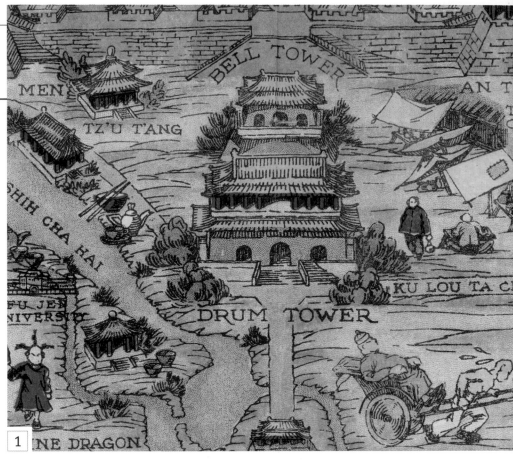

▲ **SUMMER PALACE** Dorn cheats the scale of his map here; the Summer Palace is 6 miles (10 km) west of the city, which places it far beyond the limits of his map. However, as one of Beijing's most important and most-visited sites, he could not possibly exclude it. The animals to the right represent the zoo that visitors would pass on the way to the palace.

▶ **THE FORBIDDEN CITY** The depiction of the central palace complex is highly detailed, illustrating all the major structures. In the south is the Meridian Gate, facing onto the tree-filled square now know as Tiananmen. Progressing from here through the Gate of Supreme Harmony leads to the vast Hall of Supreme Harmony, with the northern Gate of Heavenly Purity behind.

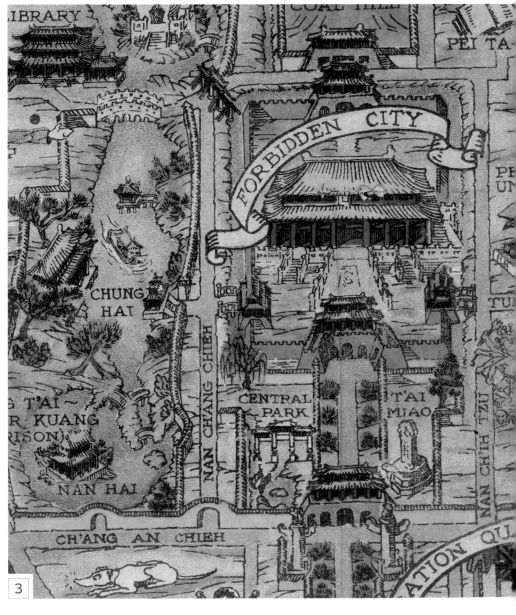

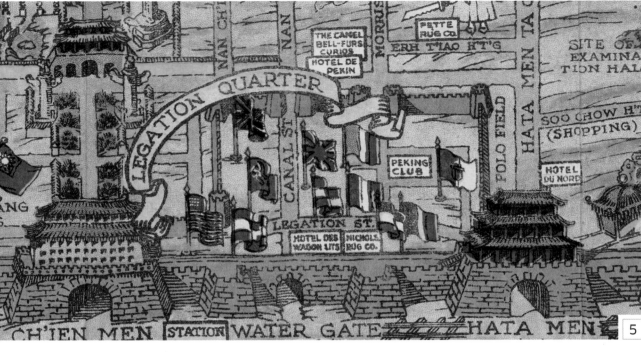

5

6

4

▲ **THE TEMPLE AND ALTAR OF HEAVEN** These two monuments, part of a single complex, appear disproportionately large on the map, which perhaps suggests that this was a place in which foreigners in 1930s Beijing liked to spend time. The complex was—and still is—a beautiful area of parks and gardens, a place in which to find some peace and solitude in the teeming city.

▲ **LEGATION QUARTER** Following the end of the Opium War in 1860, foreign delegations were permitted to take up residence in this district. Consequently, it became home to many Western businesses, including hotels and clubs. As a US officer, it is likely that Dorn would have spent a lot of time here.

▲ **TEMPLE OF 18 HELLS** Dorn enjoyed highlighting curiosities on his map. The "Temple of 18 Hells" sounds much more enticing than Dongyue Temple, which is the name it is otherwise known by. Other intriguingly named places on the map include the "Eunuch's Cemetery" and the place of the "Pigeon Thieves."

IN **CONTEXT**

Throughout history, mapmakers have integrated pictorial elements into their work—for instance, by drawing ships in an otherwise empty area of sea. From the 1920s onward, however, there was a new trend to bring these pictorial elements to the forefront of mapping, with the cartography sketched in as a backdrop. This was a direct result of the rapid growth of mass tourism; travel—previously the preserve of the wealthy, educated elite carrying their worthy Baedeker guidebooks—was now open to all. The dawning age of tourism was about fun and leisure, and these new whimsical maps reflected this change.

▲ **William Gropper's map** *America, Its Folklore* (c.1946) with characters from American tales and legends superimposed onto an outline of the United States

Madrid, 1656

PEDRO TEIXEIRA ALBERNAZ ▪ HAND-COLORED WOODBLOCK ▪ NATIONAL LIBRARY OF SPAIN, MADRID

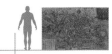

MANTUA CARPETANORUM, OR ROYAL CITY OF MADRID

SCALE

In the Middle Ages, Madrid was an unimportant and remote market town in central Spain that had grown up around a Moorish Alcázar (fortress). But in 1561 King Philip II, attracted by the town's obscurity and lack of connections, relocated the royal court to the town, kickstarting a gradual transformation of its street plan and infrastructure that continued until the 18th century under his successors. This fine, highly accurate 17th-century map of the city, which by this time was Spain's capital and the heart of its global empire, was created by Pedro Teixeira Albernaz, a cosmographer in service to the royal court. It clearly shows the city's medieval core and the grand urban development that had since taken place around it.

A cartographic celebration of a regal city

The Plaza Mayor, the large square seen in the center of the map, was built in the early 17th century to provide Madrid with a center for trade and the staging of important events. Around the same time, the medieval city walls were replaced with new ones, complete with grand fortified gates; Teixeira's detailed rendering allows the viewer to scrutinize these, along with private gardens, tree-lined promenades, and curving streets, many of which are named. He also depicts all of Madrid's parishes, its monasteries and hospitals, including their names in an index, while major monuments are itemized in the lower-left corner of the map. Madrid was founded on rich farmland, and many parks, market gardens, and orchards—seen around the perimeters of the map—were developed outside the city.

PEDRO **TEIXEIRA ALBERNAZ**

c.1595–1662

Born to a notable family of Portuguese cartographers, Pedro Teixeira Albernaz worked in Spain from 1610. He served as court cosmographer to Philip III and his successor, Philip IV, creating two works on an ambitious scale for the Crown.

In collaboration with his brother João, Teixeira Albernaz produced, in 1634, the enormous *La descripción de España y de las costas y puertos de sus reinos* (*The Description of Spain and of the Coasts and Ports of Her Kingdoms*), which comprised nautical surveys and plans of harbors and coasts. His overhead map of Madrid, which blended cartographic science with artistic flourishes, was first printed in black and white in 20 individual folios. It shows evidence of very detailed measurement and surveying, and the application of the skills required in nautical charting. As an authoritative city map, it remained unsurpassed until Giambattista Nolli produced his map of Rome a century later (*see pp.22–25*).

I left Granada, and I came to see the great city of Madrid, this new Babylon, where you will see varieties and hear tongues to confuse the most subtle wit

PEDRO CALDERÓN DE LA BARCA, FROM HIS PLAY *EL HOMBRE POBRE TODO ES TRAZAS*, 1641

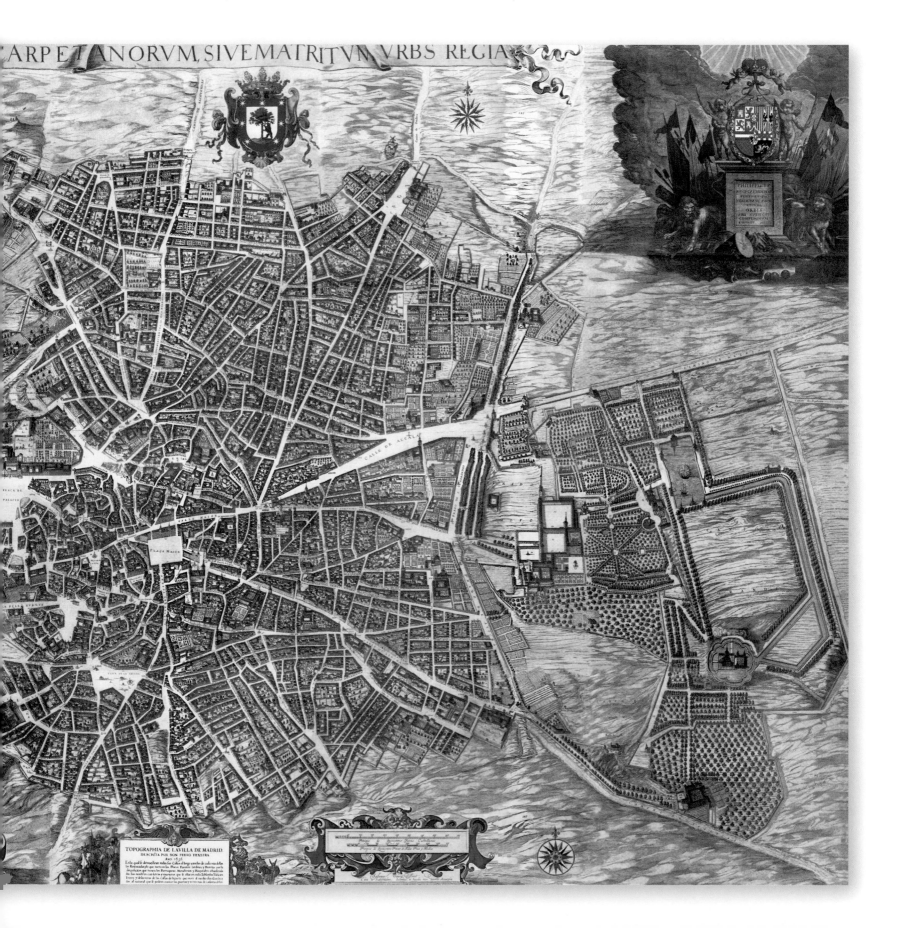

Visual tour

KEY

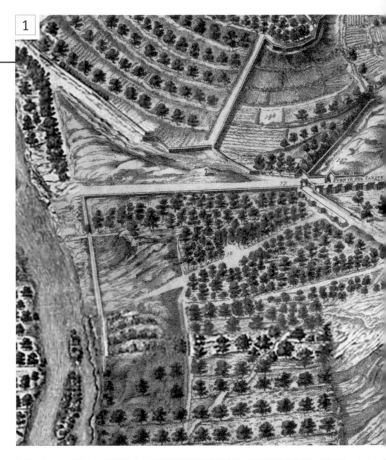

▶ **THE ALCÁZAR** The former Moorish fortress, with its ornamental gardens, was set on the western edge of the city, at its highest point. When King Philip II extended the site as a royal palace, he created large plazas to its east and south.

▼ **WEST OF THE ALCÁZAR** The gardens and orchards running down the steep incline to the Manzanares River, and across on the west bank, provided a suitably regal and uninterrupted view from what would eventually become Madrid's royal place, the Palacio Real.

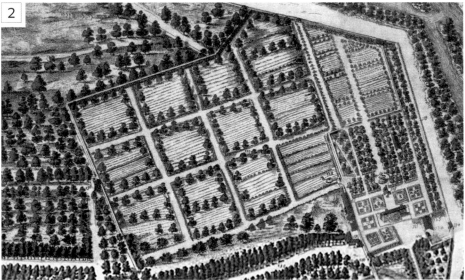

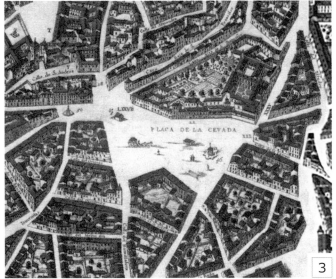

▲ **THE ARABIC QUARTER** The southwestern section of the city comprised the original Moorish (Arabic) quarter, which, in spite of Philip II's reorganization, retained much of its original cultural and topographic qualities. The narrow streets and markets seen here still remain today.

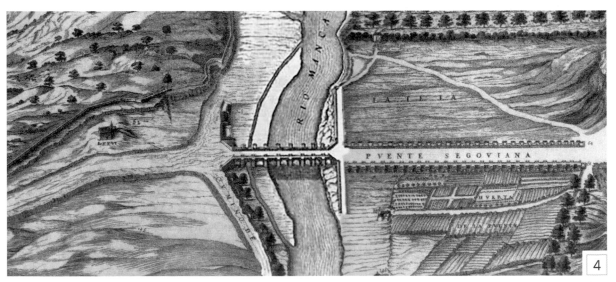

◀ **BRIDGE OF SEGOVIA** The granite bridge depicted here, commissioned by Philip II and built in 1582–84, was the main bridge across the Manzanares River. It led west then south to the historically important city of Toledo, once home to the royal court, then on to the ports of Seville and Cadiz.

▼ **PLAZA MAYOR** The city's central plaza, located near the Alcázar, was surrounded by grand buildings that contained apartments for the royal court. The square was multifunctional, serving as a processional space; an arena for public proclamations, bullfights, and executions; a market place; and a meeting place.

▼ **PUERTA DEL SOL** The "Gate of the Sun," built in the Middle Ages, was once the eastern gate of the city. By the time this map was made it had evolved into a crossroads of most of the major roadways and other routes in and out of the city; to this day it remains a busy transportation hub.

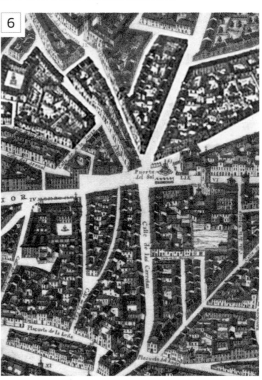

IN **CONTEXT**

Madrid's small 9th-century fortress, or Alcázar, had been built by Arab invaders on a rocky outcrop overlooking the Manzanares River. During the 16th century, it was extended as an imperial palace by King Charles I and his son Philip II. In 1636, a Renaissance façade was added by Spanish architect Juan Gómez de Mora, creating a unique fusion of Islamic, medieval, and contemporary Spanish styles. The palace remained a ceremonial and official royal residence until it burned down in 1734. The construction of a new neoclassical palace was completed between 1738 and 1755.

▲ **The Alcázar**, with its original Moorish walls (left) and its 17th-century south façade (right)

▲ **PARQUE DEL BUEN RETIRO** The park now known as El Retiro was, in the 17th century, still a walled royal— and former monastic—retreat. It was uncontained to the east, with a modest summer palace, a large lake, orchards, and tree-lined walkways. To the west, the Plaza de Cibeles and the Paseo del Prado, which would divide the city from the park, had yet to be built.

◄ **ATOCHA** At the time of this map the southern quarter of the city, Atocha, which occupied a flattish lowland, was dominated by working-class blocks and dwellings. It would later be developed into a relatively industrial, wealthy area.

Madrid, 1861

FRANCISCO PÉREZ BAQUERO ▪ STEEL ENGRAVING ▪ NATIONAL LIBRARY OF SPAIN, MADRID

UNKNOWN

THE WIDENING OF MADRID

In the three centuries following its foundation as Spain's imperial capital in 1561, Madrid expanded enormously and the population escalated. In 1860, the city's council, recognizing the urgent need to improve living conditions for all of its citizens, instructed its chief engineer, Carlos María de Castro, to devise a proposal for the future expansion of the city and its infrastructure. Castro's ambitious plan, the *Ensache de Madrid* (widening of Madrid), was very modern for its time, and was structured around a strict grid and major axes. This engraving of the *Ensache* shows the original city in 1861 (represented in dark tones) and Castro's proposed expansion (shown in orange).

The area to the north of "old Madrid," originally occupied by market gardens and a peasant suburb, gradually became an upper-class, exclusive neighborhood featuring broad avenues and grand houses. To the northeast, a more densely developed area of apartment buildings came into existence. Skirting the eastern edge of the old city, the Calle Serrano road linked the new fashionable suburbs of the north with the more commercial urban and administrative center of Recoletos.

Visual tour

KEY

▶ **ATOCHA STATION**
Originally built as the Estación de Mediodía in 1851, Madrid's first railroad terminal became known as Atocha station due to the proximity of the church Our Lady of Atocha. The first building was largely destroyed by fire, but was rebuilt and reopened in 1892.

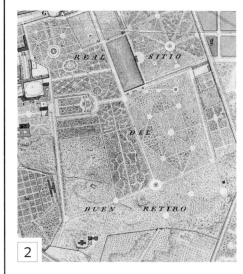

▲ **EL RETIRO** This vast, landscaped green space, once owned by Spain's monarchy, was redeveloped in the 1860s as a public recreational area with scenic lakes, fountains and statuary, cafés, pavilions, lawns, and tree-lined avenues. It remains a park today.

▲ **PASEO DEL PRADO** Forming the fashionable heart of the city in the 19th century, this two-lane boulevard fronted the Prado Museum and the Botanical Gardens, as well as a general hospital that now houses the Reina Sofía art museum.

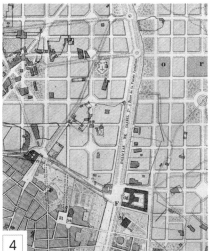

▲ **CALLE SERRANO** At its junction with the Puerto de Alcalá monument, this road continues south as Calle de Alfonso XII, marking the western edge of El Retiro. The two roads were key elements in Castro's plan to modernize Madrid's streetplan.

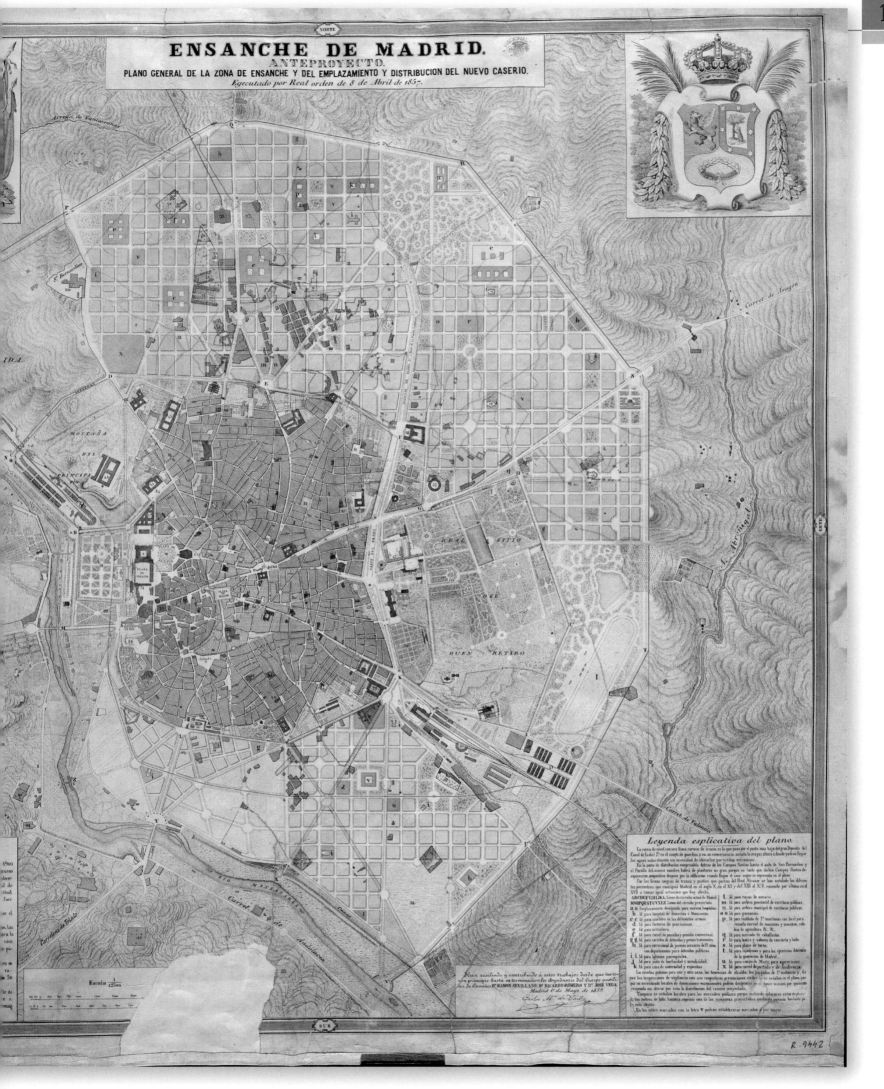

ENSANCHE DE MADRID.
ANTEPROYECTO.
PLANO GENERAL DE LA ZONA DE ENSANCHE Y DEL EMPLAZAMIENTO Y DISTRIBUCION DEL NUEVO CASERIO.
Egecutado por Real orden de 8 de Abril de 1857.

Kyoto, c.900–1100

UNKNOWN ARTIST ▪ GOLD, INK, AND COLORS ON JAPANESE PAPER, MOUNTED ON A SIX-PANEL FOLDING SCREEN ▪ PRIVATE COLLECTION

THE KYOTO SCREEN

SCALE

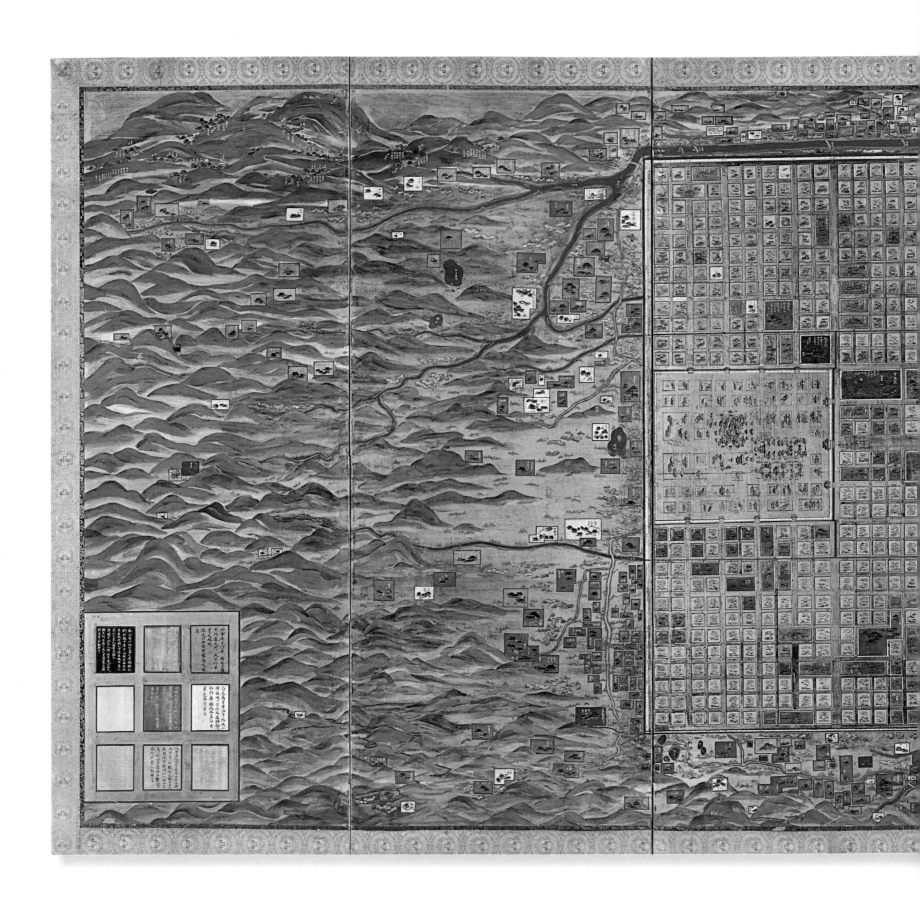

This beautiful, ornate map of the capital of imperial Japan was mounted onto a folding screen, and was never intended to be used as anything other than decoration. Painted in the 17th century, it shows Kyoto as it appeared in the 10th–11th centuries. The map is extraordinarily detailed—the number and width of each street is noted, and it even labels individual trees. The color-coded key in the lower left differentiates buildings according to their use—by the imperial household, magistrates, Shinto and Buddhist clergy, military retainers, and commoners. The map is oriented with north to the left, and the box within a box at the north end of the city is the imperial Heian Palace, built after Kyoto became capital of Japan in 794. The palace burned down in 1227 and was never rebuilt.

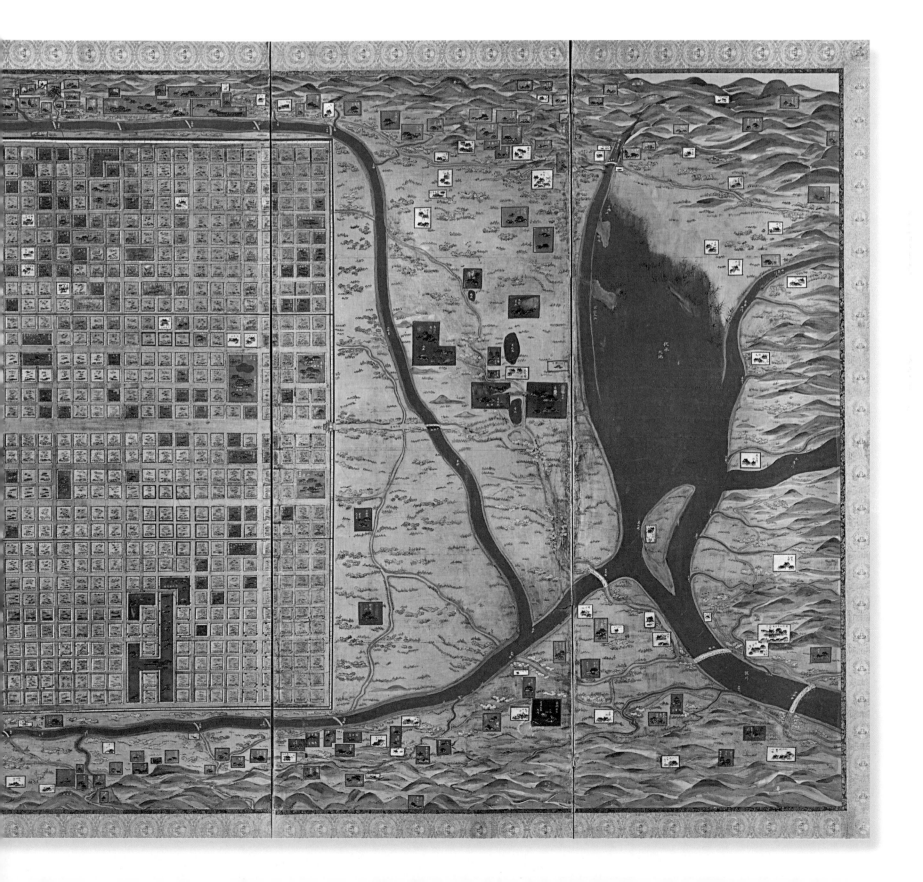

Kyoto, 1863

UNKNOWN ARTIST ▪ HAND-COLORED WOODBLOCK PRINT ▪ NUMEROUS COPIES EXIST

MAP OF KYOTO

SCALE

This map of the imperial Japanese capital, Kyoto, was produced at a time when Japan had been isolated from the wider world under the Tokugawa Shogunate for 250 years. This seclusion was a pragmatic decision, intended to reinforce the authority of the shogun, the military ruler. The map is therefore the product of a highly advanced mid-19th-century preindustrial society. It was produced not long after the "golden age" of Japanese cartography (from the 1600s to around 1855), and contains many of the features associated with this era—topography is shown in profile, and the text is written toward the center of the map, rather than having a directional orientation. The city's major buildings and grid-pattern streets are clearly shown, as are the rivers and canals that surround and flow through it. In contrast to Western maps from this period, however, there is no scale, and the emphasis is as much on visual impact as cartographic content.

Visual tour

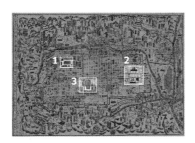

KEY

▶ KYOTO IMPERIAL PALACE Although the map shows and names the compound housing and walled complex of buildings that made up the Imperial Palace, the Kyoto Gosho, it does not show the palace buildings themselves. In the same way, buildings around the palace, the residences of officials and other nobles, are indicated but not drawn.

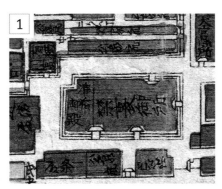

1

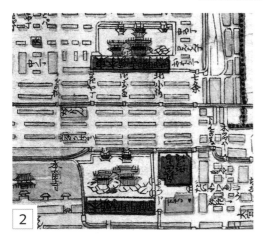

2

▲ TEMPLES OF THE ORIGINAL VOW Kyoto was the religious capital of Japan. In 1602, the shogun, Tokugawa Ieysau, ordered two Buddhist temples— the Western and Eastern Temples of the Original Vow—to be built. This was a political, not pious, move designed to dilute any challenge to his rule.

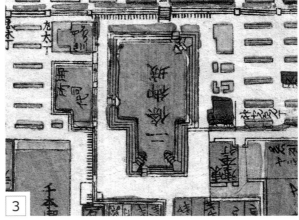

3

▲ NIJO CASTLE Between about 1570 and 1630, in response to the European introduction of firearms to Japan, 200 huge stone castles were built across the country. The castle in Kyoto was typical: supremely elegant and almost entirely impregnable. The map shows no details of the structure other than the double moats enclosing it.

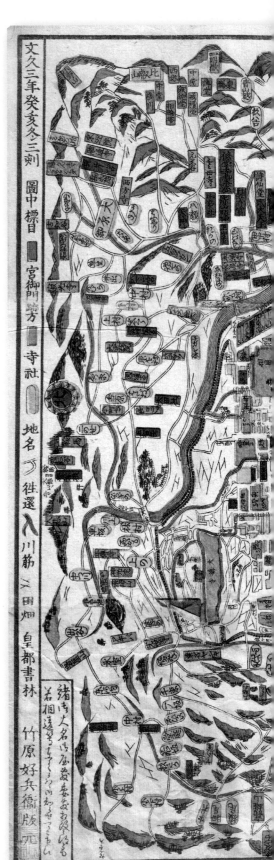

Even in Kyoto
Hearing the cuckoo's cry
I long for Kyoto

MATSUO BASHŌ (1644–94), JAPANESE POET

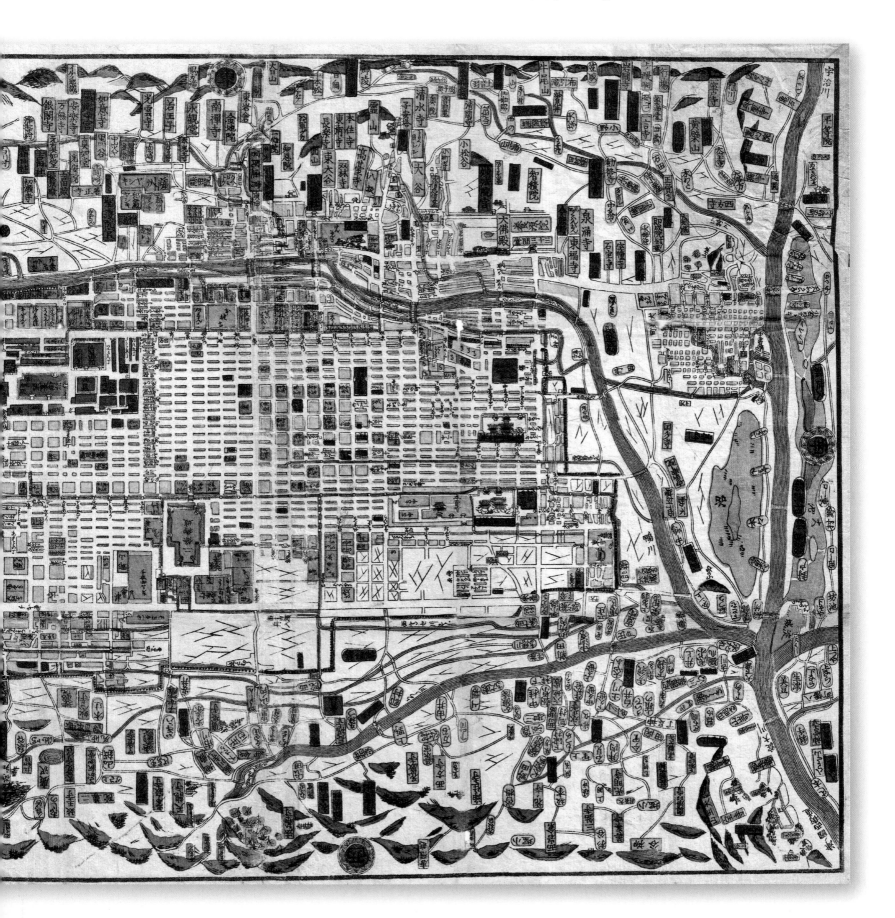

Berlin, 1688

UNKNOWN ARTIST AFTER JOHANN BERNARD SCHULTZ ▪
HAND-COLORED WOODCUT BASED ON A COPPER ENGRAVING ▪
ORIGINAL ENGRAVING: STATE LIBRARY, BERLIN, GERMANY

SCALE

MAP OF BERLIN

The modest medieval origins of Berlin, capital of Brandenburg-Prussia
in northern Germany, are scarcely apparent in this sunlit, late 17th-
century view of the city astride the Spree River. The three islands that
comprised the city are plainly shown: Berlin at the top, Cölln in the
center, and Friedrichswerder at the bottom, all three emerging simply
as Berlin in 1710. Their regular, ordered street plans were the work
of the man who sowed the seeds not just of Berlin's but of Prussia's
future greatness, Frederick William—the "Great Elector"—ruler of
Brandenburg-Prussia from 1640 to 1688, the year of this map.

The Great Elector

By the end of the Thirty Years' War (1618–48), a destructive conflict
involving many of Europe's major powers, Brandenburg-Prussia was
reduced to a shattered ruin: 50 percent of its population was dead,
and entire towns had been destroyed. Inspired by the lessons
provided by his near-direct contemporary, King Louis XIV of France,
Frederick William painstakingly rebuilt both state and city. His goal
was not just to make Brandenburg-Prussia a model state but to
provide it with an ideal capital, the rival of any in Europe.

   Among much else, the map shows Frederick William's imposing
palace, the Berliner Stadtschloss, at the left end of Cölln, as well
as the attached Lustgarten, which had been transformed from a
kitchen garden into formal grounds with fountains and geometric
paths. The architectural additions that made Berlin as defensively
strong as possible—the mighty fortifications—are depicted as precisely
as the tightly packed buildings on the islands, while the Spree River
appears as a kind of moat.

▲ **AN EXPANDING CITY** The engraving on which this map is based—by Johann Schultz, a
medallion maker and cartographer from Berlin—shows a much wider area. On the left, it clearly
depicts the new settlement of Dorotheenstadt, named after Frederick William's wife, Sophie-
Dorothea. Begun in 1670, this residential area, which was planned on a grid pattern, precipitated
a rapid expansion of the city to the west, which later became the administrative center of Berlin.

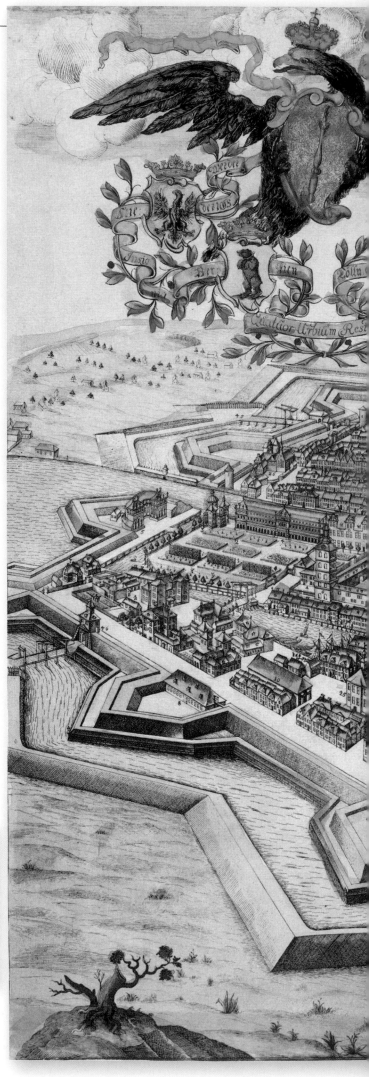

Visual tour

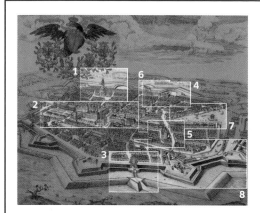

KEY

> **MARIENKIRCHE**
Begun around 1270, and completed in the 14th century, the sturdily handsome Church of St. Mary has a pitched, red roof dominated by a soaring square tower. In the entrance hall is a large fresco showing the city's inhabitants–rich and poor–"dancing with death": it was painted in 1485 during an outbreak of bubonic plague.

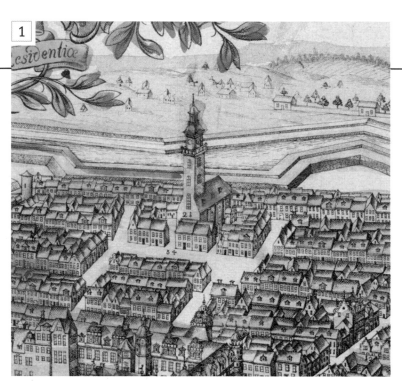

> **BERLINER STADTSCHLOSS**
The city's main royal palace was constructed in the 15th century, and progressively rebuilt and enlarged in a variety of classical styles by a succession of Brandenburg and Hohenzollern rulers, including Frederick William. Facing it is the Lustgarten, Berlin's first formal gardens, geometrically laid out in exact imitation of those at Louis XIV's Palace of Versailles in France.

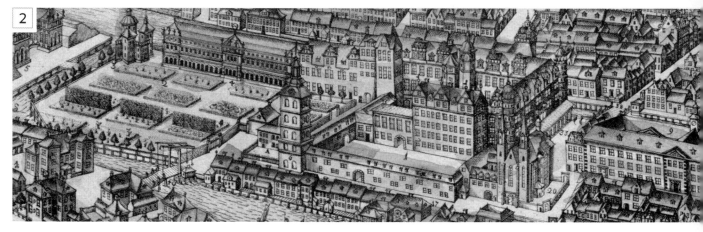

▲ **LEIPZIG GATE** So named because it led to the road running southwest to Leipzig, this gate was constructed from 1688 by Frederick William's successor, Frederick III–from 1701, Frederick I of Prussia. Exuberantly Baroque, it was a suitable symbol of the emerging might of Brandenburg-Prussia; it was demolished in the late 18th century.

▼ **KLOSTER KIRCHE** This Franciscan monastery church was constructed in the early Gothic style in 1250; it was substantially enlarged a century later. In the 19th century it was effectively rebuilt, only to be bombed in World War II. A ruined shell, it is now being painstakingly reconstructed.

▼ **PETRI KIRCHE** Since its foundation in 1230 in the center of Cölln, St. Peter's Church had been a major place of worship, its tapering spire a prominent landmark in the city. St. Peter was originally a fisherman, and the church's name showed the importance of fishing to the island's inhabitants. Nearby was the Rathaus, or City Hall.

▼ **NIKOLAIKIRCHE** The early 13th-century Church of St. Nicholas was one of the first places of worship in the city, located in its oldest district. It was altered, structurally and stylistically, several times over the centuries: in this view it has a fortified exterior and a single tower—a second one was added in the 1870s.

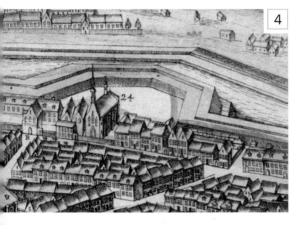

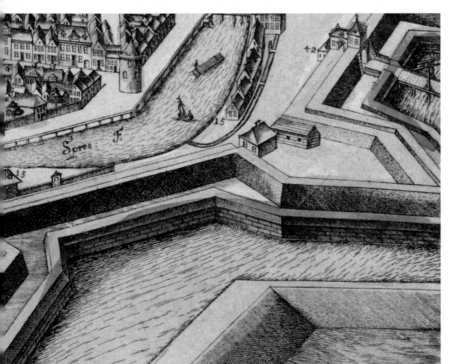

▲ **FISH MARKET** Cölln, the city's central island, was originally called Fischerinsel, or Fisher Island, after the colony of fishermen established at its southern end in the 13th century. At the time the map was made, Cölln was still the site of the city's fish market, but the area had become poor and overcrowded.

◄ **FORTIFICATIONS**
The first defensive wall around the city was built in approximately 1250 and was only around 6½ ft (2 m) high. By the mid-17th century, much of the old medieval wall had become incorporated into the fabric of the city, and in the aftermath of the Thirty Years' War (1618-48), strong new fortifications were built.

IN **CONTEXT**

From the Middle Ages onward, there was almost no major continental European city that did not seek shelter behind defensive walls. Other natural strongpoints, such as waterways, were similarly exploited, in an attempt to render such cities more impregnable still. The fortifications seen on this map of late 17th-century Berlin are typical of the scientific defence works that developed in the period. They are characterized not simply by huge masonry walls designed to resist bombardment, but by projecting, star-shaped bastions that gave defenders overlapping fields of fire, so they could subject attackers to maximum destructive force.

▲ **The remains** of Berlin's old medieval city walls

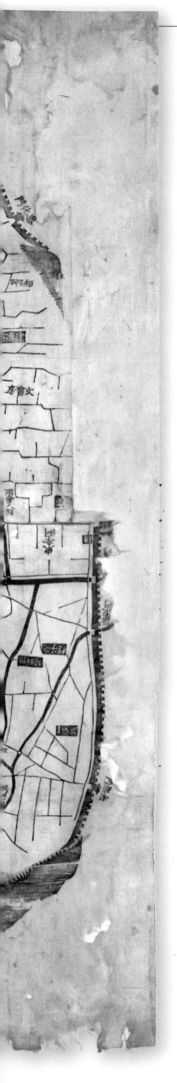

Seoul, undated

UNKNOWN ARTIST ■ BRUSH AND INK ON PAPER ■ NATIONAL LIBRARY OF KOREA, SEOUL

SCALE

HANSŎNG CHŎNDO

Korea, the "Hermit Kingdom," did not open up to the powers of the West until the 19th century, so its cartography drew inspiration from sources closer to home, notably China, the country's powerful and influential neighbor to the west. While the Koreans used many Chinese methods of mapmaking, they added one notable tradition of their own: *hyongsedo*. Similar to the Chinese idea of *chi*, this concept emphasizes the vitality of the land and views the landscape as alive with energy and life forces. When Seoul was chosen as the location for a new capital in 1394 by the newly established Joseon dynasty (1392–1910), it was because of its auspicious

setting—the area was surrounded by a chain of sheltering mountains and was crisscrossed by watercourses. Topography is prominent in this undated map of the city, which shows rivers running through the map like arteries; water was an important element in Korean mapping. As for the city itself, the encircling gate-studded walls are clearly visible, passing over the mountains of Bugaksan to the north and Namsan to the south. Also easy to pick out are the walled enclaves that contain the royal palaces of Gyeongbokgung and Changdeokgung, and the shrine of Jongmyo, all established in the first decades of the Joseon dynasty.

Visual tour

KEY

▶ **CHANGDEOKGUNG** Completed in 1412 during the reign of King Taejong, the third ruler of the Joseon dynasty, this was the seat of the royal family until 1872. After Korea was annexed by Japan in 1910, the last Korean emperor ended his days here.

1

2

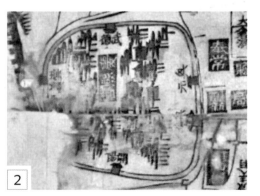

3

4

▲ **DEOKSUGUNG** The last of five grand palaces to be built in Seoul, Deoksugung was completed in 1592. It became the seat of power in the same year, after the Japanese destroyed Gyeongbokgung and burned all the other palaces, but only until Changdeokgung was rebuilt in 1618.

▲ **JONGMYO** This was a shrine where the dead rulers of the Joseon dynasty were honored. It originally took the form of two large wooden buildings containing wooden blocks in which the deceased were said to reside.

▲ **GYEONGBOKGUNG** The "Palace of Shining Happiness" was commissioned by King Taejo. Completed in 1399 it was a complex of more than 400 buildings and it was the seat of the royal throne for more than 200 years.

Prague, 1820

JOSEPH JÜTTNER ▪ HAND-COLORED ENGRAVING ▪ NUMEROUS COPIES EXIST

SCALE

GROUND PLAN OF THE ROYAL CAPITAL PRAGUE

This early 19th-century map of Prague, the historical capital of Bohemia (and today the capital of the Czech Republic), is believed to be the first accurate plan of the city. It was made using scientific principles and printed at a size of almost 11 square feet (a meter square), which was large enough to allow every street, courtyard, and block of buildings to be shown clearly. One reason such a detailed map had not been published previously was that the ruling Austrian Empire had been embroiled in the long-running Napoleonic Wars (1792–1815), and military officials were eager to prevent topographic data from falling into enemy hands.

A revolutionary plan

When it was agreed that the mapping of Prague should proceed, the man assigned the task was military engineer Joseph Jüttner (1775–1848). He conducted trigonometric surveys supported by astronomical observations, completing his work in 1816. The surveys were combined onto one large black-and-white manuscript map, of which two additional colored copies were then made, one for the Austrian emperor, the other for the Supreme Burgrave, the highest official in Bohemia. The latter authorized Jüttner's map to be published, but with one caveat: details of the fortifications surrounding Prague had to be rendered only in the vaguest of ways. Graphic artist Josef Alois Drda engraved the plan on

two copper tablets, after which it was printed on two map sheets in an edition published by the Czech National Museum in 1820. Jüttner's plan became the basis for all maps of Prague published for several decades, until the rapid development of the city in the second half of the 19th century rendered it outdated.

IN **CONTEXT**

Jüttner's plan provided the inspiration for a unique piece of art. Using the map as a base but enlarging it by a factor of around 10, a young university librarian named Antonin Langweil (1791–1837) spent 11 years (from 1826) building a three-dimensional model of Prague from cardboard and wood. His extraordinary model contained more than 2,000 buildings, constructed and painted with remarkable and realistic detail.

Langweil died in poverty but his model was bought by the emperor and moved to the National Museum in 1840. As many of the buildings it depicts have long since been demolished, the model offers a priceless historical record of the city before its redevelopment at the end of the 19th and the start of the 20th centuries. It can be seen today at the City of Prague Museum.

▲ **Detailed buildings**, their façades drawn in Indian ink, from Antonin Langweil's cardboard and wood reconstruction of Prague

> The ancient **splendor and beauty** of Prague, a city that is beyond compare, **left an impression** on my imagination that will never fade.

RICHARD WAGNER , GERMAN COMPOSER, 1826

Visual tour

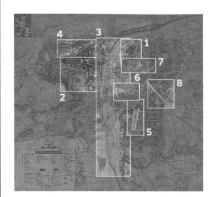

KEY

▶ **JEWISH QUARTER**
Jüttner's map was so detailed that individual buildings were identified by house numbers. The city's districts were differentiated by color (in the original black-and-white version of the map, different methods of hatching were used). Here, the area in red is labeled "Juden Stadt," or Jewish Quarter. The location of several synagogues is identified by a Star of David.

▲ **MALÁ STRANA** An old medieval neighborhood of crooked cobblestone streets, the district of Malá Strana (the Lesser Quarter) which lies between the Charles Bridge and Prague Castle, has changed little in the last 200 years. A comparison of the area's street pattern as shown on this map with a modern aerial photograph would reveal few differences.

▶ **VLTAVA** A single bridge spans the Vltava River on Jüttner's map—within the same area today there are eight bridges. What is now known as the Charles Bridge, but in the 19th century was the Pražský most (Prague Bridge), was built in 1357 during the reign of Charles IV. The only means of crossing the river until 1841, it was a vital connection between the castle and the Old Town.

▼ **PRAGUE CASTLE** Having stood for more than 1,000 years, it is no surprise that the castle as shown by Jüttner varies little from maps of it made today (although additions and alterations to the complex were being made well into the 20th century). Particularly elegant is the hachuring (small strokes depicting slope orientation) representing the steep wooded slopes around the castle.

▼ **BOULEVARDS** In 1784, Prague's four municipalities—Malá Strana, Nové Město, Staré Město, and Hradčany—were merged into a single entity. The walls that once divided them were demolished, creating broad, tree-lined avenues, such as here between the new and old towns of Nové Město and Staré Město.

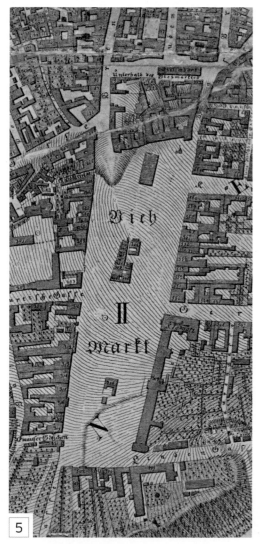

▲ **CHARLES SQUARE** Founded in 1348, this was once the largest city square in Europe. Originally it housed a cattle market and was the site of Charles IV's relic fair, where once a year crowds would come to view sacred items in the hope of being healed. During the 1860s, the central part of the square was turned into a public park.

▲ **OLD TOWN SQUARE** This was the main marketplace of Prague's Old Town (Staré Město), and the site of the Old Town Hall and the Orloj, the famous 15th-century astronomical clock (which still awes visitors today). The square was also the venue for the execution of criminals and a place where religious martyrs were burned at the stake.

◄ **HORSE MARKET** At the beginning of the 19th century the city boundaries were more or less the same as in medieval times. This would soon change, as Prague was about to outgrow its city walls. The broad diagonal avenue seen here was known as Horse Market (it was renamed Wenceslas Square in 1848); by the end of the 19th century it terminated in the grand National Museum rather than green fields.

Moscow, 1617

GEORG BRAUN AND FRANZ HOGENBERG ▪
HAND-COLORED ENGRAVING ▪
NUMEROUS COPIES EXIST

SCALE

MOSCOW, CAPITAL CITY OF WHITE RUSSIA

In 1480 Ivan III, ruler of a rapidly expanding Grand Duchy of Moscow, proclaimed himself "czar of all the Russias" and in 1525, the Russian monk Philotheus of Pskov ringingly asserted that "Moscow is the third Rome." Almost a century later, as this map from *Civitates Orbis Terrarum* (*see p.48*) shows, Moscow had several structures worthy of its new imperial status. At the center is Ivan's 90-acre Kremlin, or fortress (the upper of the two walled areas). Inside are depicted his three great churches, the cathedrals of the Assumption, of the Archangel, and of the Annunciation. In reality each church had a gilded dome, not the blue that is shown on this version of the map. The other central walled area, separated from the Kremlin by what is now Red Square, is the merchant quarter of Kitay-gorod. Yet despite the magnificence of these central areas, a contemporary account described the city as "full of filth," its streets "crooked and confused."

Visual tour

KEY

1

▲ **ST. BASIL'S CATHEDRAL** With soaring, multicolored onion domes around a central, tapering tower, St. Basil's is unique. Built by Ivan IV (also known as Ivan the Terrible) and completed in 1561, it has no precedent in Russian religious architecture.

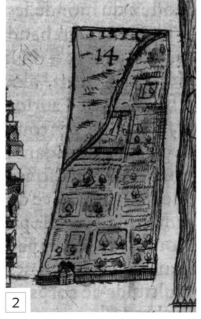

2

▲ **ROYAL GARDENS** The swampy area on the south side of the Moskva River was developed as a royal garden in the 15th century. With the building of the Vodootvodny Canal in 1786 it became, as it remains, an island in the city center.

OVIA VRBS METROPOLIS TO=
tius Rufsiæ Albæ.

16

HoBam Seroam

14

13

5

6   6   17

8

18 Intima pars vrbis dicta Kitaigorod   19

9   11   12

Secunda pars vrbis, suo circumdata muro, dicta Bielgorod

Tertia pars vrbis versus Septentrionem vocata Skorodum.

MERID. OCCID.
ORI. SEPT.

MOSCVÆ VRBS
LOCA INSIGNIORA.

1. Magni Ducis arx, dicta
   Czargorod.
2. Magni Ducis conclauia noua.
3. Ecclesia S. Michaelis.
4. Aula ſiue atrium vel Pa=
   latium Patriarchæ.
5. Conclaue, ſeu cænaculum è
   latere exstructum, è quo
   magnus Dux populo se con=
   ſpiciendum præbet, aut
   unde Principis Edicta po=
   pulo proclamantur.
6. Tabernæ ſiue pergula, in
   quibus diuerſi generis a=
   nimalium pelles, alicæque
   merces diuenduntur.
7. Curia ciuium, et Cancel=
   laria prope quas Vnguea=
   torum officinæ ſeu Phar=
   macopoliæ.
8. Legatorum externorum
   Aula ſue Hoſpitium.
9. Carceres ſeu Cuſtdiæ reorum
10. Tabernæ pictorum
11. Externorum Mercatorum
    Aula ſiue Hoſpitium.
12. Forum in quo fœnum et
    diuerſi generis tentoria
    ſeu domunculæ venduntur.
13. Aquæ calidæ ſeu Thermæ
14. Magni Ducis hortus.
15. Poganiſki ieſoro ſeu lacus.
16. Equile M. Ducis.
17. Armamentarium.
18. Forum equarium.
19. Domus Fuſoria.
20. Glinſki aula.

ПЛАНЪ
Императорскаго
Столичнаго города
МОСКВЫ
сочиненной
подъ смотрѣнiемъ
Архитектора Ивана
Мичурина
въ 1739 году.

Москва РѢКА

Moscow, 1739

IVAN FYODOROVICH MICHURIN ▪ HAND-COLORED COPPER ENGRAVING ▪ NUMEROUS COPIES EXIST

SCALE

PLAN OF THE IMPERIAL METROPOLIS MOSCOW

Drawn up under the direction of Dutch-trained Russian architect Ivan Michurin, this is the first geodetic map of Moscow (meaning that its features are placed on the map relative to their real-life coordinates). The map's scientific credentials are underlined by the prominent compass rose and an exact scale, and it also adopts the Western convention of showing north at the top. That said, many of the outlying areas are projections of future developments, not actual buildings. Around the city center two sets of walls can be seen, which roughly correspond to ring roads that encircle Moscow today. The figure in the elegant map title, pictured in an idealized landscape, is an allegory of the Moskva River. By the time this map was produced, Peter the Great had moved the Russian capital from Moscow to his new, ideal city of St. Petersburg.

Visual tour

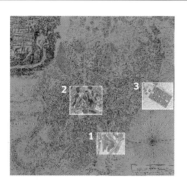

KEY

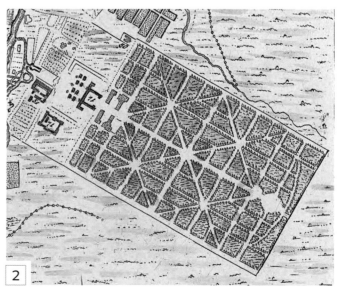

◀ **TANNERY DISTRICT** From the 17th century onward, Russian leather was considered the finest in the world. Saturating it in birch oil, a process unique to Russia's leather workers, made it durable and supple, with a dark red color. Its distinctive, rich odor pervaded the city's tannery district.

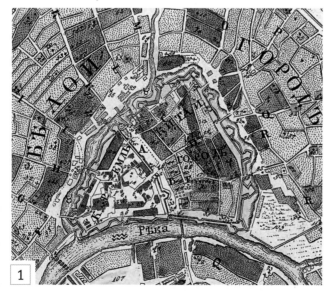

▲ **THE KREMLIN** By the time of this map, the central walled area of Moscow, the Kremlin, had fallen into disrepair. Its former glory would only be restored with the accession to the Russian throne of Catherine the Great in 1762.

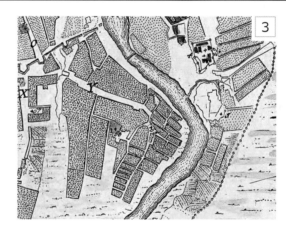

▲ **LEFORTOVO PARK** The spacious and orderly Lefortovo Park was laid out in 1701 by Feodr Galovin, one of Peter the Great's generals. Set on the banks of the Yauza River, the park precisely emulated Western—specifically French—models.

COLONIAL CITIES

CHAPTER 4

Colonial Cities

The expansion of European overseas trade from the 15th century presented huge challenges, both nautically— accurate charts and measurements were crucial, but establishing precise longitude was not solved until 1761— and cartographically: unknown coastlines and the topography of newly discovered continents had to be mapped, and the colonies that explorers and pioneers were establishing had to be represented informatively.

The main sources of information for maps were the ship's navigators, or the military surveyors and natural scientists who regularly formed part of a ship's company. Cartographically skilled navigators, such as Britain's James Cook, who charted much of the coastline and many of the archipelagos of the Pacific in his three major voyages (1768–1780), proved invaluable.

Nevertheless, mapping the full extent of the Americas, Australia, the Northwest and Northeast passages of the Arctic Ocean, and the elusive "Southern Continent"– Antarctica–proved a lengthy and laborious process: the latter was not fully completed until the 20th century.

In the 17th and 18th centuries, hungry for further trading opportunities and new goods and raw materials, the Spanish, French, British, Portuguese, and Dutch became embroiled in a competitive land-grab around the globe.

The first colonies

Eager to gain a foothold or beachhead on unfamiliar but commercially promising territories, European navigators sought out suitable-looking bays, anchorages, and natural harbors; in many cases they then pushed upstream along the major river systems to found colonies in the interior (as the French did in Canada, the British in North America and Africa, the Spanish in the south and southwest of North America, and the Portuguese in Brazil). In so doing, the colonists encountered (to their eyes) alien landscapes and peoples; thus indigenous cultural architecture and motifs often influenced the style of their maps.

Some colonial territories developed over and around existing native villages and towns, but many, such as Rio de Janeiro, Cape Town (*see pp.180–81*), and Australia's

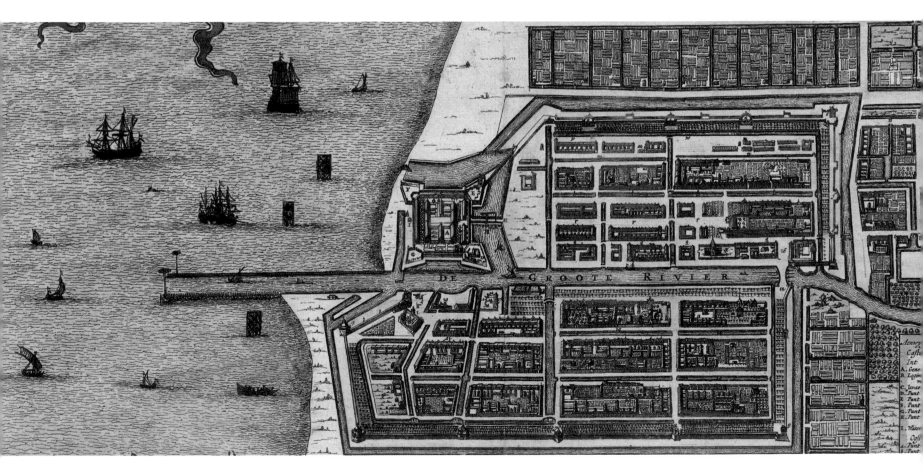

▲ **BATAVIA, 1669** This colony (now Jakarta) on the island of Java was a fine example of the Dutch using the skills they had learned while surveying, draining, and populating the Netherlands to adapt to an utterly foreign environment. The map shows with great precision the development of the port and its defenses.

> Now when I was a little chap I had a passion for maps. I would look for hours at South America, or Africa, or Australia, and lose myself in all the glories of exploration. 99

JOSEPH CONRAD, *HEART OF DARKNESS*, 1899

Port Jackson (*see pp.164–65*), which later evolved into the city of Sydney, expanded so rapidly that all traces of the original settlement and their inhabitants were lost.

Mapping colonial territories

The maps Europeans made of their international colonies and trading settlements, among them Santa Domingo in the West Indies (*see pp.178–79*), Batavia in the East Indies (*see pp.174–75*), and the extreme outposts in Australasia, served as progress reports for governments and monarchs back home, illustrating the growth and development of their "possessions." However, they also reveal the paucity of information available to mapmakers

and the degree of imaginative invention they had to employ; cartographic representations of many early colonial territories drew on "travelers' tales" of exotic beasts, plants, and colorful indigenous peoples.

By the mid-18th century there were numerous opportunities overseas for European cartographers, surveyors, and architects, as colonial settlements sprang up all around the globe. New cities had to be designed, accurately mapped, and recorded: not least for the merchant banks and trading companies back in Europe. Mapping became a means of not only demonstrating governance, but also of communicating vital information for commerce, the military, and navies.

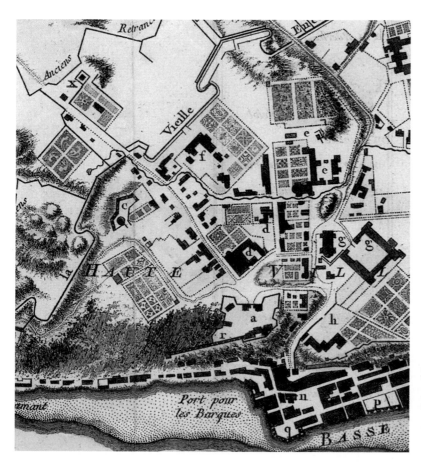

▲ **QUEBEC, 1744** Having forged up the St. Lawrence River toward the Great Lakes in the late 1500s, the French founded Quebec. This early map of the city shows a balance of defenses, commercial and residential areas, and parks at key points.

▲ **CAPE TOWN, 1884** The 19th-century rush for land, gold, and diamonds in South Africa saw the rapid creation of almost cookie-cutter Dutch and British cities that had to be mapped often to keep abreast of burgeoning immigration and commerce.

Sydney, 1788

FRANCIS FOWKES ■ HAND-COLORED ENGRAVING ■ NATIONAL LIBRARY OF AUSTRALIA

SCALE

PORT JACKSON IN THE COUNTY OF CUMBERLAND

The full title of this map is "Sketch & description of the settlement at Sydney Cove Port Jackson in the County of Cumberland taken by a transported convict on the 16th of April, 1788, which was not quite 3 months after Commodore Phillips's landing there." When this title is combined with the map's annotations ("Mens Camp," "Womens Camp," "Marine Guard House"), the document almost tells a complete story. Commodore Arthur Phillip was a British Royal Navy officer who became the first Governor of New South Wales when he established the earliest penal colony in Australia at Port Jackson– which would later become the city of Sydney.

The making of a colony

Although it is not a particularly accurate geographical representation of the area, this map provides a lot of information about the settlement, with a Governor's Mansion already in place, as well as a flourishing farm and several gardens. The map's key also identifies a bake house, a smithy, a quarry, and multiple saw pits for the cutting of large pieces of lumber, such as those used in building. This is a settlement in the making.

The 11 ships of the First Fleet, which transported the convicts, crew, and officials to Australia, are depicted anchored in the harbor, and their names are given in a separate key at the top left. When the ships departed the colony in 1789, the map was taken back to England with them, and published in London.

FRANCIS **FOWKES**

BIRTH AND DEATH DATES UNKNOWN

The creator of the map, sometimes known as the Port Jackson Painter, is identified only by the initials F. F., which, from an examination of the names of the transported convicts, led researchers to identify him as Francis Fowkes.

The records of the Old Bailey, London's central criminal court, record that Fowkes, a former navy midshipman, was convicted for stealing a greatcoat and a pair of leather boots from a pub in Covent Garden, London. He was sentenced to "transportation" on December 13, 1786, arriving at Port Jackson in Australia on the naval ship *Alexander*. There he was employed as a clerk. Fowkes was granted land on expiry of his sentence in 1797, but three years later he departed the colony for the Cape of Good Hope in South Africa, where he became a settler. Little else is known about him.

Ships Names

Sirius	Charlotte
Prince of Wales	Scarbro'
Fishburn	Lady Penryn
Golden Grove	Friendship
Alexander	Borrowdale

Supply Armed Brig

Shingling Party

Brick Field

Shingling Party

References

A	The Observatory	M L	'Geo Iohnsons the
BB	House & Garden of L.t		Gov.r Aid du Camp
	Ball of the Supply	N	Rev.d M.r Iohnsons
CC	General Hospital &	O	Survey or Generals
	Garden		Marquee
D	The Bake House	P	Gov.r Temporary House
EE	M.r Clark's Agent for	Q	Governor's Kitchen
	the Contractor Marquee	R	Store House for Bale Goods
FF	Provision Store Houses	S	Commissary's Marquee
G	The Master Builders	T	Store House for Bale Goods
	(now bel.n another)	V	Marine Guard House
H	Cap.t Campbells	U	The Smithey
II	Marine Barracks	X	Provosts Marshals
K	Lieu.t Gov.r Marquee	Y	Stone Quarry
LL	The Marine Officers		
	Marquees		The small Squares
M	Cap.t David Collins		with Figures are the
	the Judge Advocate		Saw Pits

We had the **satisfaction** of finding the **finest harbor** in the world, in which **a thousand sail of the line** may ride in the **most perfect security.**

ARTHUR PHILIP, FIRST GOVERNOR OF NEW SOUTH WALES, MAY 15, 1788

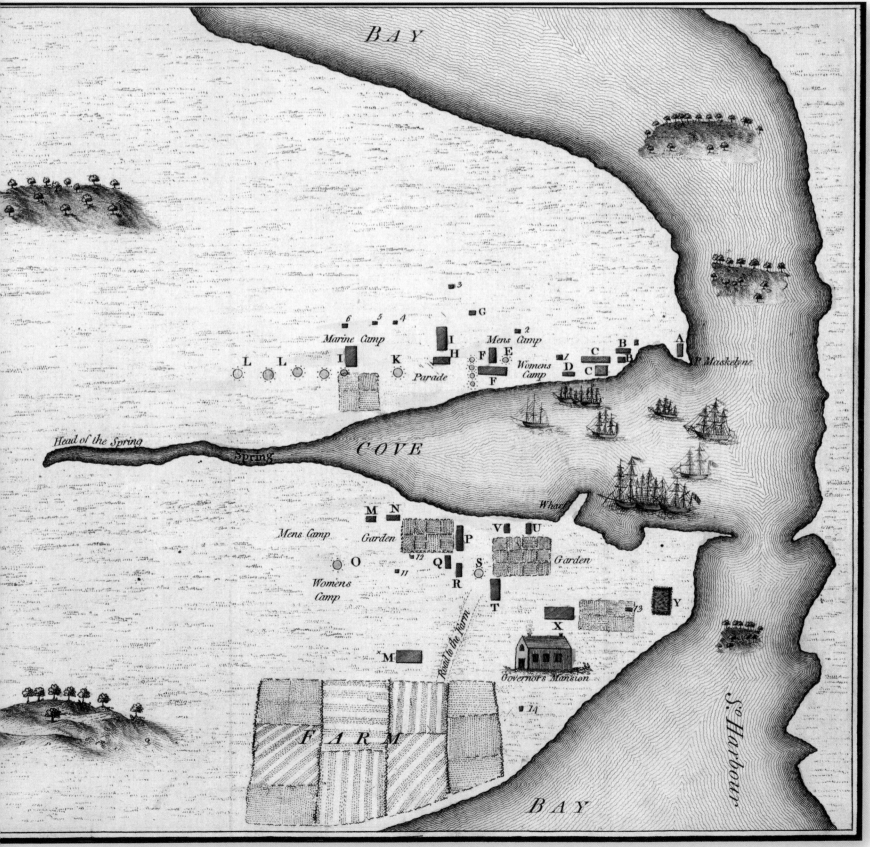

Sydney, 1888

M. S. HILL ▪ CHROMOLITHOGRAPH ▪ NATIONAL LIBRARY OF AUSTRALIA, CANBERRA

THE CITY OF SYDNEY

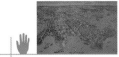

SCALE

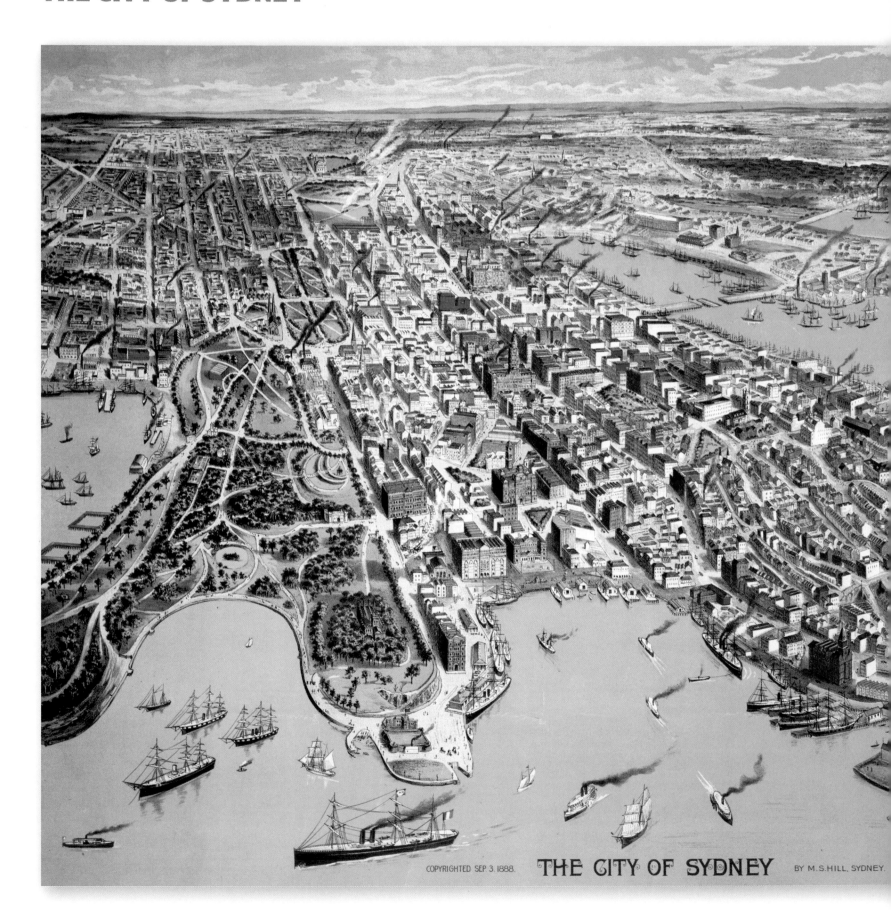

COPYRIGHTED SEP. 3. 1888.   THE CITY OF SYDNEY   BY M. S. HILL, SYDNEY

> The celebrations that are being held in Sydney this week illustrate… the substantial oneness of what is rapidly becoming… the nation of Australia.

THE SOUTH AUSTRALIAN ADVERTISER, THURSDAY JANUARY 26, 1888

To mark the centenary of European settlement, celebrations were held across Australia in January 1888. The former penal colony at Port Jackson (*see pp.164-65*) had by now become the booming city of Sydney, with a population approaching a quarter of a million. This colorful panorama, attributed to the otherwise anonymous "M. S. Hill," was intended to show off the confident metropolis. Taking a bird's-eye view from above the harbor, with Circular Quay at its center, it illustrates in extraordinary detail the industrial, commercial, and civic achievements of the far-flung British outpost. The waterways and moorings are full of steamships, and chimneys of countless factories belch smoke, but the map also shows a city of wealth and refinement. There are many grand buildings, including the recently rebuilt Customs House, which takes center stage on Circular Quay, and the imposing town hall—although its dominant clock tower would not actually be completed until the following year.

Visual tour

KEY

1

▲ **FORT MACQUARIE** The tiny fortress on the tip of Bennelong Point was completed in 1821 and equipped with cannon to guard the harbor approach. By 1888 it was largely redundant and was pulled down to make way for tram sheds soon after. These in turn were demolished in 1959 to make way for Sydney Opera House.

2

◀ **THE ROCKS** This area, known as The Rocks for its sandstone buildings, had a rough reputation. However, by 1888 its waterfront was becoming grander, with new additions such as the red ASN (Australian Steam Navigation) Building (center right), which was built in 1884.

San Francisco, 1859

OFFICE OF THE COAST SURVEY ▪ ENGRAVING ON PAPER ▪ NUMEROUS COPIES EXIST

SCALE

CITY OF SAN FRANCISCO AND ITS VICINITY, CALIFORNIA

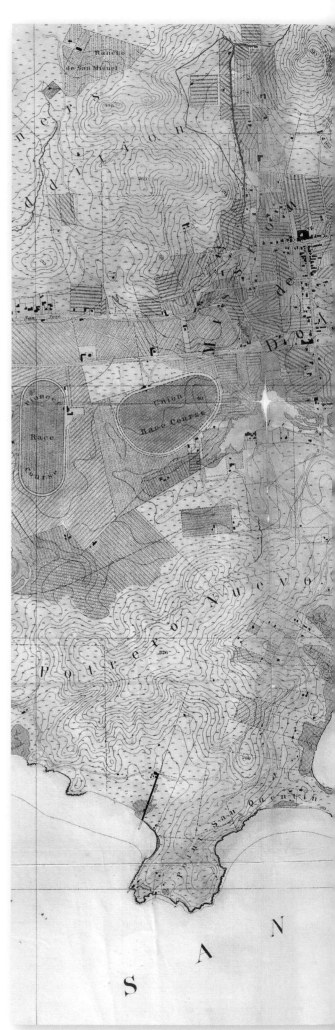

The California Gold Rush, which began in January 1848, drew a flood of fortune seekers to the western territories of America. Many arrived via the entrance port of San Francisco, recently annexed from Mexico, raising the population of the settlement from 1,000 in 1848 to 25,000 by the end of 1849. This rare map, prepared by the US Coast Survey, depicts the city 10 years later, by which time the population stood at around 70,000 inhabitants. At this point San Francisco had changed from a city of tents and flimsy shacks to one of brick and stone buildings. The map shows how the extent of the city stretched 12 blocks back from a waterfront lined with wharfs and piers, where new immigrants were still arriving daily.

At the heart of the built-up district on the map can be seen a block that is empty of buildings. This is Portsmouth Square, the civic center of the new city. Also known as The Plaza, it was the location of the new City Hall until the 1870s. It is from here that horse-drawn omnibuses would depart for all parts of the city, including the Mission de Delores (in the top left quadrant of the map). This area is now a small district known as the Outer Mission, but in 1859 it was only connected to the growing city by a single road that crossed over sandy hills. Mission de Delores was popular for its race courses, visible on the map, which were laid out during the Gold Rush years.

▲ **BEFORE THE GOLD RUSH** This view of San Francisco from the bay was drawn in 1847, the same year that the formerly Mexican settlement changed its name from Yerba Buena to San Francisco, and just one year before the Gold Rush that would transform it from a sparse frontier outpost to a booming city.

San Francisco, 1914

C. MERRIMAN PETER ■ PHOTOLITHOGRAPH ■
NUMEROUS COPIES EXIST

SCALE

PETER'S SAN FRANCISCO LOCATOR

Ostensibly the Panama–Pacific International Exposition of 1915 was held to celebrate the completion of the Panama Canal, but its real purpose, as far as residents of the host city were concerned, was to announce the rebirth of San Francisco in the wake of the cataclysmic 1906 earthquake. So while this souvenir map includes a site plan of the exposition identifying its various palaces and pavilions, it also showcases the greater city beyond.

The devastation wrought by the earthquake was seized on as an opportunity to regenerate San Francisco. Streets were widened and more arterial thoroughfares created; the city gained a new civic center complex, as well as the Stockton Street and Twin Peaks tunnels, the latter the world's longest streetcar tunnel. Both are marked on the map, even though the latter was not completed until 1918. The tunnels facilitated the expansion of the new electric streetcar network, which crucially allowed streetcars to run from downtown to the new Marina district, the site of the International Exposition.

IN **CONTEXT**

There had been magnificent world's fairs in London in 1851, Chicago in 1893, and Paris in 1900; in 1915 it was the turn of San Francisco. The intention of the Panama–Pacific International Exposition was to showcase achievements in technology, science, industry, and the arts. The event drew more than 18 million visitors, who could watch the assembly of a pair of Levi's jeans or of a brand new Ford. When the fair ended on December 4, 1915, almost all of its buildings were dismantled. Only the Palace of Arts was left standing, which became an exhibition hall, then a tennis center, then a storage depot, and eventually a museum.

▲ **The Tower of Jewels**, at a height of 435 ft (132 m) the centerpiece of the exposition, covered with 102,000 pieces of cut glass that were illuminated by searchlights at night

SAN FRANCISCO, 1914

...RN PACIFIC   THE DISTINCTIVE SAN FRANCISCO LINE   DIRECT ROUTE PANAMA PACIFIC EXPOSITION 1915

PACIFIC OCEAN

PETER'S
SAN FRANCISCO
LOCATOR
THE BIRDS-EYE-VIEW MAP
OF THE
EXPOSITION CITY
Published By LOCATOR PUBLISHING CO.
417 LICK BLDG   PHONE GARFIELD 7060

LEGEND

Railroads
Street Railways
Street Railway Transfer Points
Post Office Stations — indicated by letter in black circle thus
Post Office Sub Stations ○
Theatres — indicated by letter in black square thus
500-1000-etc-Street Address block numbers

Numbers run 100 to each block; Thus 1 to 99 are in the first block, 100 to 199 in the second block, 2100 to 2199 in the twenty-second block, etc. All streets running out of Market from Guerrero street to the Ferry Station number from Market Street.

PANAMA-PACIFIC INTERNATIONAL EXPOSITION 1915

DIRECTORY

No.
1—Palace of Fine Arts
2—Palace of Horticulture
3—Palace of Education and Social Economy
4—Palace of Food Products
5—Palace of Liberal Arts
6—Palace of Agriculture
7—Palace of Manufactures
8—Palace of Transportation
9—Palace of Varied Industries
10—Palace of Mines and Metallurgy
11—Festival Hall
12—Palace of Machinery
13—Ferry Building
14—California Building

No.
16—State Buildings
17—Foreign Pavilions
18—Live Stock Exhibit
19—Race Track and Athletic Field
20—U. S. Government Exhibit
21—South Gardens
22—North Gardens
23—Amusement Concessions
24—Van Ness Avenue Entrance
25—Fillmore Street Entrance
26—Scott Street Entrance
27—Baker Street Entrance
28—Presidio Entrance
29—Laguna Street Entrance

The grounds comprise 635 acres, divided into three sections. In the center are grouped the eleven great Exhibit Palaces and Festival Hall. To the west, spreading fan-shaped along the bay, are located the pavilions of foreign nations and the imposing buildings of the States, while still beyond these are the Live Stock Exhibit Buildings and Race Track covering 65 acres, the Aviation Field, and the Drill Grounds, capable of showing ten thousand troops in drill at one time. To the east of the Exhibit Palaces lie the sixty-five acres devoted to the Amusement Concessions.
This Exposition represents an outlay of approximately $50,000,000.

The city of San Francisco covers an area of 46½ square miles and has a population of 530,000, which together with adjoining and trans-bay communities (as shown in small map) within a radius of 15 miles contain about 1,000,000 people.

RAILWAY DEPOTS

Northwestern Pacific, Union Ferry Depot, 13-B
Oakland, Antioch and Eastern, Union Ferry Depot, 13-B
Ocean Shore, 14-J
Santa Fe, Union Ferry Depot, 13-B
Southern Pacific, Valley Route, Union Ferry Depot, 13-B
Southern Pacific, Coast Route, 9-N
Western Pacific, Union Ferry Depot, 13-B

THEATERS

Key
A — Columbia—High Class Productions 15-M
B — Alcazar—Stock Company 15-M
C — Tivoli—Grand Opera (Movies Between Seasons) 15-M
D — Orpheum—Vaudeville 15-M
E — Cort—High Class Productions 14-M
F — Gaiety—Musical Comedy and Movies 15-N
G — Savoy—15-K
H — American—14-K
I — Imperial—Movies 14-L
J — Empress—Vaudeville 14-L
K — Pantages—Vaudeville 15-L
L — Portola—Movies 14-N
M — Republic—Vaudeville and Movies 20-J
N — Princess—Vaudeville and Movies 19-I
O — Valencia 18-I
P — Wigwam—Vaudeville and Movies 10-H

POINTS OF INTEREST

Affiliated Colleges 18-F
Alamo Square 17-I
Alta Plaza 17-J
Appraisers Building 16-P
Auditorium 15-J
Aviary (Golden Gate Park) 29-F
Baker's Beach 28-G
Balboa Park 13-O
Bernal Park 8-G
Buena Vista Park 16-G
Cemeteries 7-B
City Hall 15-J
Civic Center 15-J
Cliff House 27-C
Coliseum 17-H
Columbia Park 11-L
Conservatory (Golden Gate Park) 20-F
City and County Hospital 7-I
Custom House 16-P
Dreamland Pavilion 20-J
Duboce Park 16-H
Ewing Field (Baseball Park) 20-H
Fishermen's Wharf 25-P
Fort Mason 26-N
Fort Miley 27-E
Fort Point 32-I
Franklin Square 10-J
Garfield Park 8-H
Golden Gate 33-I
Golden Gate Park 23-E
Great Highway and Beach 21-C
Hall of Justice 17-O

Hamilton Square 20-E
Holly Park 8-F
Jackson Park 9-K
Jefferson Square 17-J
Land's End 26-E
Lake Merced 15-C
Library 15-K
Lincoln Park 27-E
Mission Park 13-H
Murray's (Ingleside) Beach 18-C
Museum (Golden Gate Park) 21-F
Music Stand (Golden Gate Park) 21-F
Pavilion 20-I
Portsmouth Square 17-O
Presidio 28-H
Presidio Golf Links 25-G
Public Golf Links 27-E
Recreation Park 12-I
San Francisco Golf and Country Club 15-C
Seal Rocks 27-D
South Park 15-L
Stadium (Golden Gate Park) 23-E
Strawberry Hill (Golden Gate Park) 21-F
Sutro Baths 27-D
Sutro Heights 26-D
Sutro Forest 17-E
Ten Gardens (Golden Gate Park) 21-F
Twin Peaks 15-F
Twin Peaks Tunnel 15-F
Union Square 19-L
U. S. Mint 14-L
U. S. Sub Treasury 15-O
Washington Square 20-P

SEAL ROCKS
CLIFF HOUSE
SUTRO BATHS

LAKE MERCED
MURRAY'S BEACH
S.F. GOLF & COUNTRY CLUB
INGLESIDE TERRACE
ST. FRANCIS WOOD
FOREST HILL
SUNSET
TWIN PEAKS
SUTRO FOREST
EUREKA VALLEY
AFFILIATED COLLEGES
GOLDEN GATE PARK
RICHMOND DIST.
FORT MILEY
PUBLIC GOLF LINKS
LINCOLN PARK
LAND'S END
PRESIDIO GOLF LINKS
BAKERS BEACH
PRESIDIO
U.S. MILITARY RESERVATION
FORT POINT
GOLDEN GATE
MISSION PARK
MISSION DOLORES
RECREATION PARK
BUENA VISTA PARK
MASONIC ASS'N
ODD FELLOWS ASS'N
EWING FIELD
CALVARY
LAUREL HILL
PRESIDIO HEIGHTS
PRESIDIO TERRACE
ALAMO SQUARE
HAYES VALLEY
WESTERN ADDITION
JEFFERSON SQUARE
ALTA PLAZA
PACIFIC HEIGHTS
LAFAYETTE SQUARE
AUDITORIUM
CIVIC CENTER
CITY HALL
LIBRARY
POST OFFICE
U.S. MINT
NOB HILL
RUSSIAN HILL
FORT MASON
U.S. TRANSPORT DOCKS
GENERAL DEPOT WESTERN PACIFIC HILLS BUILDING
CHINATOWN
HALL OF JUSTICE
SUB TREASURY
LATIN QUARTER
TELEGRAPH HILL
CUSTOM HOUSE
APPRAISERS BLDG
FISHERMEN'S WHARF
PROPOSED WESTERN PACIFIC FREIGHT SLIP
40—HICKS-HAUPTMAN CO.
41—J. R. HANIFY CO.
42—CHAS. R. McCORMICK CO.
WESTERN PACIFIC FREIGHT DELIVERY TRACKS
BELT LINE R.R.
UNION FERRY STATION
THE EMBARCADERO
WESTERN PACIFIC FREIGHT SLIP

TO W.P.
CALIFORNIA NAVIGATION & IMPROVEMENT CO.
PETALUMA-SANTA ROSA RY. CO.
CALIFORNIA TRANSPORTATION CO.
SOUTHERN PACIFIC CO.
PACIFIC NAVIGATION CO.
NORTH PACIFIC S.S. CO.
KOSMOS LINE
NAPA TRANSPORTATION CO.
POLLARD S.S. CO.
OCEANIC S.S. CO.
C.A. SMITH CO.
E.J. DODGE CO.
CHAS. H. HIGGINS, SWAYNE & HOYT
SUDDEN & CHRISTENSON
UNION S.S. CO.
MONTICELLO S.S. CO.
PACIFIC COAST S.S. CO.

BAGGAGE
SOUTHERN PACIFIC TO OAKLAND
SOUTHERN PACIFIC TO ALAMEDA
SOUTHERN PACIFIC TO BERKELEY
KEY ROUTE TO OAKLAND
KEY ROUTE TO BERKELEY
SANTA FE TO RICHMOND
NORTHWESTERN PACIFIC

SAN FRANCISCO BAY

C. MERRIMAN PETER
1914

Visual tour

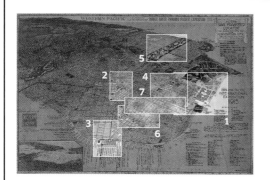

▶ **EXPOSITION GROUNDS** Laid out on landfill on the northern shore of the Golden Gate, the Panama–Pacific International Exposition covered 635 acres (257 hectares). At the center were 11 grand exhibition palaces and the Festival Hall. To the west were the international pavilions and racetrack; to the east, beside Fort Mason, was "The Zone," an area of popular amusements and concessions featuring scale models of Yellowstone National Park, the Grand Canyon, and even the biblical Creation.

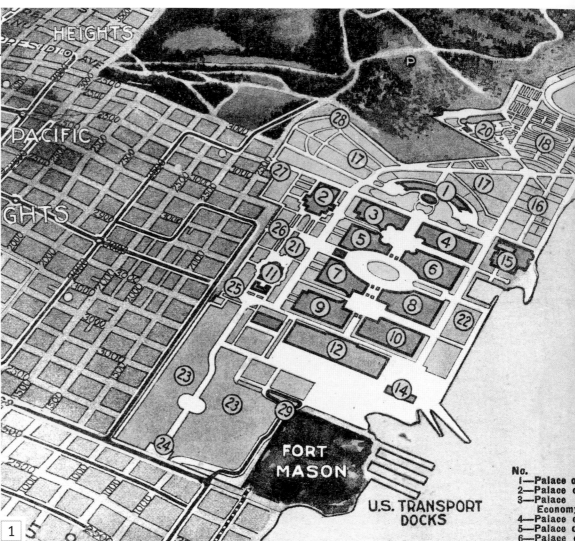

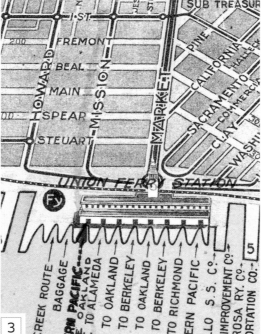

▲ **CIVIC CENTER** After the earthquake, almost the entire downtown district was rebuilt between 1906 and 1912. The architects favored a Beaux-Arts style, which looked back to buildings from ancient Europe. At the heart of the area was a Roman-inspired civic center with a new City Hall, completed in 1915—just in time for the Panama–Pacific Exposition. The library and auditorium, included on the map, came later.

▲ **UNION FERRY STATION** The city's grandest, busiest, and most iconic building was inspired by the 12th-century Giralda bell tower in Seville, Spain. The Ferry Building was topped by a 245-ft- (75-m-) tall clock tower with four clock faces. It was completed in 1898, and served the commuters who traveled to and from San Francisco by ferry across the East Bay. It survived the earthquake largely unscathed.

▲ **PACIFIC HEIGHTS** During the urbanization of the city in the late 19th century, the rich built their mansions in the neighborhood of Nob Hill, but this area was completely destroyed in the earthquake. When the time came to rebuild, the money moved west to Pacific Heights, a scenic area on a hill overlooking the Bay. The location even had its own microclimate, with clearer weather than much of the rest of the city.

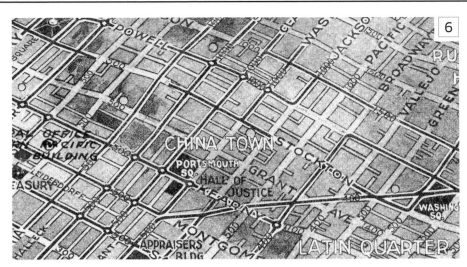

◄ 6 CHINATOWN The Chinatown neighborhood was completely destroyed by the fires that came in the wake of the 1906 earthquake. In the aftermath, city officials and developers looked to move the Chinese out to less valuable land on the southern edges of the city. Ironically, this proposal was defeated because of local regulations restricting where the Chinese could settle, and Chinatown was rebuilt in the same place.

▼ STREET TRANSPORT San Francisco's extensive system of streetcars and cable cars are clearly shown on this map. The black lines running along the streets follow their routes, with the black circles representing the stops. Many of the cables had to rebuilt after the earthquake in 1906 (*see below*).

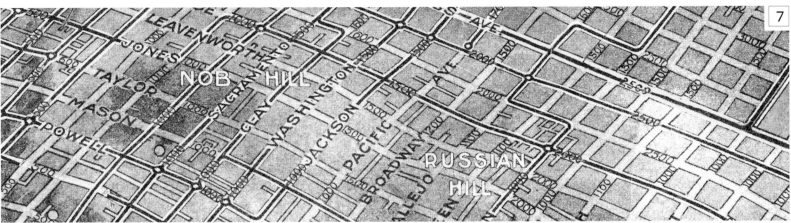

7

▲ 5 GOLDEN GATE PARK This was San Francisco's answer to Central Park, but it was 20 percent bigger than its New York cousin. Laid out in the 1870s to encourage urbanization of the sparsely populated western districts, the park stretched 3 miles (4.8 km) east to west and half a mile (0.8 km) across. Following the 1906 earthquake, it became partly urbanized itself, hosting a makeshift town of tented housing for some of the tens of thousands made homeless.

IN **CONTEXT**

On April 18, 1906, San Francisco suffered a colossal earthquake. At 5:12 a.m., tectonic plates shifted far below the ocean floor. The shock waves raced toward the city, hitting just a few seconds later. The ground rippled like waves. Buildings that survived the initial devastation were then subject to several days of raging fires caused by broken gas pipes and torn electric cables. More than 80 percent of the city was destroyed and approximately 3,000 people died, while up to 300,000 people of a total 400,000 population were left homeless. However, the city quickly and completely rebuilt itself, which was cause for immense civic pride. The Panama-Pacific International Exposition of 1915 celebrated the city's rejuvenation.

▲ Ruins of the Grand Hotel, situated at the corner of Market and Montgomery streets, after the 1906 earthquake

Batavia, 1669

UNKNOWN ARTIST ▪ HAND-COLORED
COPPERPLATE ENGRAVING ▪ PRINCETON
UNIVERSITY LIBRARY, NEW JERSEY, USA

SCALE

MAP OF BATAVIA

The growth of the Dutch East India Company from the beginning of the 17th century heralded the start of a golden age of Dutch cartography, particularly in the field of sea charts and maps documenting the nation's mastery of trade in East Asia. This particular map is of Batavia, the Dutch colonial capital in the East Indies, which would eventually grow into the modern Indonesian city now known as Jakarta. The plan of the settlement is probably based on log entries made by a Dutch embassy on its way to Japan sometime between 1649 to 1661, which were later published in Amsterdam.

At the time this map was drawn, the colony was precisely 50 years old. The new settlement was under constant threat of attack from the local Javanese population, so, in around 1630, it had been enclosed with the defensive walls and moat that are clearly visible on the map. The quarters that can be seen within were laid out on a grid plan, crisscrossed with canals in the fashion of cities such as Amsterdam back in the Dutch homeland. The houses inside the walls were grand and belonged to wealthy Dutch merchants, some of whose ships are illustrated out in the bay. Outside the walls the native quarters were far more cramped; these areas also contained the housing for the Chinese workmen the Dutch had brought to Batavia as labor.

IN **CONTEXT**

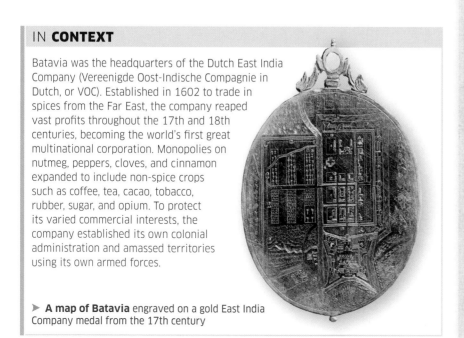

Batavia was the headquarters of the Dutch East India Company (Vereenigde Oost-Indische Compagnie in Dutch, or VOC). Established in 1602 to trade in spices from the Far East, the company reaped vast profits throughout the 17th and 18th centuries, becoming the world's first great multinational corporation. Monopolies on nutmeg, peppers, cloves, and cinnamon expanded to include non-spice crops such as coffee, tea, cacao, tobacco, rubber, sugar, and opium. To protect its varied commercial interests, the company established its own colonial administration and amassed territories using its own armed forces.

▶ **A map of Batavia** engraved on a gold East India Company medal from the 17th century

Wegens het Casteel ende Stadt BATAVIA
groot Eylant JAVA Anno 1669.

DE GROOTE RIVIER

Cam. privil.
S. C. M^{tis}

Eschale van 180 Rhynlantsche Roeden.

denwysinge van de principale plaetsen des
Casteels ende Stadt BATAVIA.

Int Casteel
A. Generaels huys.
B. Logiment van de Raden van India.
C. Javaensche corps du garde.
D. Punt Diamant.
E. Punt Robyn.
F. Punt Sasier.
G. Punt de Parel.
H. Punt enbruch vant Casteel.
I. Waterpoert vant Casteel.

Ossey der Stadt
a. Punt Amsterdam.
b. Punt Middelburgh.
c. Punt Rotterdam.
d. Punt Delft.
e. Punt Gelderlandt.
f. Punt Orangien.
Nieuwe poert.
g. Punt Hollandia.
h. Punt Grimbergen.
Amsterdamsche gracht.
i. Tygers gracht.
m. Raynsins gracht.
k. Malle baers gracht.
l. Leeuwe gracht.
Groene gracht.
q. Bebere straet.
p. Prince straet.

s. Prince steech.
t. Bruch straet.
v. Bandanees quartier.
w. Malle baers quartier.
x. Nieuwe Kerck.
y. 't Stadt huys.
z. 't Hospitael.

Westzy der Stadt.
1. Redout byren.
2. 't Viercant
3. Punt Cuylenburch.
4. Punt Zeeburch.
5. Punt Groeningen.
6. Punt Overyssel.
7. Punt Westvrieslandt.
8. Punt Uytrecht.
9. Punt Zeelandia.
10. Punt Nassauw.
11. Punt Diest.
12. Punt Uytrecht.
13. Straet Uytrecht.
14. Redout van Capt Silvernagel.
15. Punt Hollandia.
16. Cinees Siecken huys.
17. Timmerwerf der Chyneesen.
18. Vismarckt.
19. Timmerwerf van de Company.
20. 't Spinhuys.
21. De Jonckers Straet.

Quebec, 1744

JACQUES-NICOLAS BELLIN ▪ HAND-COLORED COPPER ENGRAVING ▪ NUMEROUS COPIES EXIST

MAP OF THE TOWN OF QUEBEC

SCALE

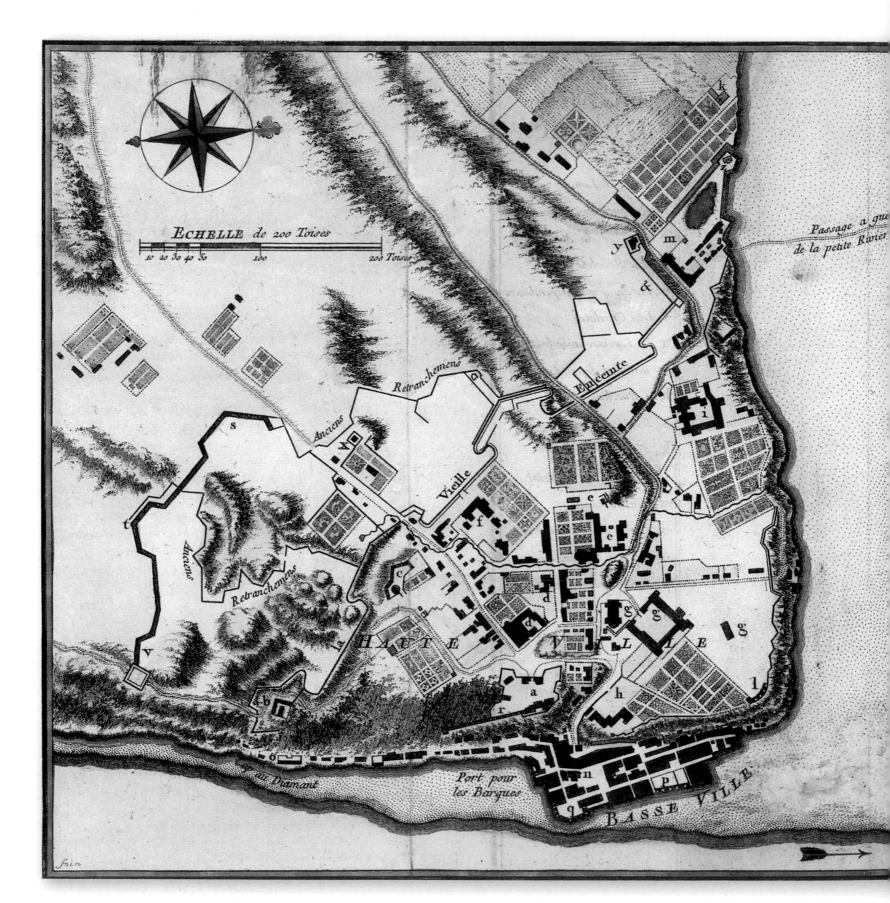

> Thus the fortifications began at the palace . . . ran along to the Upper Town . . . and terminated on the mountain toward Cape Diamond.

PIERRE FRANÇOIS XAVIER DE CHARLEVOIX, *HISTORY AND GENERAL DESCRIPTION OF NEW FRANCE*, 1744

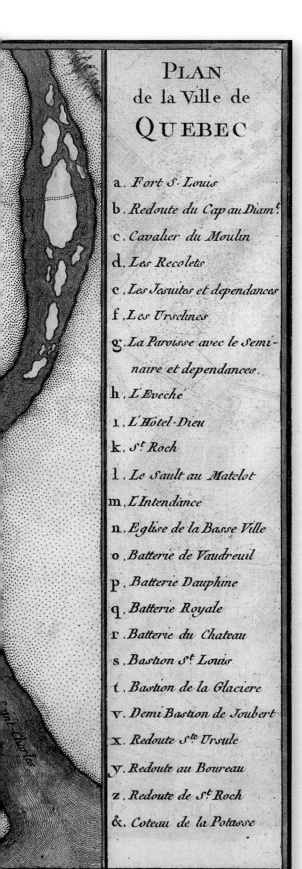

PLAN de la Ville de QUEBEC

a . *Fort S. Louis*
b . *Redoute du Cap au Diam.*
c . *Cavalier du Moulin*
d . *Les Recolets*
e . *Les Jesuites et dependances*
f . *Les Urselines*
g . *La Paroisse avec le Seminaire et dependances.*
h . *L'Eveche*
i . *L'Hôtel-Dieu*
k . *S.t Roch*
l . *Le Sault au Matelot*
m . *L'Intendance*
n . *Eglise de la Basse Ville*
o . *Batterie de Vaudreuil*
p . *Batterie Dauphine*
q . *Batterie Royale*
r . *Batterie du Chateau*
s . *Bastion S.t Louis*
t . *Bastion de la Glaciere*
v . *Demi Bastion de Joubert*
x . *Redoute S.te Ursule*
y . *Redoute au Boureau*
z . *Redoute de S.t Roch*
&. *Coteau de la Potasse*

France became a colonial power in North America in the early 17th century as French settlers established short-lived territories along the Atlantic seaboard and, more lastingly, in the Gulf of St. Lawrence, creating "New France." In 1608 explorer Samuel de Champlain founded the first permanent French base in Canada at Quebec, which grew as a fortified fur-trading post; in 1663 the strategically vital town became New France's capital. This fine, detailed plan of Quebec, which by 1744 housed around 2,000 people, is oriented with west at the top. It was created by a leading French cartographer, Jacques-Nicolas Bellin (1703–72), for inclusion in the monumental *History and general description of New France* compiled by Jesuit priest Pierre François Xavier de Charlevoix; it was also sold separately. Major structures appear in the key, and the Haute and Basse villes (Upper and Lower towns) and the fortifications are labeled.

Visual tour

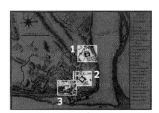

KEY

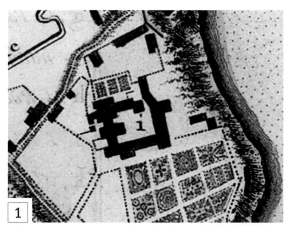

▶ **HÔTEL-DIEU** The first purpose-built hospital in North America was opened in 1644 by Augustinian nuns; their successors ran it until 1962. Today it is a teaching hospital, and the building seen here still stands.

1

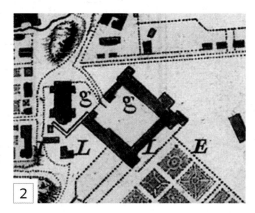

2

▲ **PARISH CHURCH AND SEMINARY** Religious orders played a key role in the settlement of New France. The Seminary of Quebec, founded in 1663, trained new priests during the drive to convert native peoples to Christianity.

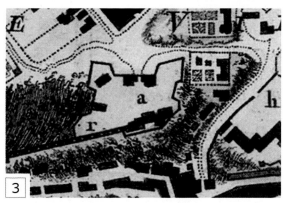

3

▲ **FORT ST. LOUIS** Set high on a cliff overlooking the port, the 1648 fort was the residence of New France's governor. It was substantially enlarged in the early 1700s, but destroyed by fire in 1834. In 1893, what is still Quebec's most imposing hotel opened on the site.

Santo Domingo, 1589

GIOVANNI BATTISTA BOAZIO ▪ HAND-COLORED ENGRAVING ▪
LIBRARY OF CONGRESS, WASHINGTON, D.C., USA

SCALE

MAP OF SANTO DOMINGO

Pirate, explorer, and scourge of Spain, Sir Francis Drake—among Elizabethan England's most noted seafarers—led the largest English fleet yet to the New World in 1585-86. With open warfare declared between England and France in 1585, the fleet's goal was to disrupt and plunder Spain's settlements to enrich the English crown, Drake's financial backers, and Drake himself. Four raids took place—that against Santo Domingo on the Spanish island of Hispaniola was the second, in January 1586. It took the Spaniards entirely unawares. Drake's forces remained in Santo Domingo for a month, gleefully looting and raiding the settlement, and deliberately terrorizing its citizens.

The first published account of the voyage, illustrated with five maps by Boazio, an Italian who worked extensively in England, was a work of anti-Spanish propaganda. Boazio's richly colored view of Santo Domingo is as much an illustration of the raid as a map of the city and its lush, tropical surroundings. Events that occurred at different times—a raiding party landing at lower left, the Spaniards fleeing the city, the destruction of the Spanish fleet—are shown simultaneously. The cartographer's interest in the exotic sea life of the New World is also evident.

Visual tour

KEY

1

2

▲ **CATHEDRAL OF SANTA MARÍA LA MENOR** Begun in 1512 and completed in 1540, Santa María la Menor is the oldest cathedral in the New World. Although Drake used it as his headquarters, he also extensively looted the cathedral to persuade the Spaniards to buy off his forces. What could not be removed was destroyed.

▲ **DESTROYING THE SPANISH FLEET** The Spaniards had approximately 30 ships in Santo Domingo. Drake made off with three as replacements for ships in his own 21-strong fleet, about 20 were burned to the waterline, and one, a galley, sunk. Boazio's cartographic license is apparent in his depiction of the narrow Ozana River as a wide waterway.

We broke into the gates with a great rush and
with our full **exertion**, and entered the city
together with the enemy **pell-mell**.

CONTEMPORARY ENGLISH ACCOUNT OF THE FALL OF SANTO DOMINGO, 1588

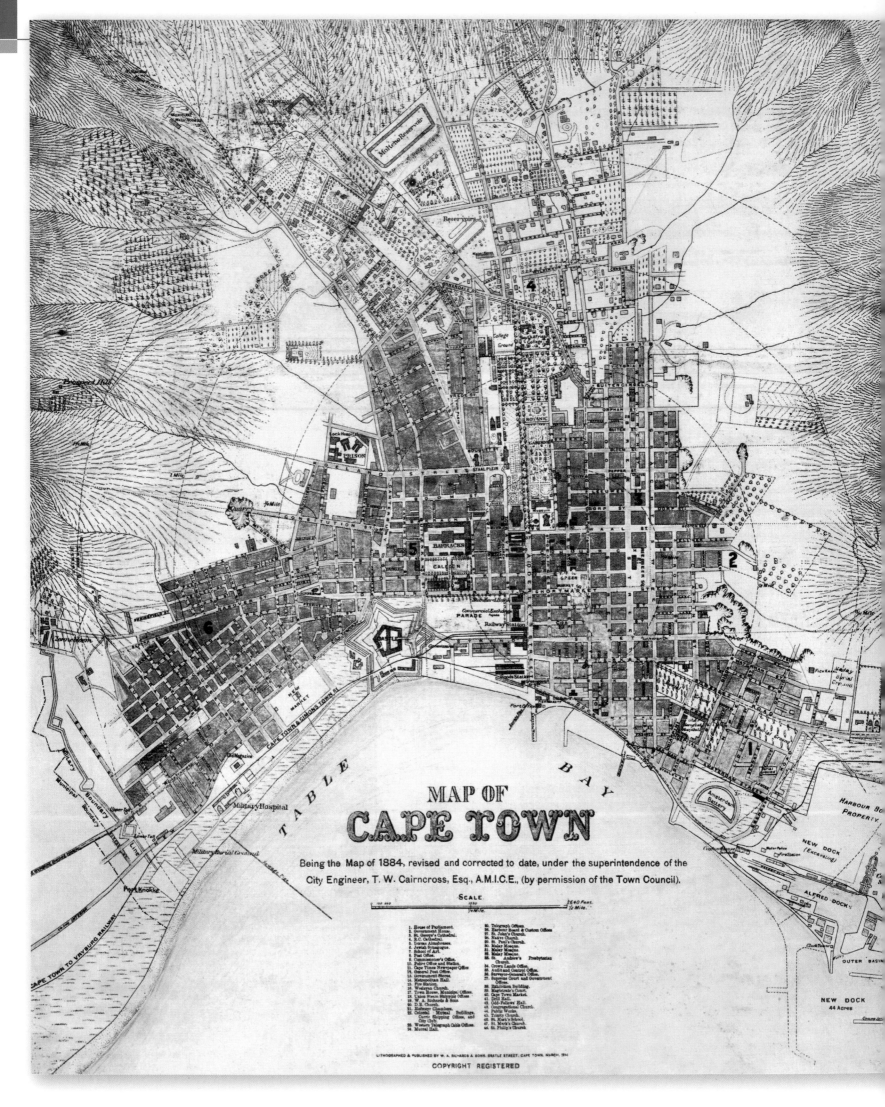

MAP OF
CAPE TOWN

Being the Map of 1884, revised and corrected to date, under the superintendence of the
City Engineer, T. W. Cairncross, Esq., A.M.I.C.E., (by permission of the Town Council).

SCALE

1. House of Parliament.
2. Government House.
3. St. George's Cathedral.
4. R.C. Cathedral.
5. Lutheran Almshouses.
6. Jewish Synagogue.
7. School of Art.
8. Post Office.
9. Commissioner's Office.
10. Police Office and Station.
11. Cape Times Newspaper Office
12. General Post Office.
13. Government Stores.
14. Metropolitan Hall.
15. Fire Station.
16. Wesleyan Church.
17. Town House, Municipal Offices.
18. Union Steam Shipping Offices
19. W. A. Richards & Sons.
20. D.R. Church.
21. Mechanics' Chambers.
22. Colonial Mutual Building,
    Currie Shipping Offices, and
    City Club.
23. Western Telegraph Cable Offices.
24. Mutual Hall.

25. Telegraph Offices.
26. Harbour Board & Custom Offices
27. St. John's Church.
28. Native Church.
29. St. Paul's Church.
30. Malay Mosque.
31. Malay Mosque.
32. Malay Mosque.
33. St. Andrew's Presbyterian
    Church.
34. Crown Lands Office.
35. Audit and Control Office.
36. Surveyor-General's Office.
37. Supreme Court and Government
    Offices.
38. Exhibition Building.
39. Magistrate's Court.
40. Cape Town Market.
41. Drill Hall.
42. Odd-Fellows' Hall.
43. Congregational Church.
44. Public Works.
45. Trinity Church.
46. St. Mary's School.
47. St. Mark's Church.
48. St. Philip's Church.

LITHOGRAPHED & PUBLISHED BY W. A. RICHARDS & SONS, CASTLE STREET, CAPE TOWN, MARCH, 1891.

COPYRIGHT REGISTERED

TABLE BAY

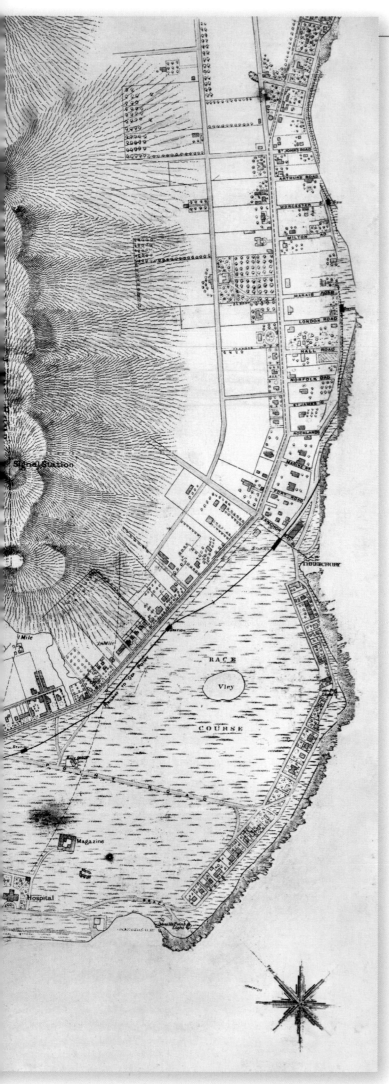

Cape Town, 1884

T. W. CAIRNCROSS ■ LITHOGRAPH ■ NUMEROUS COPIES EXIST

UNKNOWN

MAP OF CAPE TOWN

Late 19th-century Cape Town was a city in rapid transition, enjoying a sudden economic boom after the discovery of diamond fields to the north of it. In this 1884 map of the capital of the British Cape Colony—which is unusually oriented with southwest at the top— the grid plan of the original Dutch settlement is still clearly visible. However, the city was poised to expand dramatically, in part as a consequence of much-improved transportation links; the small and simple structure of the relatively new railroad station, only built in 1861, can be seen at the center of town, near the coast.

The shoreline as shown in this map is dramatically different from that of the city today. This is particularly obvious in the positioning of the Dutch-built Castle of Good Hope, now well inland as a result of extensive land reclamation programs in the 1930s and '40s, but shown here as it was originally built, directly next to the sea.

Visual tour

KEY

▶ **BOTANIC GARDENS** Laid out in 1652, the botanic gardens known as the Company's Garden were originally intended to produce vegetables and fruit for Dutch ships. The area was opened to the public as a pleasure garden from 1848 and is still in use as such today.

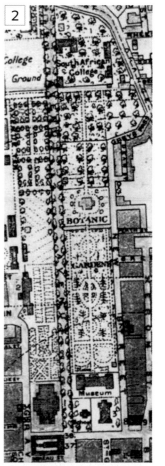

▼ **CASTLE OF GOOD HOPE** Constructed by the Dutch East India Company, the star-shaped Castle of Good Hope was the most important military installation in southern Africa.

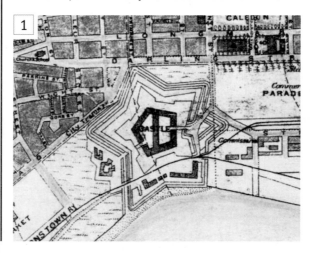

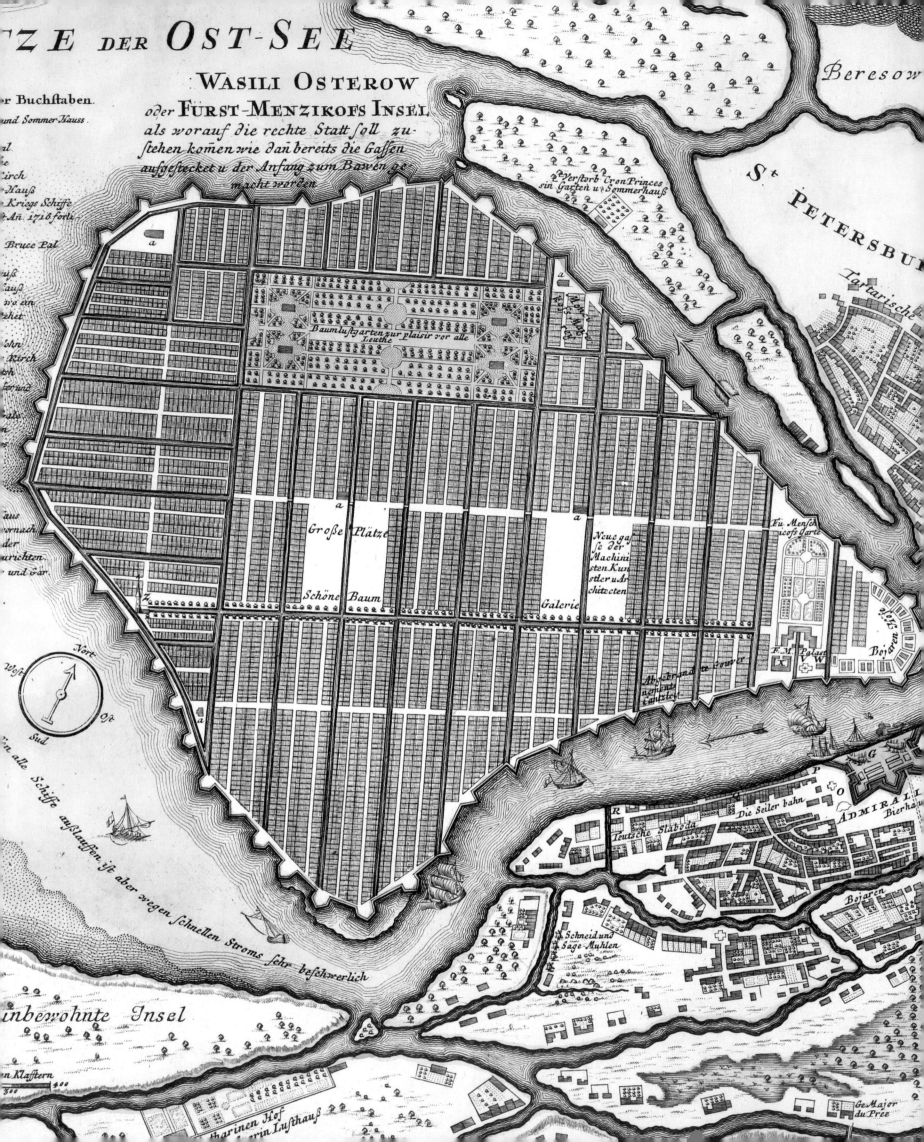

ZE DER **OST-SEE**

WASILI OSTEROW
oder **FURST-MENZIKOFS INSEL**
als worauf die rechte Statt soll zu-
stehen komen wie dan bereits die Gaßen
aufgestecket u der Anfang zum Bawen ge-
macht worden

Beresow

S.t PETERSBU

Tortarische

Verstorb Cron Princes
sin Garten u. Sommerhauß

Baumlustgarten zur plaisir vor alle
Leuthe

Große Plätze

Schöne Baum

Neue gas
se der
Machini
sten Kun
stler u. Ar
chitecten

Galerie

Fu Mensch
icofs Garte

Abgebrandte Cour
Cantzley

F. M. Palast

Bojaren

Nort

West

Ost

Sud

in alle Schiffe außlauffen ist aber wegen
Schnellen Stroms sehr beschwerlich

Die Seiler bahn

ADMIRAL
Bierhau

Teutsche Sloboda

Schneid und
Säge-Muhlen

Bojaren

inbewohnte Insel

Klafftern
400
300

tharinen Hof
rin Lusthauß

GeMajor
du Pree

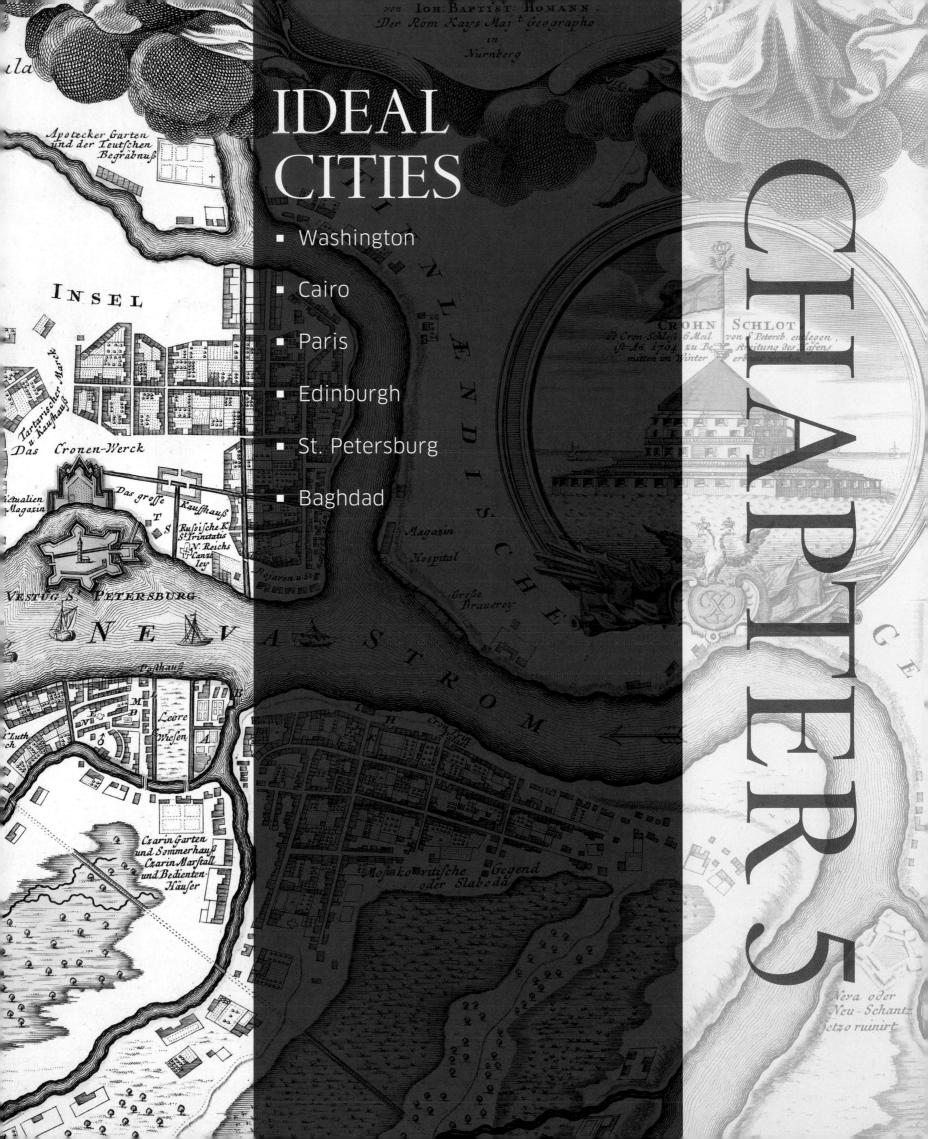

IDEAL CITIES

- Washington
- Cairo
- Paris
- Edinburgh
- St. Petersburg
- Baghdad

CHAPTER 5

Ideal Cities

The concept of an "ideal" city is not new. The philosophers Plato in his *Republic* (c.380 BCE) and Thomas More in *Utopia* (1516) had outlined their concepts of the perfect urban environment: not too large, civically manageable, and to be designed as a healthy, sanitary, and morally inspiring environment. In ancient times, attempts had also been made (at el-Armana in Egypt c.1341 BCE and by the Abbasid caliph al-Mansur at Baghdad in 764) to reinvent Heaven upon Earth, with designs frequently informed not just by scriptures, but by stellar astronomical observations.

Planning ideal cities

Establishing new capitals had the advantage of being able to start with a clean slate. In the 18th century, the Russian ruler Peter the Great moved his capital from Moscow to the new city of St. Petersburg in 1712. Johann Baptist Homann's map of the city (*see pp.208-09*)—created in 1721, the same year that Peter became Emperor of All Russia—is a blueprint for the emperor's vision of the capital, as the city was still under construction. Similarly, the first map to be produced of the new capital of the United States, Washington, D.C., showed a city that did not as yet exist (*see pp.186-87*). This ideal plan of Washington would not be fully realized until the beginning of the 20th century, when landscaping and building work on the city's National Mall brought this central area closer to the original vision for the nation's capital (*see box p.191*).

Expanding medieval centers

Many existing cities, which had grown organically throughout the medieval period, were also replanned to create an improved layout and living environment. Towns such as Berlin, Dublin, and Edinburgh—and later, Madrid, Barcelona, and Mexico—were greatly enlarged, often by creating idealized new extensions and suburbs while preserving much of the historical heart of the old city. John Ainslie's map of Edinburgh (*see pp.206-07*) from 1804 highlights the formality of the layout for the residential area known as New Town—a masterpiece of urban planning designed in the late 18th century—when compared to the ramshackle streets and alleys of the Old Town's medieval quarter.

▲ **CAIRO, 1521-26** Now one of the world's fastest growing megacities, Cairo was founded in 968 as a new capital for the Fatimid dynasty and planned as a center of learning and government set alongside the fertile banks of the Nile River.

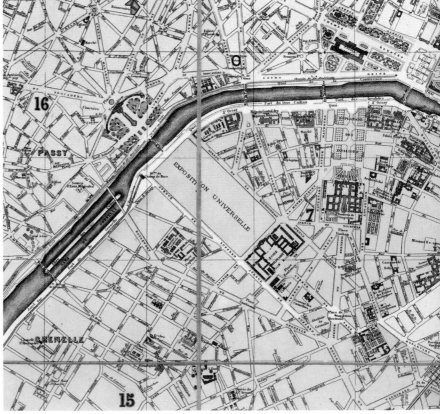

▲ **PARIS, 1878** By 1870, Haussmann has restructured Paris to address water and gas supply, transportation flow, and gas lighting systems. It had also been ordered into new administrative districts—the color-coded *arrondissements* seen on this map.

> # The materials of city planning are: sky, space, trees, steel and cement; in that order and in that hierarchy
>
> **LE CORBUSIER**, SWISS-FRENCH ARCHITECT

Medieval cities were also reshaped by catastrophe. The Lisbon earthquake of 1755 devastated the capital (*see box p.104*), but it allowed planners to create a more ideal city center (*see pp.106–07*). In London, however, plans for rebuilding in the wake of the Great Fire of 1666 (*see box p.72*) were never realized. It was not until the early 19th century that London was improved by the addition of new green spaces and suburbs (*see pp.76–79*).

Creating modern cities

In France, social and urban reform underpinned plans to rebuild the capital, Paris. Although kings such as Henry IV and Louis XIV had made additions to the medieval center, it was the radical restructuring under Georges-Eugène Haussmann that made Paris into an enduring modern city. Detailed maps after Haussmann's renovation demonstrate these reforms, and the expanded administrative structure provided by the *arrondissements* (*see pp.202–05*).

In the early decades of the 20th century, modernist visionaries such as the Italian Futurist architect Antonio Sant'Elia and the urban planner Le Corbusier were radically questioning the infrastructure and topography of the city. However, with the rise of totalitarian states across Europe, social engineering came to the forefront of notions of the "ideal" city. Hitler's favorite architect, Albert Speer, drew up visionary plans for transforming Berlin into the capital of a new Europe. It was a model of "ideal" planning that also occurred in Stalin's Russia and Mussolini's Italy.

The 20th century also saw examples of cities built from scratch. Brasília in Brazil and Canberra in Australia were defined by expensive architectural conceits and landscaped environments. However, their success as ideal cities is debatable; while they are functional administrative centers, it has been argued that they have little urban "soul."

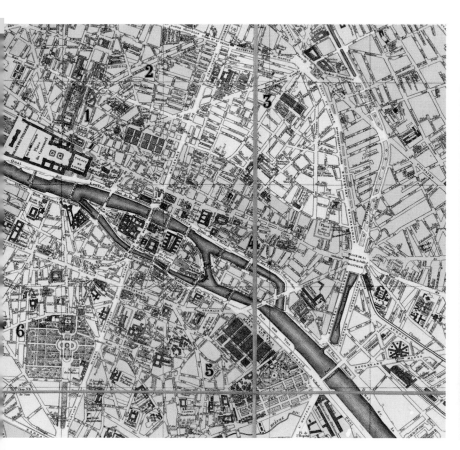

▲ **WASHINGTON, D.C., 1880** By the late 19th century, the US capital city was being celebrated in widely distributed popular prints, providing an image of the center of government to citizens across a vast country.

Washington, 1792

SAMUEL HILL ▪ HAND-COLORED ENGRAVING ▪
LIBRARY OF CONGRESS, WASHINGTON, D.C., USA

SCALE

THE ELLICOTT PLAN

Many cities have founding myths, yet very few have specific founding dates, as is the case with Washington. On July 9, 1790, the United States Congress passed the Residence Act approving the creation of a national capital on the north bank of the Potomac River. Then on December 9, 1791, the commissioners overseeing the capital's construction named the city in honor of President George Washington (1732–99). Andrew Ellicott's "Plan of the City of Washington," published the following year, is not just the first official map of the new US capital, it is its blueprint.

Selling the city

Unlike all the other maps in this book, which at least purport to be representations of existing cities, this is a map of somewhere that had yet to be built. This is apparent in the way that all the blocks on the map are numbered, to facilitate the sale of land for the new enterprise. In addition to being a blueprint, Ellicott's plan was also a sales brochure for developers to buy off-plan. The text on the map describes various aspects of the city, such as: "The grand avenues and such streets as lead immediately to public places, are from 130 to 160 feet wide, and may be conveniently divided into foot ways, walks of trees, and a carriage way."

This plan was engraved and published in two versions, one by the firm of Thackara & Vallance in Philadelphia and another, reproduced here in a colored version, by Samuel Hill in Boston.

> At a Public Sale of Lots in the City of Washington, George Washington, President of the United States of America became purchaser of Lots 12, 13 & 14 in Square 637 ”

CERTIFICATE FOR LOTS PURCHASED IN THE DISTRICT OF COLUMBIA,
SEPTEMBER 18, 1793; SQUARE 637 IS JUST SOUTH OF THE CAPITOL BUILDING

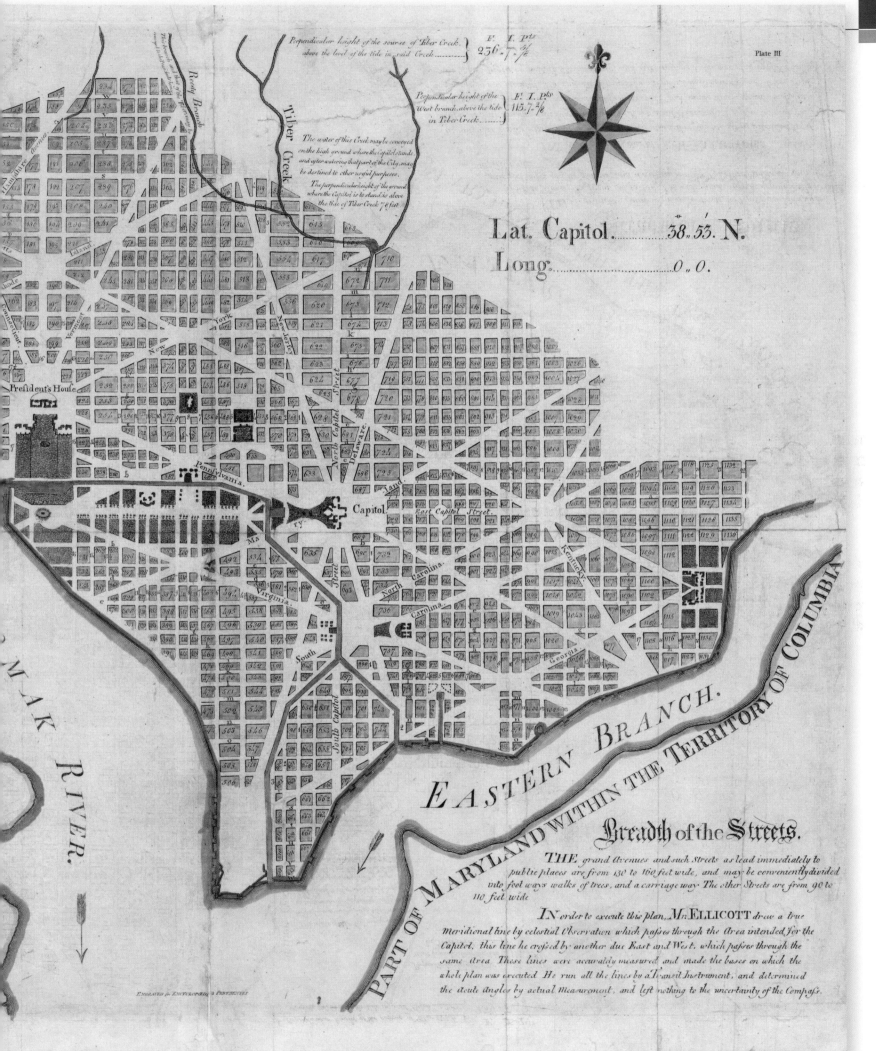

Plate III

Perpendicular height of the source of Tiber Creek F. T. Pts
above the level of the tide in said Creek ...... } 236..7..⅝

Perpendicular height of the F. T. Pts
West branch above the tide } 115..7..⅔
in Tiber Creek ......

The water of this Creek may be conveyed
on the high ground where the Capitol stands,
and after watering that part of the City, may
be destined to other useful purposes.

The perpendicular height of the ground
where the Capitol is to stand is above
the tide of Tiber Creek 78 feet.

Lat. Capitol ...... 38..53. N.

Long. ...... 0..0.

President's House

Capitol

East Capitol Street.

EASTERN BRANCH.

PART OF MARYLAND WITHIN THE TERRITORY OF COLUMBIA

POTOMAK RIVER.

Breadth of the Streets.

THE grand Avenues and such Streets as lead immediately to
public places are from 130 to 160 feet wide, and may be conveniently divided
into foot ways walks of trees, and a carriage way. The other Streets are from 90 to
110 feet wide.

IN order to execute this plan, Mr. ELLICOTT drew a true
Meridional line by celestial Observation which passes through the Area intended for the
Capitol, this line he crossed by another due East and West, which passes through the
same Area. These lines were accurately measured and made the bases on which the
whole plan was executed. He run all the lines by a Transit Instrument, and determined
the acute angles by actual Measurement, and left nothing to the uncertainty of the Compass.

ENGRAVED for ENCYCLOPÆDIA PERTHENSIS

Washington, 1880

C. R. PARSONS ■ LITHOGRAPH ■ NUMEROUS COPIES EXIST

THE CITY OF WASHINGTON

SCALE

Printmaking firm Currier & Ives, based in New York City from 1834 to 1907, described itself as "the Grand Central Depot for Cheap and Popular Prints." In its 72 years of operation, it published more than 7,500 lithographs (prints made using a greasy substance, such as wax crayon) to adorn homes across the United States. Popular subjects included historical scenes, still lifes, and images of ships and railroads, as well as landscapes and cityscapes.

This cityscape was one of an extensive series celebrating the great American city during an era of rapid expansion. It was drawn by one of the publisher's regular artists, Charles R. Parsons (the "R" distinguished him from his father, who was also named Charles Parsons and drew maps, some of which were also published by Currier & Ives). Charles R. Parsons worked on a large number of such city views during the period from 1872 to 1892, including Boston, Chicago, Philadelphia, San Francisco, Brooklyn, and several of New York City.

Washington from above

Drawn from the air, this panoramic city view illustrates Washington from above the Potomac River looking north. It shows landmarks—such as the US Capitol and Washington Monument—in the foreground, but neglects background areas. Panoramic maps like this often depict major monuments in detail but are inaccurate in other respects. This view of Washington holds some curiosity value because shortly after it was drawn the city was remodeled, following the 1902 McMillan Plan (*see p.191*).

There is something good and motherly about Washington, the grand old benevolent National Asylum for the helpless.

MARK TWAIN, *THE GILDED AGE*, 1873

Visual tour

KEY

▶ **THE US CAPITOL** Construction of the Capitol building began in 1793. This seat of the US Government was constantly expanding during its first 70 years to accommodate the growing number of representatives. After the Statue of Freedom was lowered onto its dome in 1863, building paused for a time and the Capitol stayed in the form seen on this map. Work resumed four years later with the creation of marble terraces to the north, south, and west of the building. The small white building below the Capitol's steps is the first greenhouse of the US Botanic Garden, constructed in 1867.

1

2

▲ **DUPONT CIRCLE** This plaza was one of many open spaces included in Ellicott's "Plan of the City of Washington" (see pp.186-87) published in 1792. By the time of Parson's map, it was at the heart of a fashionable neighborhood. The map includes the turreted mansion known as Stewart's Castle, built in 1873, on the north of the Circle. The depiction of the equestrian statue of Samuel Francis Du Pont, not installed until 1884, would have been based on plans.

▶ **THE WHITE HOUSE** An original feature on the Ellicott plan (see pp.186-87), the presidential residence was completed in 1800, but rebuilt in the form seen here after being damaged in the War of 1812 with the British. The West and East Wings were added in the 20th century, but the central residence has changed little.

3

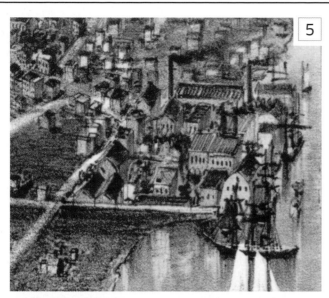

5

◄ **NAVY YARD** The oldest shore establishment of the US Navy was inaugurated in 1799. It became the navy's largest shipbuilding and shipfitting facility, constructing more than 20 vessels. In 1886, just six years after this map was produced, the Yard was designated the manufacturing center for all naval artillery.

6

◄ **LINCOLN SQUARE** Now known as Lincoln Park, this area was originally conceived to hold a monumental column from which all distances in America would be measured; however, this plan was never executed. During the Civil War it was the site of Lincoln Hospital, and later became Lincoln Square, which from 1876 was graced with a statue of the former president, as shown on this map.

7

◄ **THE SMITHSONIAN** The headquarters of the Smithsonian Institution, which was founded "for the increase and diffusion of knowledge among men" in 1846, was sited on Washington's prestigious Mall. Construction of a gothic-styled building began in 1847 and was completed five years later. A second building, built to serve as a national museum, was under construction while this map was drawn, but is shown here completed.

4

▲ **WASHINGTON MONUMENT** The building of the world's tallest obelisk began in 1848. Work was halted from 1854–77 due in part to lack of funds and in part to the Civil War. When this map was drawn the monument was still under construction, but in 1892 the map was reissued showing the completed structure, which had opened in 1888. However, the reflection of the obelisk in the Potomac was not amended, so the later map shows a complete obelisk casting half a reflection.

IN **CONTEXT**

One hundred years after the founding of Washington, legislators decided that the development of the capital needed a change of direction. A new plan—named for the senator, James McMillan, who commissioned it—proposed relandscaping the ceremonial heart of the city. This involved replacing trees and parks with lawns and pools to open up grand views. It also proposed using reclaimed land from the river to extend the area and to site the imposing monument that would be the Lincoln Memorial. A height limit of 160 ft (50 m) was set to maintain a skyline of steeples, domes, and monuments. The plan would also clear slums, introduce new zoning, and establish a series of parks. The McMillan Plan is the blueprint for Washington today.

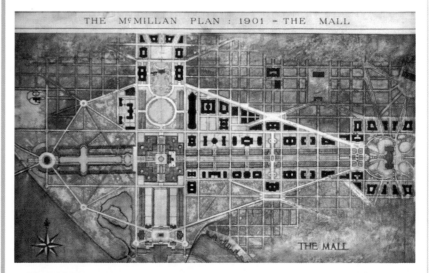

▲ **The McMillan Plan** of 1901, which redesigned Washington's National Mall

Cairo, 1521–26

PIRI REIS ▪ INK AND PIGMENTS ON PAPER ▪ THE WALTERS ART MUSEUM, BALTIMORE, USA

SCALE

MAP OF CAIRO

Egypt was ruled by the Mamluk Sultanate from 1250 until the early 16th century. The Mamluk state was eventually overthrown by the Ottoman Empire in 1517, bringing this part of North Africa under the rule of its sultan at Constantinople. The author of this map, the Turkish sea captain Piri Reis (*see p.42*), was a part of the naval supply fleet supporting the Ottoman army that defeated the Mamluks. It is quite possible that he personally visited the city–the map is certainly accurate enough to suggest that this may have been the case.

Cairo was a walled city separated from the Nile by a broad flood plain. A single road connected the main city gate with Bulaq, the city's riverside port. To the south–which is at the top on this map–a grand aqueduct supplied water to the Citadel, the city's fortified seat of power. To the east, beyond the city walls, were large areas of cemeteries and then the rocky bluffs of the Moqattam Hills, which the Ottoman army had used to ambush the Mamluk forces. The map also correctly depicts the main north-south thoroughfare through the walled city, lined by a series of grand mosques. The placing of some of these buildings is not accurate, however, and the mosques appear more Turkish than Mamluk in style, suggesting that the map may not have been drawn "on the ground" but compiled from sketches, notes, and reports at a later date.

> I swear that if it were possible to put Rome, Venice, Milan, Padua, Florence, and four more cities together, they would not equal in wealth and population half that of Cairo.

RABBI MESHULAM OF VOLTERRA, 1481

Visual tour

KEY

▶ **RAWDAH** Piri packs this island in the Nile with detail: at its southern tip is the Nilometer, used since ancient times to measure the annual rise of the river, while to the north are the gardens that give the island its name (rawdah is Arabic for "garden").

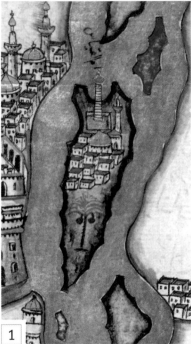

1

2

◀ **THE PYRAMIDS** The mapmaker cheated a little here: although the three Pyramids of Giza do lie to the southwest of Cairo as drawn, in reality they were far out in the desert. Piri brought them closer to the Nile in order to include them on his map.

▼ **BULAQ** A single road ran from the busy river port of Bulaq to the main city gate. The map shows vegetation on the flood plain surrounding the road, which was inundated regularly during the annual flooding of the Nile until the building of dams in the 19th century.

3

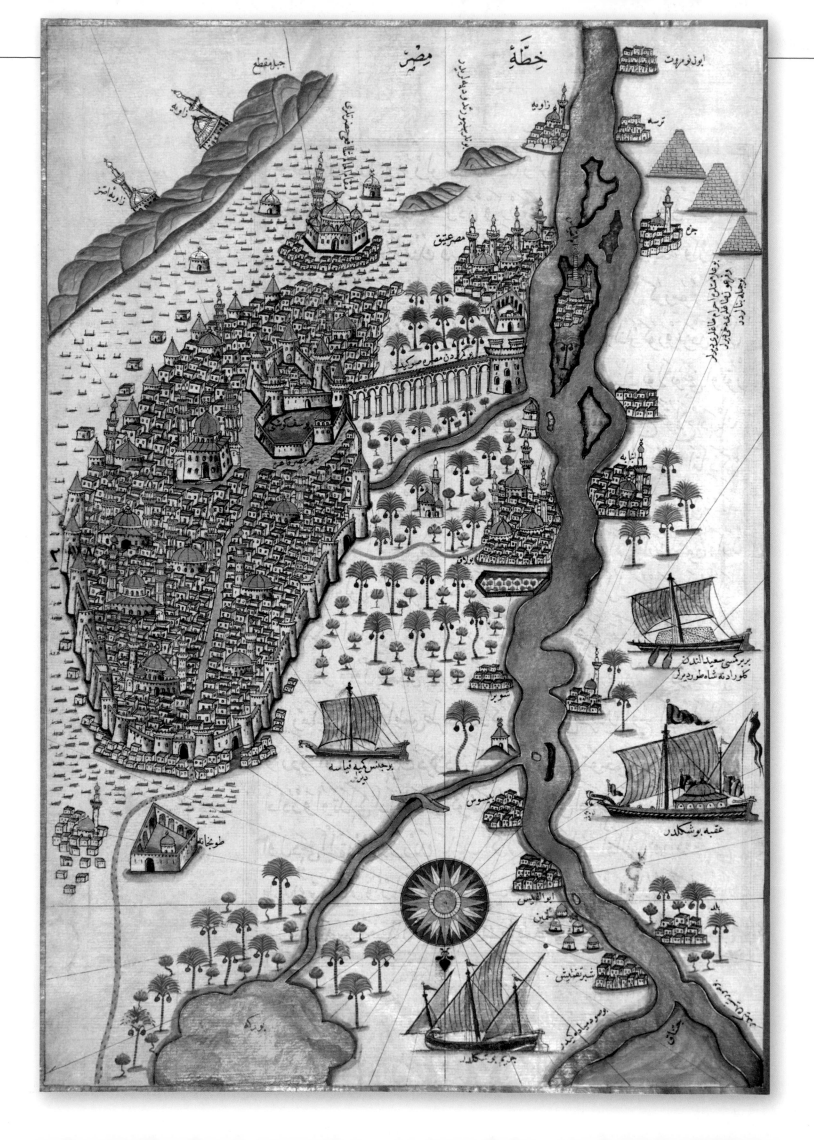

Paris, 1615

MATTHÄUS MERIAN ▪ HAND-COLORED ENGRAVING ▪ NUMEROUS COPIES EXIST

SCALE

THE MERIAN MAP OF PARIS

Some features of this beautiful document, which was created by, and named after, the Swiss engraver Matthäus Merian, immediately identify it as a map of Paris: for example, the Île de la Cité, connecting to the right and left banks of the river via the arches of the Pont Neuf, or the well-known grand Gothic frontage of Notre Dame. In many other respects, however, it bears little resemblance to the city as it is known today. The map, oriented with east at the top, shows us a compact city wrapped around by muscular walls. In fact, as can be seen in the foreground, there are two sets of walls: an inner ring built in the late 14th century by Charles V and his son and successor, Charles VI, and an outer ring of earthen bastions with a moat, erected in the late 16th century. These fortifications were not just for show; as recently as 1590, the city had successfully endured a prolonged siege by Protestant Huguenot forces under Henry IV during the French Wars of Religion, albeit with the loss of about 30,000 citizens who died of starvation.

A map of improvements

Since 1598 there had been peace and Paris, still the largest city in Europe, was in recovery. Its commercial center was the port on the right bank, at the Place de Grève, and the main market, Les Halles, was close by. The Louvre was the main royal residence. From here, in the early years of the 17th century, when Merian's map was made, Henry IV embarked on a grand plan to overhaul parts of the medieval city, creating grand new public spaces and buildings, including laying out the Place Royale (now the Place des Vosges), inaugurating the Pont Neuf, and extending the Louvre. Merian's plan is the first map to show either the Pont Neuf or the Place des Vosges.

MATTHÄUS **MERIAN**

1593–1650

Born in Basel in Switzerland, Merian (often called Merian the Elder to distinguish him from his son) studied drawing and engraving in Zurich. He was obviously a gifted student as he drew his map of Paris when he was still in his early 20s.

In 1618, Merian relocated to Frankfurt where he worked for the publisher Johann Theodor de Bry. He married de Bry's daughter and after his father-in-law's death, took over the de Bry family business. He completed works left unfinished on de Bry's death including *Collectiones Peregrinationum in Indiam* (Collections of Travels in India), but his greatest work was the *Topographia Germaniae*, a 16-volume set on the topography of German, French, and Italian territories. The engravings in these volumes, which were executed by several artists including Merian and his sons, often depicted bird's-eye or panoramic views of cities, accompanied by text written by the German scholar Martin Zeiler (1589–1661).

> This city is another world / Therein a flowerful world, /
> Of people very powerful / To whom all things abound.

MATTHÄUS MERIAN, VERSE IN THE CARTOUCHE AT THE BOTTOM LEFT OF THE MAP

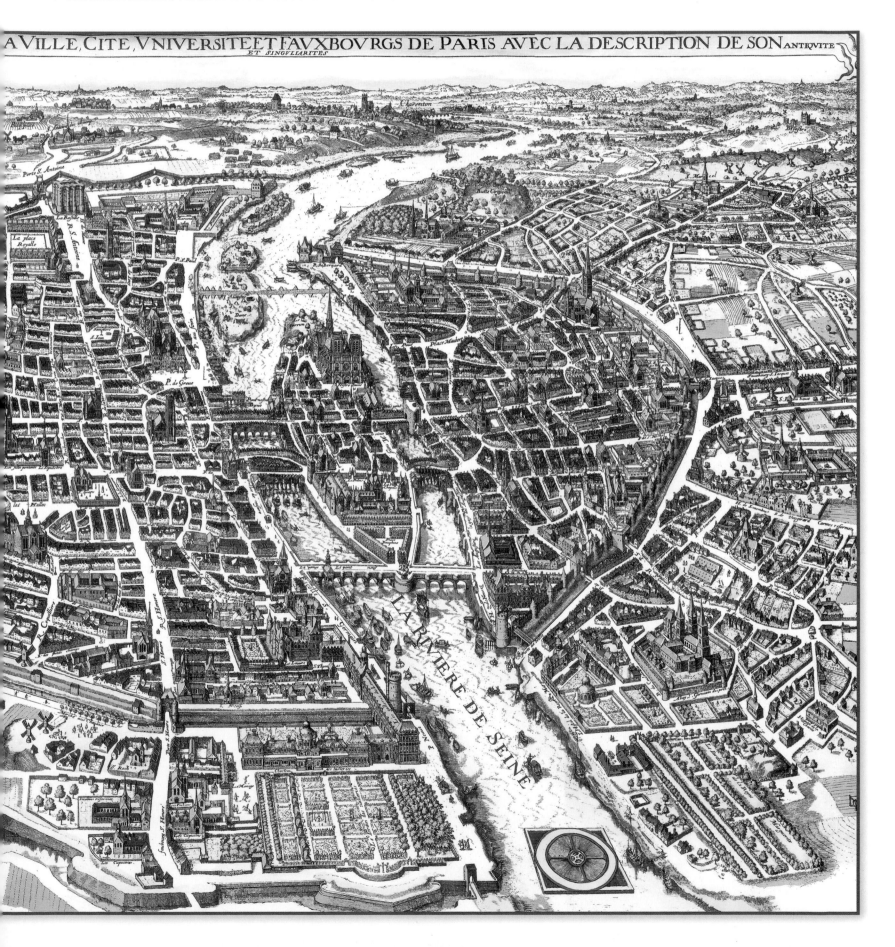

A VILLE, CITE, VNIVERSITE ET FAVXBOVRGS DE PARIS AVEC LA DESCRIPTION DE SON ANTIQVITE
ET SINGVLIARITES

LA RIVIÉRE DE SEINE

Visual tour

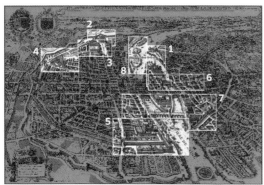

KEY

▶ **NOTRE DAME** By the time Merian came to draw his map, the cathedral at the heart of Paris was already a venerable structure. Completed in 1345, it was by this time 270 years old. Following the traditional technique of the time for depicting major civic and religious buildings, Merian has exaggerated the size of the cathedral to emphasize its importance.

▼ **THE BASTILLE** Built in approximately 1370–80, the Bastille underwent significant changes in the century prior to Merian's map. A southern entrance to the fortress had been created (visible on the right, crossing a moat); neighboring Porte Saint-Antoine had its drawbridge replaced with a fixed bridge; and large earthwork bastions were formed projecting eastwards (seen on the map in a V-shaped form).

▼ **PLACE ROYALE** Built under the patronage of Henry IV from 1605 to 1612, the Place Royale was the first planned square in Paris, featuring house frontages that were all built to the same design, as Merian's drawing makes clear. Since 1800 it has been known as the Place des Vosges.

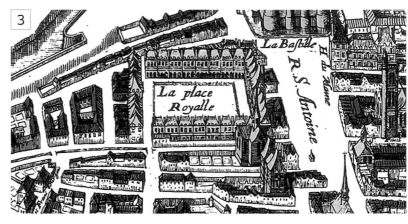

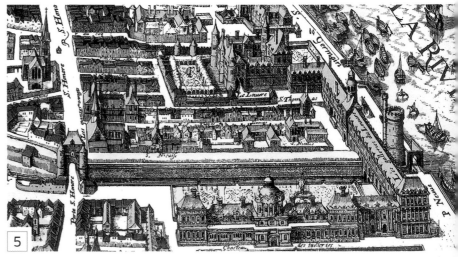

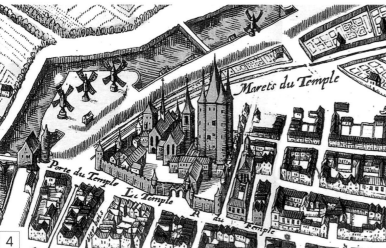

▲ **THE TEMPLE** Originally built as the fortified headquarters and monastery of the Knights Templar in France, this building was used as a prison after the order was disbanded in 1312. As drawn by Merian, it is a sizeable complex, dominated by the massive turreted Great Tower. Napoleon Bonaparte had the tower and complex demolished in 1808 and nothing remains today.

▲ **THE LOUVRE** In the mid-16th century, Catherine de Medici built a chateau just outside the city walls that became known as the Tuileries Palace. Henry IV linked this to the nearby royal Louvre Palace by means of a Grande Galerie, running parallel to the Seine. At more than a quarter of a mile long, it was at the time of its completion the longest building in the world.

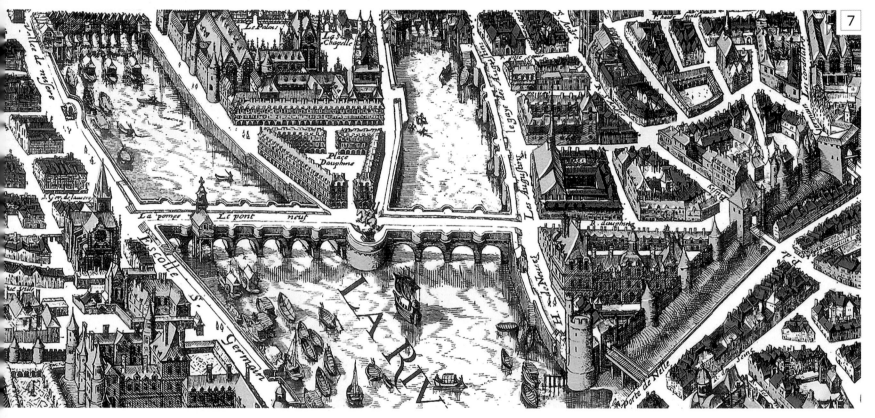

◄ RUE ST JACQUES This one street conveys a sense of how it might have been to visit Paris at the turn of the 17th century. The buildings here are densely packed, culminating in the clustered dwellings on the Petit Pont, with their suggestion of overcrowded, close-quarter living.

▼ PONT NEUF Shown to advantage by the orientation of the map with east at the top, the Pont Neuf, completed in 1606, was the city's first stone bridge. It was also the first bridge that was not topped by buildings, allowing citizens to appreciate its views of the city. Beside it, Henry IV also created the grand Place Dauphine, a regal triangular "square."

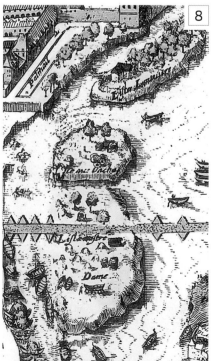

◄ ÎLE SAINT-LOUIS The two islands east of the Île de la Cité were used for the grazing of cattle, as the map shows. However, the fact that there are two separate islands suggests that some of the drawings for the map may have been done before 1615, because in 1614 the ditch between the islands was filled in. Between 1620 and 1650, the land was covered with streets and buildings, and named the Île Saint-Louis after Louis IX.

IN **CONTEXT**

Henry IV was responsible for the first great civic replanning of Paris, perhaps to make amends for having bombarded the city with artillery during the French Wars of Religion (1562–98). He had laid siege to the city in 1590 in an attempt to capture it from the Catholic League. The Protestant king-in-waiting failed so instead elected to convert to Catholicism in order to win over Paris and claim the French throne. Once peace was restored, he embarked on a program of modernization and beautification of the city, with the aim of establishing Paris as the focal point of a unified French state. He picked up some of the projects his predecessors had left unfinished and to these added new plans of his own. The Louvre, the Place Royale, the Pont Neuf, and Place Dauphine were all part of an urban regeneration project that would be unmatched in Paris for more than two centuries.

▲ **Equestrian statue of Henry IV** on the Pont Neuf, at the point where the bridge crosses the Île de la Cité

Paris, 1739

LOUIS BRETEZ ▪ ENGRAVING ON BRASS PLATES ▪
NUMEROUS COPIES EXIST

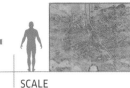

SCALE

THE TURGOT PLAN

One of the most elaborately detailed early isometric projection maps, which represent the three-dimensional nature of places, is the Turgot Plan of Paris. It takes its name from Michel-Étienne Turgot, who held the mayorlike office of Prévôt des Marchands de Paris ("Master of the merchants of Paris") from 1729 to 1740 and who, in 1734, commissioned this great work. Turgot's aim was to show his city as orderly and well governed—the map is filled with wide, clear streets, and the buildings are crisp and pristine—but in reality the Paris of the 1730s was a raucous, teeming city of slums and considerable squalor.

Compiling the plan

The surveying and drawing of the map was led by a sculptor and painter named Louis Bretez. Issued with a permit to enter every building and court in Paris, Bretez and his team produced thousands of sketches that were collected to prepare the final drawings. It is recorded that the task took two years; it took a further three years for the engravers to make the printing plates. The completed plan was finally published in Paris in 1739, consisting of 20 double-page sheets, originally issued in a bound folio. The double pages could be assembled into one large sheet of roughly 8 ft by 10 ft (2.5 m by 3.2 m). The finished work shows every building, bridge, garden, and tree in Paris just a century before Baron Haussmann set to work demolishing many of the city's medieval streets and structures (*see pp.202–05*).

LOUIS **BRETEZ**

Bretez was a sculptor and painter, and a member of the French Académie Royale de Peinture et Sculpture. He was also an architectural draftsman, and in 1706 he published a treatise on how to draw architecture in perspective, a subject that he taught at the Academy.

Historians assume that it was Bretez's authority in architectural drawing that led Michel-Étienne Turgot to select him for the grand project of drawing this map. It is not possible that the work could have been carried out alone, and the likelihood is that Bretez employed a team of apprentices. These assistants would have been directed to allocated districts where they would have sketched façades and noted approximate measurements; it is possible that Bretez himself would then have transferred these sketches to a gridded master drawing.

Visual tour

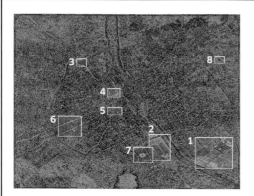

KEY

▶ **HÔTEL DES INVALIDES** Louis XIV ordered the establishment of a home for retired and injured soldiers in 1670. The site was a plain on the western edge of the city. Almost 70 years later, the area was still hardly developed but the complex had grown to include a royal chapel, the Église du Dôme, with its gilded 351-ft- (107-m-) high dome, completed in 1708.

▼ **THE TUILERIES** This royal garden had been in existence for around 180 years by the time Turgot's map was published. During that period it had been remodeled and added to on several occasions by a succession of monarchs. In 1719, early in the reign of Louis XV, the garden was relandscaped yet again into the form shown on this map.

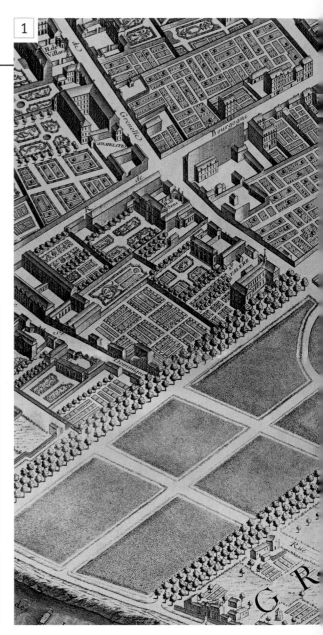

▼ **THE BASTILLE** What was originally built in the 14th century as a fortress to guard the eastern approach to Paris was turned into a prison three centuries later by Cardinal Richelieu. The Turgot Plan precisely renders this dominant and unforgiving landmark, with its towers, thick walls, and dry moat.

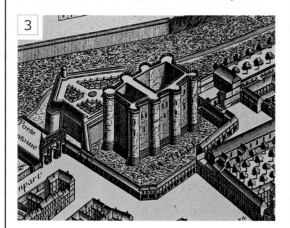

▲ **HÔTEL DE VILLE** The grand building that housed Paris's seat of governance was just over a century old when the Turgot Plan was engraved. It had taken 95 years to complete so, unsurprisingly, no changes were made to its structure for a further 200 years. It stands on the Place de Grève, which, as illustrated, served as a river port for unloading wheat and wood, and which was also a place of executions. Today it is the Place de l'Hôtel de Ville.

▲ **CEMETERY OF THE INNOCENTS** The oldest and largest cemetery in Paris lay right at the heart of the city, beside the markets of what is now Les Halles. It was founded in the 12th century, and by Turgot's time space had run out, leading to mass burials with up to 1,500 bodies buried in a single pit. One visitor in the 18th century described entering Paris as like being "sucked into a fetid sewer," picking out one stench above all others: that of the Cimetière des Innocents.

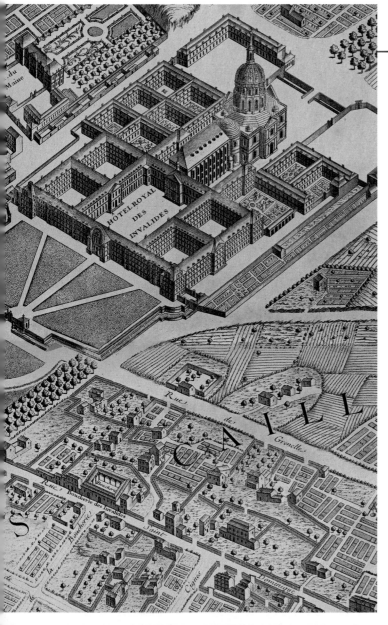

7 ◄ **PLACE VENDÔME** In the dense and irregular street pattern of 18th-century Paris, the Place Vendôme stands out as an orderly space. This grand square was laid out in 1702 as a monument to the military might of Louis XIV. A larger-than-life-size equestrian statue of the king was placed at its center, as seen here. This was later destroyed in the French Revolution and replaced in 1810 with the Napoleonic column that stands in the square today.

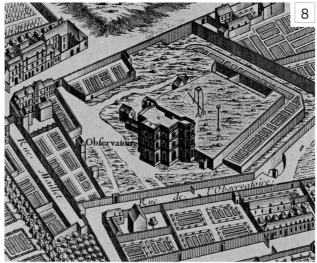

8 ◄ **OBSERVATORY** Built during the long reign of Louis XIV, which fostered numerous artistic and scientific academies in the city, the Paris Observatory was completed in 1671, four years before the Royal Observatory in Greenwich, England. Extended in 1730 and many further times over the centuries, today it is one of the largest astronomical centers in the world.

6

▲ **TREE-LINED BOULEVARDS** In 1670, Louis XIV demolished the fortified city walls built by his royal predecessors to make Paris an "open city." He replaced them with a series of tree-lined *grands boulevards*. On the site of some of the former medieval gates, he erected monuments, including this pair of triumphal arches— Portes Saint-Martin and Saint-Denis—which celebrated recent military victories on the Rhine and in Franche-Comté.

IN **CONTEXT**

The "Sun King" Louis XIV of France (reigned 1643–1715) was not very fond of Paris. As a young man he was forced to flee the city twice and he therefore distrusted its citizens, which is why he relocated the royal court from the Tuileries Palace, at the heart of the city, out to rural Versailles. At the same time, he wanted his capital to reflect his own glory, so he adorned the city with new squares, including the Place Vendôme and Place des Victoires, and with grand buildings and institutions like the Hôtel des Invalides and a rebuilt Louvre. So sure was he of France's military might, that he ordered Paris's protective city walls to be dismantled. During Louis XIV's reign several major new churches were also begun, including the Church of Saint-Sulpice. It is the glory of this city that Turgot's map seeks to reflect.

▲ **The Church of Saint-Sulpice**, built from 1646, the second-largest church in Paris after Notre Dame

Paris, 1878

EDOUARD DUMAS-VORZET ▪ HAND-COLORED
PRINT ON LINEN ▪ LIBRARY OF CONGRESS,
WASHINGTON, D.C., USA

SCALE

PARIS AND ITS SURROUNDINGS

When the French king Louis-Philippe was forced to abdicate in 1848, he departed a city that was medieval in appearance, infrastructure, and sanitary conditions. It was his successor, Napoleon III, who made upgrading public works a priority. The task of executing new construction fell to his prefect of the Seine, Georges-Eugène Haussmann, who between 1853 and 1870 orchestrated wholesale demolition of crowded neighborhoods to make way for wide avenues, squares, and parks, not to mention new sewers. Haussmann rebuilt all the bridges, installed street lighting, doubled the number of trees, and improved the supply of drinkable water. Aside from a few later landmarks, notably the Eiffel Tower, most of what is now considered quintessentially Parisian is the result of Haussmann's efforts. Work on his designs would go on until 1927, but in 1878 the grand project was sufficiently complete to be celebrated in this map, issued on the occasion of a grand Exposition Universelle (World's Fair).

New administrative districts

The different colors on this map mark the administrative districts of the city, or *arrondissements*. In 1860, Napoleon III had incorporated a number of suburban communes into Paris proper, increasing the number of *arrondissements* from 12 to 20. All were contained within the bounds of the outer set of defensive walls that surrounded the city. The annexation more than doubled the city's area and quadrupled the population, but the residents in the new suburbs were not happy with the arrangement—it meant they had to pay higher taxes.

> Most of the **streets** of this **wonderful Paris** are nothing but intestines, **filthy** and permanently wet with pestilential water.
>
> **"**
>
> **HENRI LECOUTURIER**, REFORMER, 1848

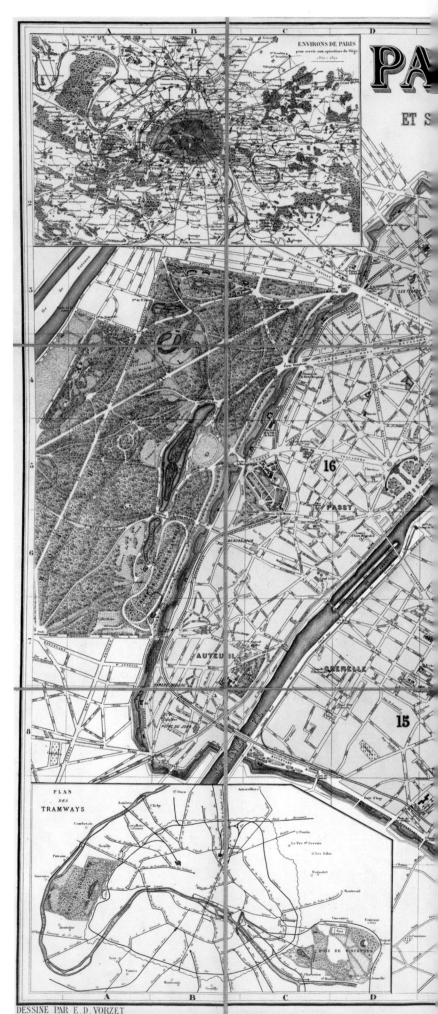

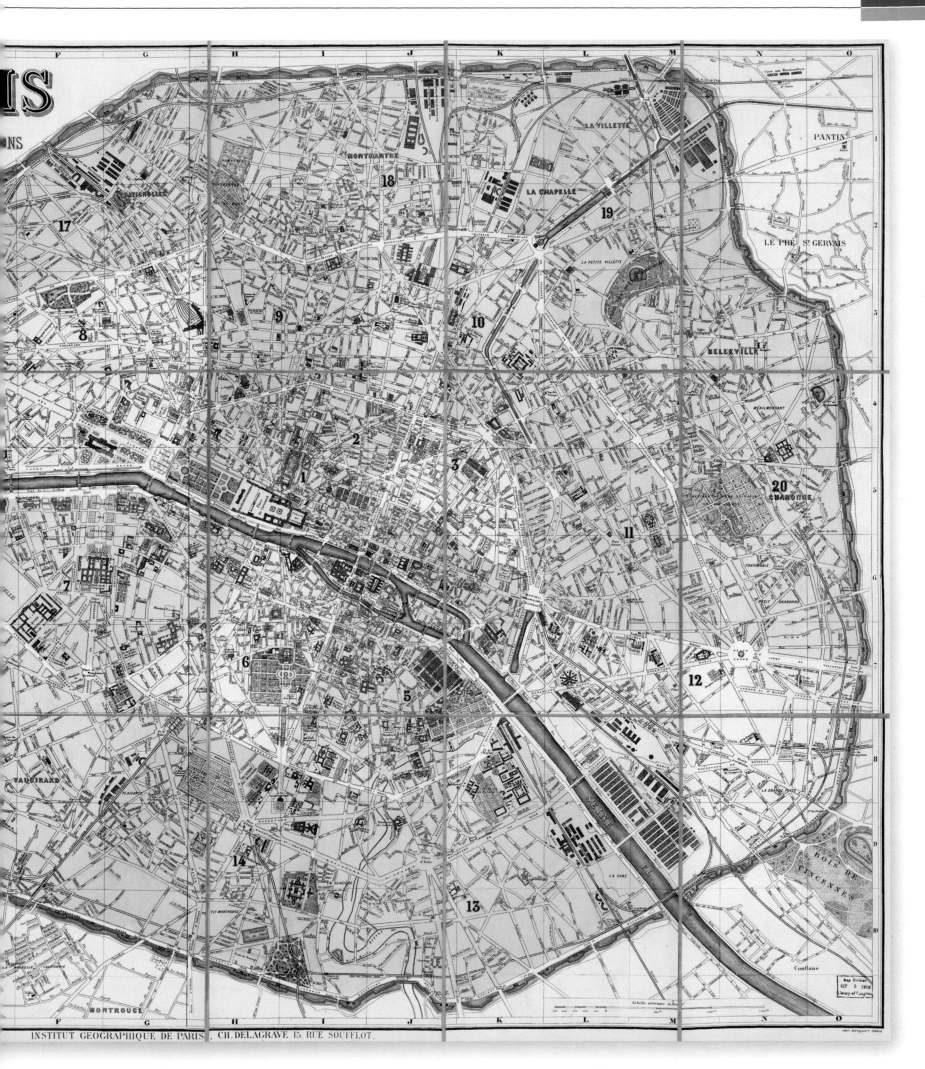

INSTITUT GEOGRAPHIQUE DE PARIS, CH. DELAGRAVE 15, RUE SOUFFLOT.

Visual tour

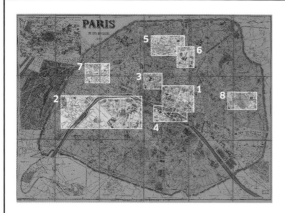

PARIS

KEY

▶ **LA CROISÉE DE PARIS**
Haussmann's first phase of renovation was to create a great cross in the center of Paris. The rue de Rivoli (at the bottom of this detail), forming the east-west axis, was widened and extended. Intersecting this, a new grand boulevard, the Sebastopol, ran north to south, cutting through some of the most overcrowded areas of the city. "It was the gutting of old Paris," wrote Haussmann in his memoirs.

▼ **EXPOSITION SPACE** The 1878 Exposition Universelle was the third World's Fair to be held in Paris. Intended to celebrate recovery from the 1870-01 Franco-Prussian War—and perhaps also to show off the great works accomplished by Haussmann—it took place on the Champ de Mars, where the Eiffel Tower would later be built in 1889.

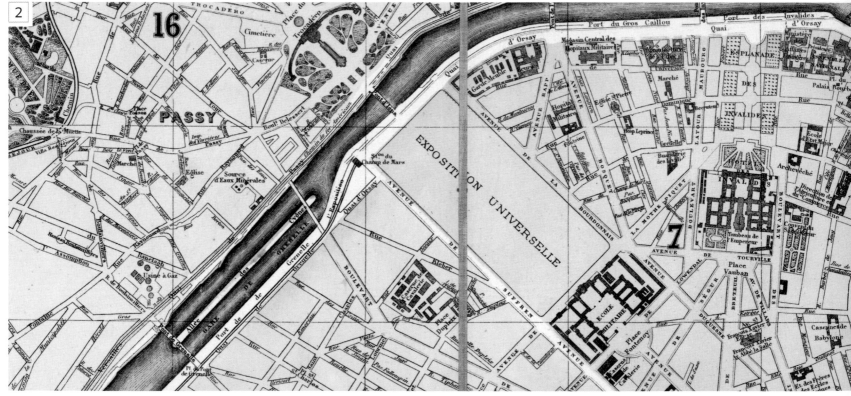

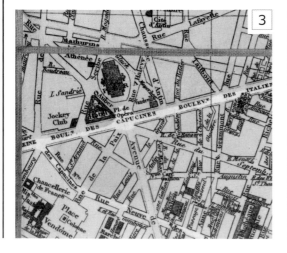

◀ **OPÉRA** Place de l'Opéra was built during the first and second phases of Haussmann's plan; the opera house itself was part of the third phase. It was designed by Charles Garnier and built between 1861 and 1875.

▶ **ÎLE DE LA CITÉ** This island in the Seine was once one of the most densely populated areas in the city. Haussmann removed many of the houses, replacing them with large public buildings. The island's narrow lanes were eradicated by creating wide transverse streets connected to bridges.

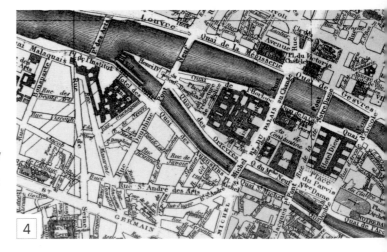

▼ **SACRÉ-COEUR** Although Sacré-Coeur Basilica appears on the map, there was no finished structure at this time, only a building site. Construction had begun on the church—sited on the highest point in the city—in 1875, and would not be completed until 1914; on the map, the area in front is labeled "Projected Square."

▼ **GARE DU NORD** Haussmann and Napoleon III saw railroad stations as the new gateways to the city and many were rebuilt, becoming bigger than before. Haussmann also created new, open squares in front of some of them, including the Gare du Nord.

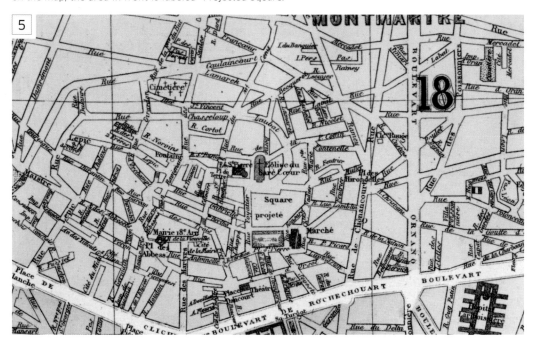

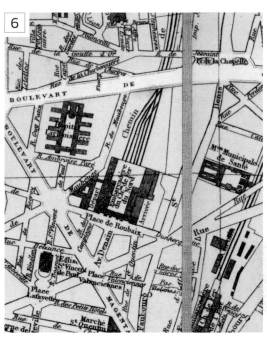

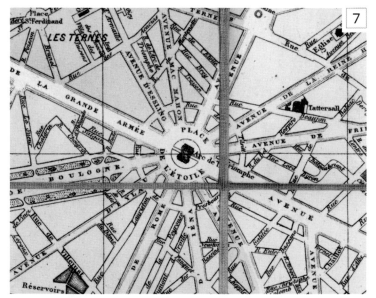

◄ **PLACE DE L'ÉTOILE** The first phase of Haussmann's renovation of Paris involved over 6 miles (9 km) of new boulevards. A parliamentary report of 1859 found that it had "brought air, light, and healthiness" to the city. The second phase, begun that same year, was even more ambitious, involving many more new boulevards and squares. Perhaps most striking of all was his redesign of the Place de l'Étoile around the Arc de Triomphe, which became the meeting point of 12 long, straight avenues.

IN **CONTEXT**

The man who revolutionized Paris, Georges-Eugène Haussmann (1809-91), was himself a native Parisian. However, he was not sentimental and even demolished the house he was born in because it stood in the way of progress (it made way for what was to become Boulevard Haussmann). His sweeping remaking of Paris met with much opposition, and Napoleon III eventually had to dismiss him in 1870. History views him more kindly and he is now generally credited as the man responsible for the beauty of modern Paris.

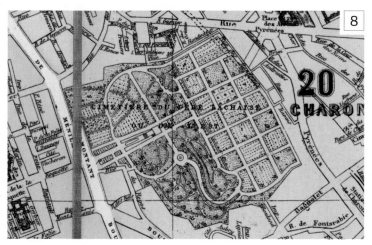

◄ **PÈRE LACHAISE CEMETERY** In the early 19th century, cemeteries were created on the fringes of the city to relieve overcrowded burial grounds in the center. Père Lachaise, in eastern Paris, was opened in 1804 and had been expanded on five occasions by the time this map was produced.

▲ **Place de l'Étoile**, encircling the Arc de Triomphe, considered one of Haussmann's finest achievements

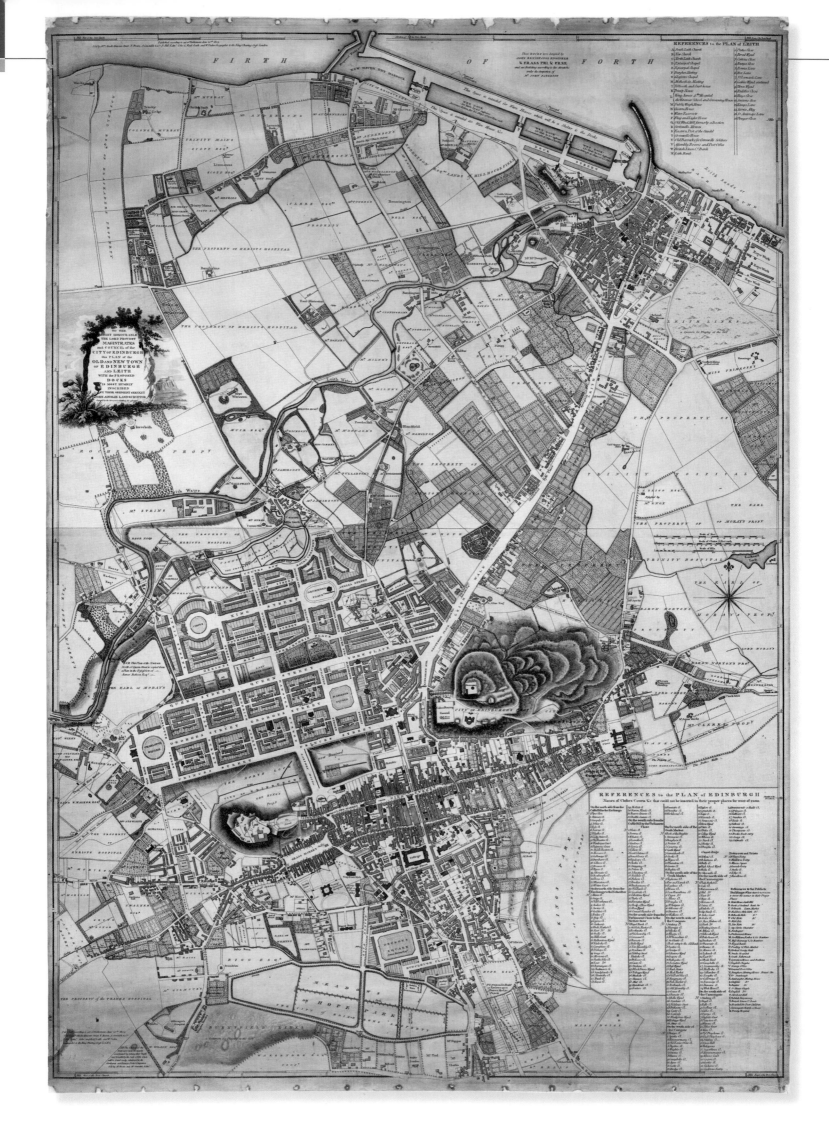

Edinburgh, 1804

JOHN AINSLIE ■ HAND-COLORED ENGRAVING ■ NATIONAL LIBRARY OF SCOTLAND, EDINBURGH

SCALE

PLAN OF THE OLD AND NEW TOWN

John Ainslie's 1804 map of Edinburgh highlights the extent to which this once-remote northern city had become one of the most imposing urban centers in Britain. Its title (in full "Old and New Town of Edinburgh and Leith with the proposed docks") makes the point. The Old Town was a tangle of tiny stone-built streets clustered around a medieval heart. By contrast, the New City to the north was a self-conscious assertion of a new Edinburgh. A series of spacious, rationally planned streets and squares, harmoniously classical, this was the Athens of the North, a precise reflection of the Enlightenment values that Edinburgh aspired to. The precision of Ainslie's map— every street exactly surveyed, every name accurately inscribed—mirrors the attention to detail that had made 18th-century Scotland so self-confidently prosperous.

The paradox was that as the city's newly rich installed themselves in the New Town, so the Old Town became more slumlike—a foul-smelling warren of deprivation.

JOHN **AINSLIE**

1745-1828

Born in Jedburgh, a Scottish town close to the English border, Ainslie spent his early career as a surveyor working principally in England, but in the 1770s he returned to his native Scotland.

Ainslie rapidly established a reputation for the accuracy of his surveying. In 1789, he produced a nine-sheet map of Scotland, the first to show the Scottish coast and islands accurately. In the 1790s, he also produced the first detailed maps of central Scotland and the Borders. A key figure in the emergence of a new, scientific school of Scottish cartography, Ainslie was a surveyor first, and a cartographer second. His *Comprehensive Treaty on Land Surveying* (1812) underlined his determination to produce maps based on precise surveying.

Visual tour

KEY

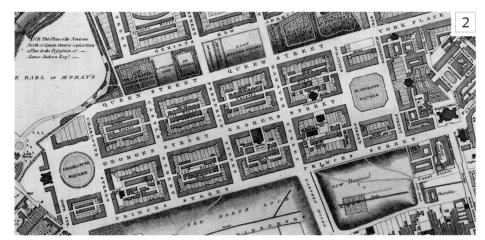

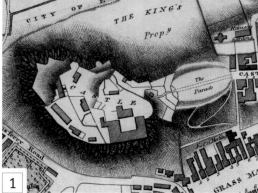

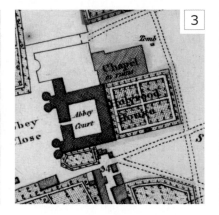

▷ **EDINBURGH CASTLE** The volcanic spur on which the brooding bulk of Edinburgh Castle sits is a natural defensive strongpoint. Commanding views over the area, the castle was the core from which the medieval Old Town below developed.

◁ **NEW TOWN** The notion that a new kind of ideal city could be created by a prosperous, self-aware community underpinned the rapid development of the city's New Town. Though it would be significantly extended after Ainslie's map, the New Town as depicted here was a late 18th-century model for a new kind of urban planning.

◁ **HOLYROOD HOUSE** Marking the eastern end of the Royal Mile— the main thoroughfare through the Old Town – Holyrood House was originally a monastery, founded in 1138. Largely rebuilt in the 1670s, at the time of the unification of Scotland and England in 1707 it became (and remains) the official residence of the British monarch in Scotland.

St. Petersburg, c.1721

JOHANN BAPTIST HOMANN ■ HAND-COLORED ETCHING
WITH LINE ENGRAVING ■ NUMEROUS COPIES EXIST

SCALE

MAP OF ST. PETERSBURG

The most dominant element on this map of St. Petersburg by the leading German cartographer Johann Baptist Homann (1664–1724) is the black-and-white engraving surrounding the title in the top-right corner. Centered on a mirrored portrait of the Russian emperor, Peter the Great, surrounded by cloud-borne figures that personify subjects such as astronomy, engineering, geography, shipbuilding, and mathematics, the image's message was unmistakable: that the new city of St. Petersburg was to be a new capital of a new Russia, created by Peter the Great and built in his name. The map itself was as much a map of expectations as it was of reality. At the time it was produced, only the outlines of the city that subsequently emerged had been completed. The idealized gridlike streets that are depicted on the northern island, Vasilyevsky, would never be more than partly realized. Tellingly, the buildings most obviously emphasized—in red—were military installations, a point reinforced by the depiction (to the right) of Kronstadt castle, the key naval defensive point to the west of the city.

Visual tour

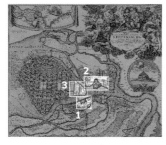

KEY

▶ **ADMIRALTY** The fortified Admiralty was the most important structure in Peter the Great's new city. As it was both a dockyard and the headquarters of Russia's Baltic Fleet, it became a vital weapon in the emperor's ongoing war with Sweden.

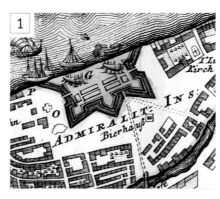

1

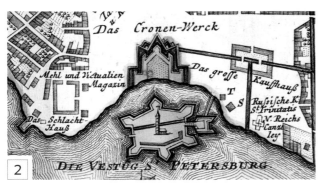

2

▲ **PETER AND PAUL FORTRESS** Begun in 1706 to the designs of the Italian architect Domenico Trezzini—who was summoned to create buildings for the new capital by Peter the Great—this fortress was successively expanded and strengthened. Its most dominant feature is the thin spire of Trezzini's Cathedral of St. Peter and St. Paul, which rises 403 ft (123 m) from the ground.

3

▲ **MENSHIKOV PALACE** The first stone building in the city, the Menshikov Palace was incomplete at the time of Homann's map. It was the home of General Alexander Menshikov, the most powerful man in Russia after the death of Peter the Great in 1725.

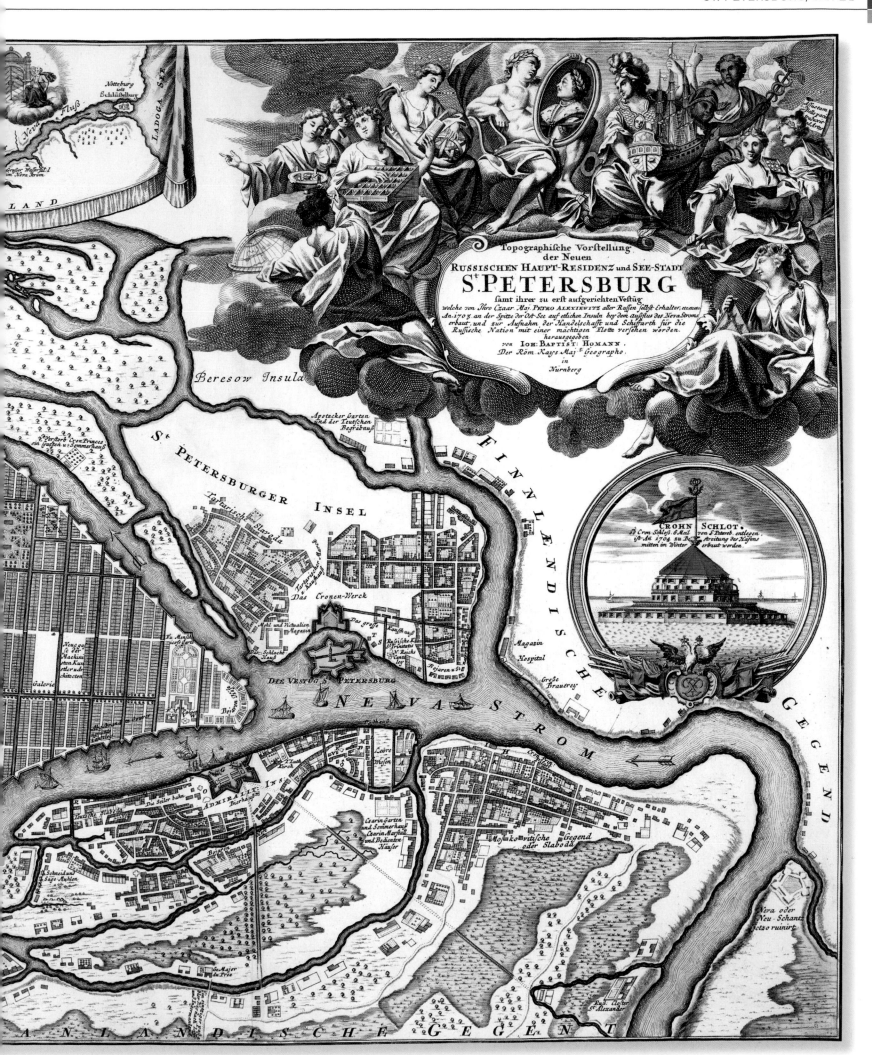

Topographische Vorstellung
der Neuen
Russischen Haupt-Residenz und See-Stadt
St. PETERSBURG
samt ihrer zu erst aufgerichten Vestüg

herausgegeben
von IOH: BAPTIST: HOMANN.
Der Röm: Kays: Maj.t Geographo.
in
Nurnberg

CROHN SCHLOT.

NEVA STROM

St. Petersburg, 1885

A. ILYIN CARTOGRAPHIC COMPANY ▪ LITHOGRAPH ▪ NATIONAL LIBRARY OF RUSSIA, ST. PETERSBURG

PLAN OF ST. PETERSBURG

SCALE

The expansion of St. Petersburg in the 180 years after its foundation, and the dramatic advances in mapmaking and printing over the same period, are captured in this detailed map of the imperial capital. By 1885 all of the city's principal monuments and public buildings had been completed, as had its major thoroughfares, parks, and numerous bridges. The Admiralty, just east of Palace Square, was rebuilt from 1806–23 and topped by a tapering gilded spire. Next to it is the even more sumptuous Winter Palace, rebuilt and enlarged several times after 1732, with its interior similarly recast after a fire in 1837.

The map highlights, too, the impact of industrialization on the city. The massively enlarged dockyard to the southwest is shown, as are three railroad stations. The most important, southeast of the city center, was Nicholaevsky station, opened in 1851 to provide a direct link with Moscow 400 miles (650 km) away. Also represented are the major industrial districts that had sprung up on the city's outskirts, home to a rapidly expanding urban population crammed into insanitary and inadequate housing. By the time this map was produced, the city's population was beginning to approach one million.

Visual tour

KEY

▶ **SMOLNY CATHEDRAL** The centerpiece of the substantial complex that comprised the Smolny Convent, constructed from 1748–64, is its startling blue-and-white Baroque cathedral. Designed by the Italian architect Bartolommeo Rastrelli, it was initially intended to be more opulent still, with a vast bell-tower.

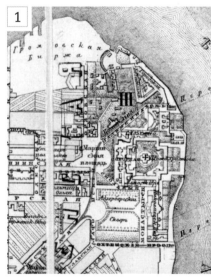

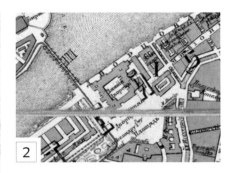

▲ **AROUND PALACE SQUARE** Palace Square is a deliberate statement of imperial splendor. To the north is the green-and-white façade of the Winter Palace. Facing it is the headquarters of the Imperial General Staff, pierced by a monumental triumphal arch. Towering over the square is the Alexander Column.

▶ **NEVSKY PROSPECT** One of three major streets converging on the Admiralty, Nevsky Prospect began life as a track driven through unpromising wastes of forest. By the early 19th century, it had become the best-known street in St. Petersburg, studded with imposing buildings and ever more fashionable shops.

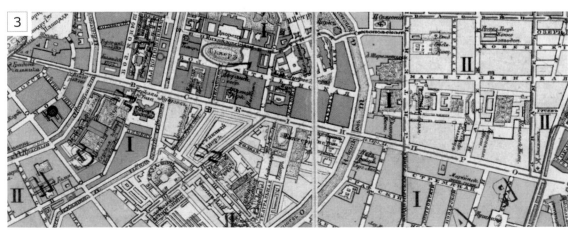

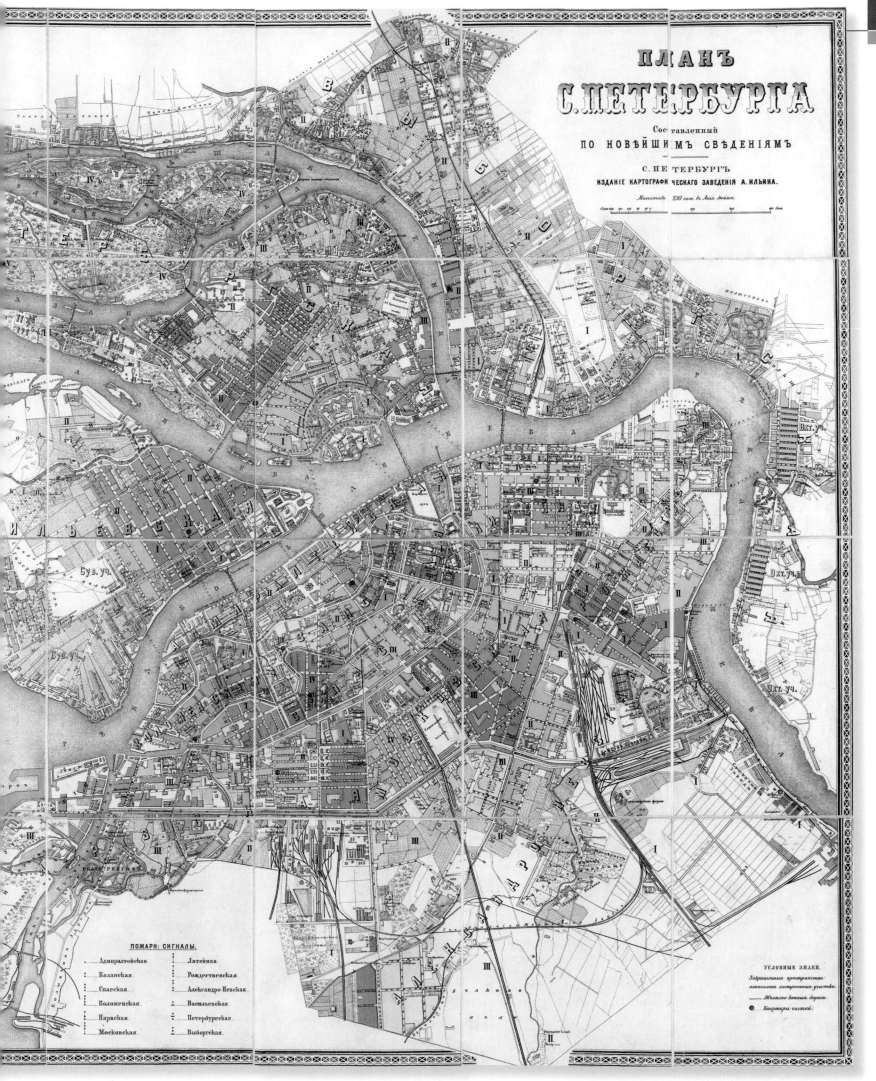

ПЛАНЪ
С.ПЕТЕРБУРГА

Составленный
ПО НОВѢЙШИМЪ СВѢДѢНІЯМЪ

С.ПЕТЕРБУРГЪ
ИЗДАНІЕ КАРТОГРАФИЧЕСКАГО ЗАВЕДЕНІЯ А. ИЛЬИНА.

Масштабъ 210 саж. въ Англ. дюймѣ.

ПОЖАРН: СИГНАЛЫ.

Адмиралтейская.	Литейная.
Казанская.	Рождественская.
Спасская.	Александро-Невская.
Коломенская.	Васильевская.
Нарвская.	Петербургская.
Московская.	Выборгская.

УСЛОВНЫЕ ЗНАКИ.

Закрашенныя пространства
означаютъ застроенныя участки.

Желѣзно-конныя дороги.

Квартиры частей.

Baghdad, 1533

MATRAKÇI NASUH ■ MINIATURE ON MANUSCRIPT ■ TOPKAPI PALACE MUSEUM, ISTANBUL, TURKEY

UNKNOWN

MAP OF BAGHDAD

The Islamic Ottoman Empire—one of the largest and most powerful states in history—reached its height during the 16th century. As conquered cities were absorbed within its expanding borders, imperial artists documented the Ottoman sultans' territorial acquisitions in exquisite miniature paintings and illuminated manuscripts.

One such artist was Matrakçi Nasuh, who painted this fresh, jewel-colored view of modern-day Iraq's capital as Suleyman I (c.1494–1566) was in the process of adding the region to his realm. Nasuh was sent on royal military expeditions and sketched the broader details of his paintings from life, but probably relied on secondary sources for creating this map of Baghdad.

A city reborn

Baghdad was founded in 762 by the Abbasid caliphs, and for the next 500 years, it was one of the world's greatest cities, and the center of Islamic culture. That incarnation was destroyed by invading Mongols in 1258, after which the city's importance waned. The Egyptian historian Al-Makrizi wrote in 1437: "Baghdad is in ruins. It cannot be called a town." By Nasuh's time, it had been refortified with walls and ditches, and was "a city of palm trees, lancelike minarets, and sun-bleached domes," an image that accords with the artist's precise and detailed view.

MATRAKÇI **NASUH**

1480–1564

Matrakçi Nasuh has been described as a polymath—an Ottoman "Renaissance man." A skilled calligrapher and painter of miniatures, he also excelled as a mathematician, engineer, scientist, historian, translator, and warrior.

Nasuh was born in the town of Visoko, in present-day Bosnia—then a part of the Ottoman Empire. He was recruited into the Ottoman navy, and while he was serving, he wrote several works on mathematics and history, and one on swordsmanship. He achieved renown when he designed two mobile citadels built from paper for the ceremony to celebrate the circumcision of Suleyman's two sons. Soldiers emerged from the citadels and staged a battle during the festivities. He was later engaged to prepare a chronicle of Suleyman I's campaigns against the Safavid Empire, in what is now Iraq, illustrating the progress of the Ottoman army. This included several panoramic views of landscapes and cities, including a famous early view of Constantinople (*see p.45*) and the map of Baghdad shown here.

Visual tour

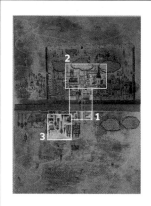

KEY

▶ **BRIDGE OF BOATS** During the Abbasid Caliphate, the two parts of Baghdad were connected by three pontoon bridges, but after the sacking of the city by the Mongols in 1258, only one remained.

1

2

▲ **EAST BAGHDAD** This became the heart of the city in medieval times, with three great mosques, portrayed here, and a citadel lodged tight against the north wall and the Tigris River.

▶ **WEST BAGHDAD** The site of the great Abbasid city was largely abandoned after the Mongol attack. By the early 16th century it was little more than a village.

3

MEGACITIES

- Rio de Janeiro

- Shanghai

- New Amsterdam & New York

- Tokyo

CHAPTER 6

Megacities

No one planned the megacity: it evolved as growing populations in urban centers forced their expansion in often uncontrolled ways. Although the number of humans on the planet has increased dramatically over the past 200 years, technological and agronomical advances have led to the depopulation of the countryside everywhere, as people have migrated to cities in search of employment.

The result has been the emergence of the megacity and the megalopolis. Of the world's estimated 7.4 billion inhabitants, around 60 percent live in cities or large urban areas. There are currently 35 officially recognized "megacities," defined as containing populations of more than 10 million people; both Tokyo and Shanghai have more than 35 million residents.

The size and scale of urban development in the last 50 years has effectively defeated the urban cartographer's traditional skills. As a relatively new phenomenon, the rise of the megalopolis – a chain of ongoing metropolitan areas – has presented many planning and management challenges, not least the hurdle of providing templates and plans for organizing sanitary living conditions, utility supplies, and communications systems. The growth of rambling shanty towns around cities such as Rio de Janeiro and São Paulo in Brazil, Cairo in Egypt, and Delhi in India, makes the problem even more difficult. Representing megacities cartographically, and usefully, has become an almost unattainable goal.

Modern city mapping

The solution has been to produce maps tailored to perform specific functions. The most ubiquitous of these are the road or street atlas and the public transportation map. British draftsman Harry Beck's brilliant and influential non-geographical map of the London Underground (*see box p.240*) may have been based on the principal of electric circuits, but it worked—and still works—very effectively. Over time, it has proved an inspiration to those tasked with designing underground network maps for other megacities, such as the 2013 "circle map" of the New York subway (*see pp.240-41*).

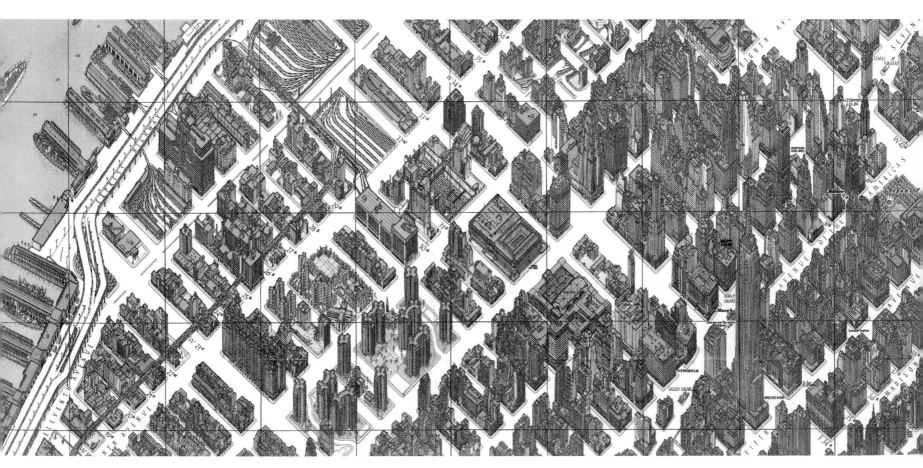

▲ **NEW YORK, 1963** Herman Bollmann's vertiginous rendering of Midtown Manhattan is drawn with astonishing detail, and attempts to deal with one of the many problems of mapping the modern city—its towering structures.

In the case of New York, it is intriguing to see how the mapping of the city has come full circle: in early maps, when it was the Dutch colony of New Amsterdam, the focus was Manhattan Island; at the time, the extent of the settlement (*see pp.224–27*). Subsequent maps pulled back to capture the city's widening boundaries, but Herman Bollmann's visionary 1963 map (*see pp.236–39*) zoomed back in again, showing only a small part of Manhattan but with the specific purpose of celebrating its vertical aspect.

A new cartographic response

Satellite-based global positioning systems (GPS) have also made the traditional city map redundant, prompting the creation of niche products such as specialized maps with such titles as *Brooklyn Bars*, *Small Shops in Paris*, and *Literary London*. These have a historical precedent in the popular illustrated city maps of the 1920s and '30s, such as Carl Crow's 1935 map of Shanghai (*see pp.222–23*)– themselves a by-product of the technological advances that enabled both cheap printing and mass tourism.

> No longer static images, **maps have become active interfaces for information exchange**… determining **where we are**… and **suggesting** where we **ought to go**.

PROFESSOR SETH SPIELMAN, UNIVERSITY OF COLORADO, USA

Today, the megacity is often presented as a dystopian nightmare: a place that we can no longer comprehend or fathom how it works or is organized. Instead of using a city map to depict order, modern artists use it to chart experiences and record observations. It seems we have given up trying to tame the 21st-century version of the city—all we can do is watch it and try to make sense of it.

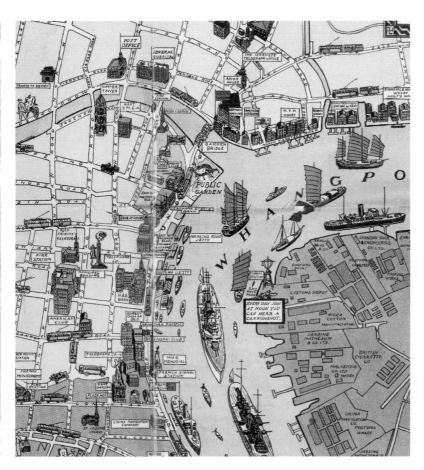

▲ **SHANGHAI 1935** Carl Crow's depiction of this Chinese trading city contains many of the features found in a modern-day tourist map, such as color-coded districts, depictions of vehicles, and buildings of interest drawn in three dimensions.

▲ **TOKYO 2014** Japanese artist Sohei Nishino takes a meticulous photo-collage approach to portraying the world's largest urban entity, in a modern and very personal exploration of the boundaries between art and cartography.

Rio de Janeiro, 1867

E. & H. LAEMMERT ▪ PRINT ON CLOTH ▪ LIBRARY OF CONGRESS, WASHINGTON, D.C., USA

NEW MAP OF THE CITY OF RIO DE JANEIRO

SCALE

The Portuguese name of Rio de Janeiro translates into English as "River of January," it was called "River" because of a mistaken belief that it stood at the mouth of a river, and "January" after the month in which the area was discovered in 1502. The colonial settlement became the focus of a burgeoning Portuguese empire based first on sugar-cane cultivation, and later on diamond and gold mining. By the time this map was produced, the city had been the capital of Brazil since 1763, a status it retained when Brazil declared its independence from Portugal in 1822.

This map, oriented with west at the top, depicts Rio in a period of rapid expansion. The more or less regular north-south grid plan of the original settlement can be clearly seen, as can the ring of forts, strategically placed on the hills—*morros* in Portuguese—overlooking the city center. The heavily wooded, hilly country around Rio is shown equally clearly. Boosted by a tram system that had been introduced in 1859, the area would soon see the growth of extensive suburbs, particularly on the relatively flat land to the northeast. Between 1820 and 1890, Rio's population boomed, rising from 113,000 to 520,000.

Visual tour

KEY

▼ **CASTLE HILL** The French founded the first European settlement in Rio on an island in the bay in 1555. By 1568, the Portuguese had driven off the French and established a new settlement inland. It was centered on one of a number of natural strongpoints, Castle Hill.

▼ **ILHA DAS COBRAS** The Isle of the Snakes lies just off Rio's central district. It has served variously as a fortress, a prison, a naval shipyard and an arsenal. Since the early 19th century, its primary function has been as a Brazilian naval base, the Arsenal de Marinha do Rio de Janeiro.

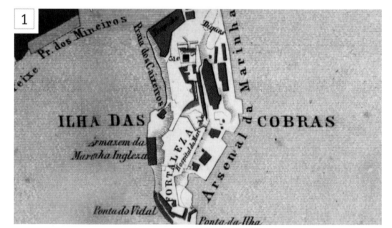

▶ **CAMPO D'ACCLAMAÇÃO** On September 7, 1822, in the spacious park known as the Campo de Santana Dom, Pedro I declared Brazil's independence. The park was renamed Campo d'Acclamaçao in honor of the event. It was in this park, too, that the Brazilian republic was later proclaimed in 1889. Just visible to the north is Rio's first railroad station, opened in 1852.

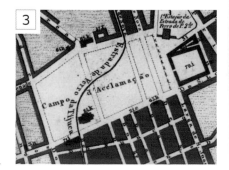

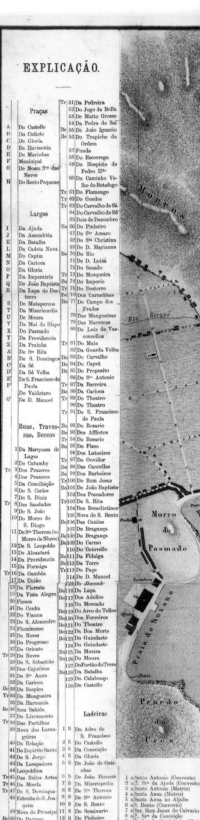

> I have **again and again** entered and quitted the
> Bay of Rio de Janeiro—it has always presented
> to me **new glories** and **new charms**.

PRINCE ADALBERT OF PRUSSIA, *TRAVELS IN BRAZIL*, 1849

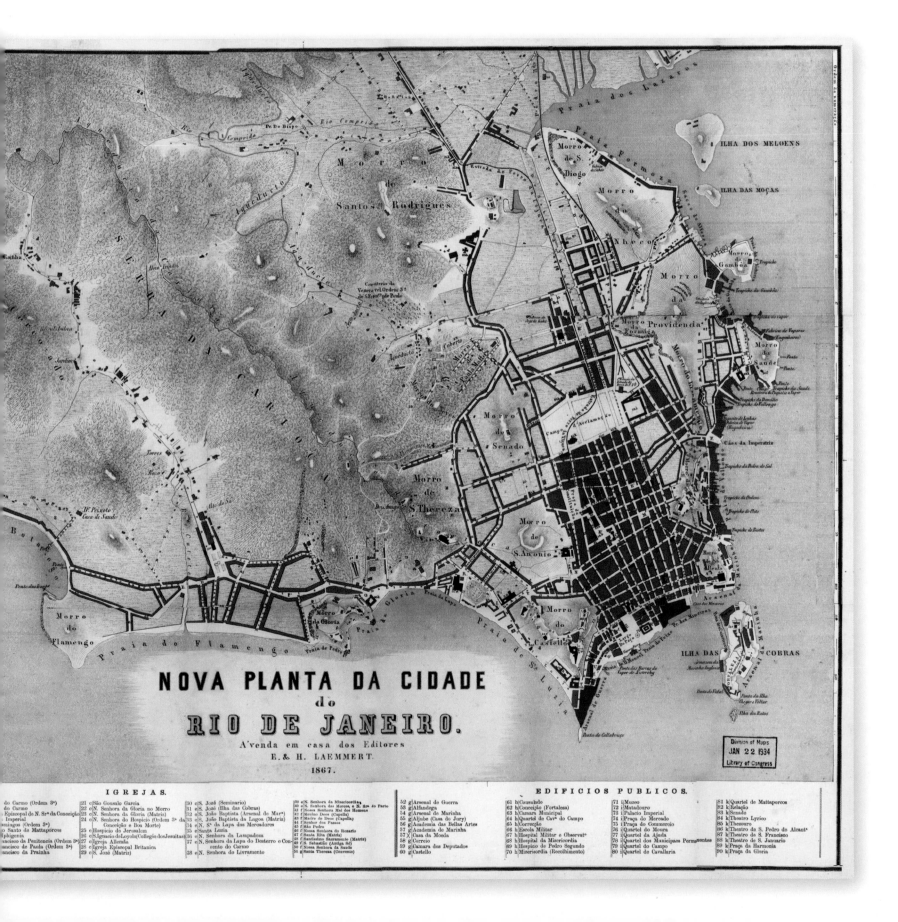

NOVA PLANTA DA CIDADE
do
RIO DE JANEIRO.
A'venda em casa dos Editores
E. & H. LAEMMERT.
1867.

Rio de Janeiro, 1929

ARTHUR DUARTE RIBEIRO ▪ MEDIUM UNKNOWN ▪ NATIONAL LIBRARY, RIO DE JANEIRO, BRAZIL

SCALE

INFORMATIVE MAP OF THE CITY OF RIO DE JANEIRO

In 1929, when this map was produced, Rio de Janeiro was among the fastest growing cities in the world. Oriented with west at the top, the map highlights this explosive growth, the pattern of which follows the city's topography, which is also detailed on the map. In 1872, the population of Rio was 280,000; by 1920, this figure had reached 1.5 million. The spread of settlement from the original core of the city in the lower left can be clearly seen, as can the route of the main rail line to and from the heart of Rio.

Improving the city

In the early years of the 20th century the government, conscious of Rio's increased status, initiated major urban improvements. Slums were flattened and swamps drained, and both of these initiatives resulted in major health improvements. What is still the city's principal avenue, Avenida Rio Branco, was also laid out. No less significant was the development of new districts to the southwest centered on Copacabana and Ipanema beaches, shallow bays that can be seen on the left of the map.

IN CONTEXT

By the early 20th century, Brazilian society was highly stratified. There was a tiny, landowning elite, a small if significant liberal-minded middle class, and a vast army of the dispossessed, many of whom were former slaves. This latter group was mainly crowded into cities, Rio in particular, in the hope of finding work. The result was social dislocation and impoverishment on an epic scale, symbolized by the construction of extraordinary shanty towns called favelas. Perched vertiginously on the dramatic hills that surround the city, these became a by-word for a new kind of urban deprivation, a disturbing backdrop to the image of Latin-American glamour Rio otherwise sought to project.

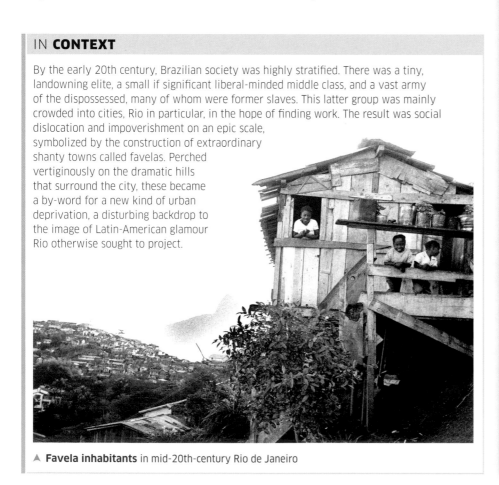

▲ **Favela inhabitants** in mid-20th-century Rio de Janeiro

By the **1920s**, the **beach** was crowned as a place of sports activity, socialization, and leisure... Copacabana was extolled as a new form of **chic modernity**.

BEATRIZ JAGUARIBE, *RIO DE JANEIRO* (2014)

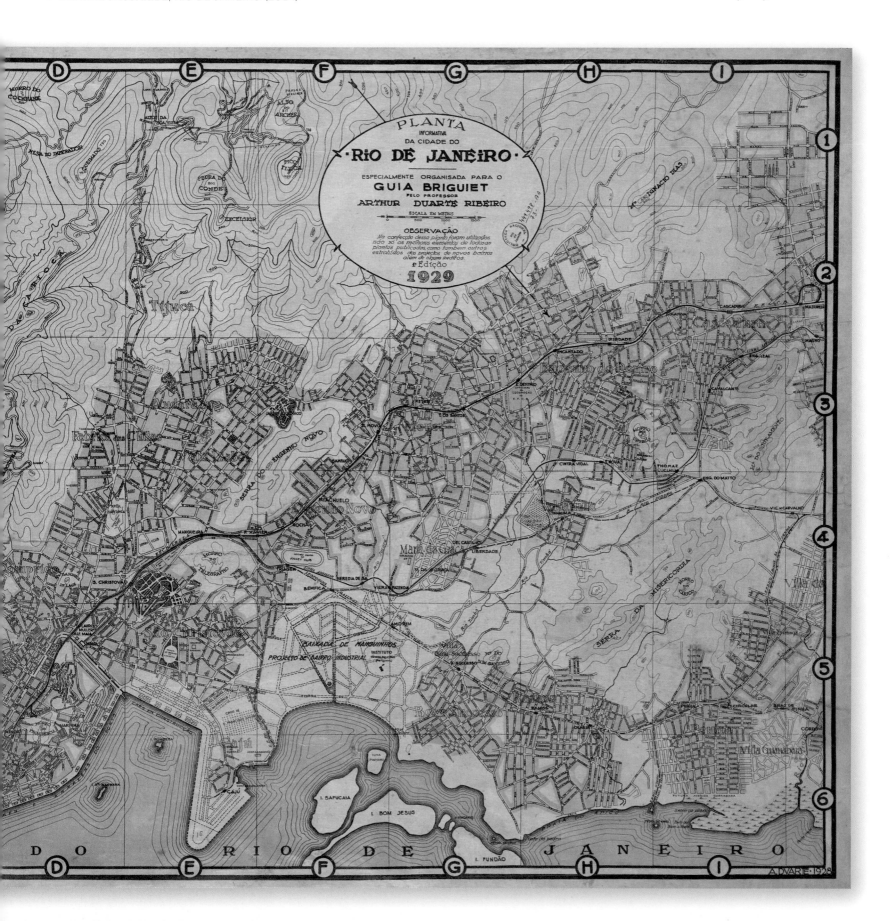

Shanghai, 1935

CARL CROW AND V. V. KOVALSKY ■ COLORED AND PRINTED DRAWING ■ BOSTON PUBLIC LIBRARY, BOSTON, USA

SCALE

MAP OF SHANGHAI

Carl Crow (1884–1945) was an American from Missouri who arrived in the Chinese city of Shanghai at age 27, where he founded the city's *Evening Post* newspaper and its first Western advertising agency. During his quarter of a century as a resident, the city was transformed from a colonial backwater to a vibrant and cosmopolitan metropolis. This was a city of opportunity, prompting Crow to author a best-selling book, *400 Million Customers*, that was aimed at encouraging other would-be businessmen to make the move to Shanghai. This map was intended to fulfill a similar function. It was commissioned by the Shanghai Municipal Council, who were looking to utilize Crow's marketing skills. His design is clear and simple, and attractively colored. To the intended viewer, it mixes the familiar (illustrations of horse racing, baseball, and Western architecture) with the Asian (chinoiserie motifs, illustrations of teahouses and sampans). It is a map that is meant to entice and at the same time reassure the viewer; on the Whangpoo River, the picturesque local junks are dwarfed by the Western cargo ships and battleships in a graphic display of who holds power in the city.

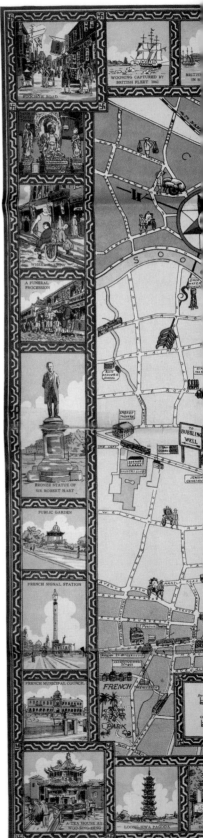

Visual tour

KEY

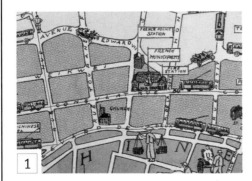

1

2

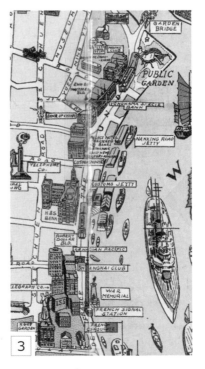

3

▲ **COLOR CODING** The city of Shanghai was largely controlled by foreign powers at the time this map was made. The yellow zone, known as the International Settlement, was administered by the British and Americans; the pink area was the French Concession; and purple areas belonged to the Chinese.

▲ **RACETRACK** Built by the British in 1862, the racetrack was the center of expat social life in Shanghai. During race season, its weekly meets were where high society gathered to drink and gossip. Out of season, it was a venue for polo and other sports.

▲ **THE BUND** A sweeping parade of ostentatious towering buildings, the Bund was once Shanghai's powerful business center. The grand edifices along the waterfront housed the headquarters of banks, shipping companies, and insurance agencies.

Shanghai... the megalopolis of continental Asia, inheritor of ancient Bagdad, of pre-War Constantinople, of 19th-century London, of 20th-century Manhattan. "

FORTUNE MAGAZINE, JANUARY 1935

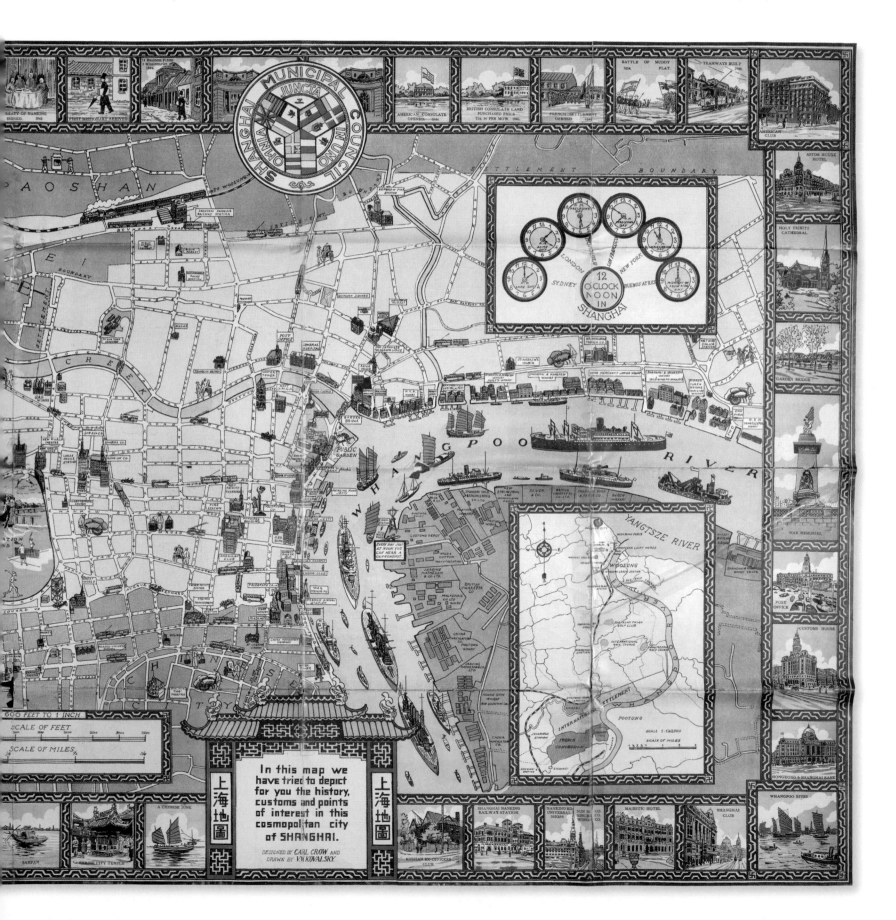

New Amsterdam, 1660

JOHN WOLCOTT ADAMS & ISAAC NEWTON
PHELPS STOKES ▪ COLOR WASH ON PAPER ▪
NEW YORK HISTORICAL SOCIETY LIBRARY

THE CASTELLO PLAN

SCALE

The Castello Plan of New Amsterdam depicts an area that now forms Lower Manhattan in New York (south is left, north is right). The map was originally created by Jacques Cortelyou, who was surveyor-general of the early Dutch colony, in 1660. It was commissioned by the provincial governors to send to the directors of the Dutch West India Company back in Amsterdam. The colony had been established under the patronage of the company in the early 17th century and this is the earliest known depiction of it in map form.

An idyllic vision

The map was sold to Cosimo III de Medici, future Grand Duke of Tuscany, in 1667. It remained in Italy and was later found in the Villa Castello (after which it was then named) near Florence, Italy, in 1900. The version shown here is a redraft of the original made in 1916 by John Wolcott Adams and Isaac Newton Phelps Stokes; the redraft was the first published version of the map. With its green pastures, neat gardens, orchards, and red-roofed homes, New Amsterdam appears idyllic but the reality was different. According to Eric Homberger in *The Historic Atlas of New York City* it was "a thinly populated, uncomfortable and muddy place with few creature comforts and much lawlessness."

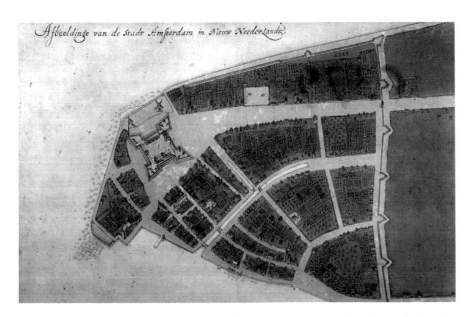

▲ **THE ORIGINAL CASTELLLO PLAN** Bound into an atlas together with other depictions of New Amsterdam, the original Castello Plan (a 1665–70 copy of which is shown here) was most likely sent to the Netherlands in around 1667, from where it passed to Cosimo de Medici.

Visual tour

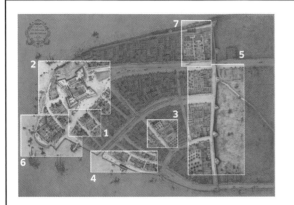

KEY

> **OFFICE OF JACQUES CORTELYOU** The man who drafted the original Castello Plan arrived in the New World in 1652 as a tutor. Five years later he was appointed surveyor-general of the province of New Netherland, of which New Amsterdam was part. He lived on Long Island but kept this small office (top left), where it is likely that his map was prepared.

> **FORT AMSTERDAM** The fort was the nucleus of the Dutch settlement. Construction began in 1625 on an elevated piece of ground, which was ringed by four stone walls, with a defensive bastion at each corner. Within the fortifications were a barracks (top), a church (bottom right), and beside it, the seat of local governance.

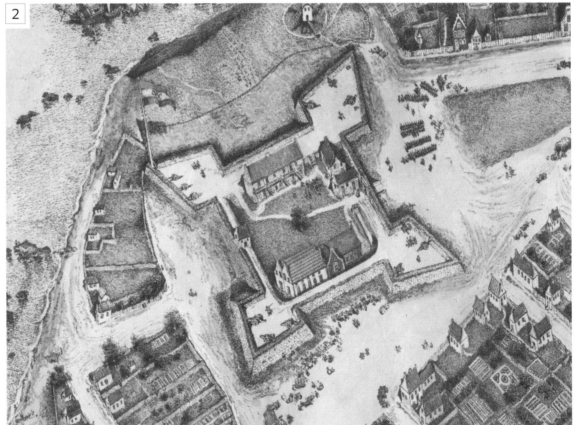

▼ **RED LION BREWERY** Built in 1633, the tile-roofed brewery shown here was one of New Amsterdam's first significant buildings. There were several breweries in the colony, which supplied around 20 taverns (and there was one tavern for every 12.5 houses). Beer was brewed using water drawn from a well in the garden, in which the malt or hops were steeped, then boiled and fermented in wooden barrels. The beer was heated to be drunk warm.

▲ **CITY HALL** This building, shown with a blue roof on the map, was originally a tavern, dating from 1642. Governor Peter Stuyvesant had it converted into a city hall (Stadt Huys) in 1653. It was eventually extended to five stories in height and a cupola was added on top, from which a flag was flown.

▲ **PETER STUYVESANT'S HOUSE** Occupying prime position on the wharf at the tip of the island was the residence of Peter Stuyvesant, the last Dutch governor of the colony of New Netherland. He lived here from 1658–65 in what appears from the plan to be the largest dwelling in the colony, backed by extensive gardens.

IN **CONTEXT**

Isaac Newton Phelps Stokes (1867–1944) was an architect and campaigner for social housing who also spent 19 years compiling a six-volume work on the early development of New York called *The Iconography of Manhattan Island*. For volume two, he had illustrator John Wolcott Adams redraw the Castello Plan. A key was also provided to the plan, on which each individual building was numbered to correspond to descriptive notes provided by Stokes. To say the notes are exhaustive is an understatement: Stokes provided the identity, occupation, and as much background as was known on every inhabitant of the approximately 370 buildings that made up the colony of New Amsterdam in the year 1660.

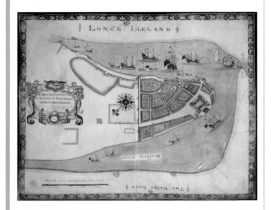

▲ **The Duke's Plan of New Amsterdam (1664)**, which appeared in the first volume of Stokes's *The Iconography of Manhattan Island* (1915)

▲ **CITY WALLS** The fortifications built to protect the settlement from attack by natives were begun in 1658, two years before this plan was drawn. They stretched from the North River (now known as the Hudson) to the East River. An earlier palisade was damaged by citizens using parts for firewood. The line of the walls survives in Wall Street today.

▲ **COMPANY GARDENS** The gardens of the Dutch West Indies Company included flowerbeds and orchards with their trees neatly arranged in rows, as shown on the map. They provided fruit, vegetables, and medicinal herbs. A gateway on the main street of Heerestraat (modern-day Broadway) opened on to a path, ending in a summerhouse close to the river.

New York, 1767

BERNARD RATZER ▪ HAND-COLORED COPPERPLATE ENGRAVING ▪ THE BRITISH LIBRARY, LONDON, UK

SCALE

THE RATZER PLAN

Bernard Ratzer (active 1756–1777) was a lieutenant in His Majesty's Royal American Regiment, a corps formed in 1756 to defend the British colonies in North America against attack by France—Britain's European rival—and by Native Americans. Ratzer was also a cartographer, one of several assigned in 1766-67 to survey America's eastern coastline in a further effort to help the British protect their territories. This map came out of that scientific work, and was published in 1770.

Positioned in the center of Ratzer's meticulously detailed plan is New York, the second-largest city of the American colonies, with a population of 18,000. By this time, the once tiny settlement had pushed way beyond the extent shown on the Castello Plan of 1660 (*see pp.224-27*), and its infrastructure was developing fast. Ratzer's map shows gridlike streets on the tip of Manhattan Island, many of which exist today, including Broadway, the Bowery, Pearl and Water streets, and Wall Street—named after a defensive wall built by the Dutch, who had founded the colony as New Amsterdam in the early 17th century.

Pre-revolutionary New York
Ratzer's coverage of Manhattan Island stretches north to roughly what is now 50th Street. Most of this is shown as a tinted patchwork of small farms and farmsteads, annotated with the names of the landowners. However, the growing colony occupies only a small portion of the map, which is more concerned with the surrounding topography and maritime access. The marshy New Jersey shores of the Hudson River, parts of present-day Brooklyn along the East River, as well as Kennedy, Bucking, and Governors islands, are all depicted. Natural features such

as hills and marshes are carefully rendered on land, and in the surrounding waterways, numbers denote the depth of the water—vital information for the defending army. Groups of buildings reveal where New Yorkers lived and worked, and the map's key marks places of interest to the military, including barracks and weapons stores, along with major public buildings, among them theaters, prisons, and the multifaith colony's numerous houses of worship.

IN **CONTEXT**

By the 1760s, New York was the commercial and military powerhouse of Britain's empire. Wars with the French had left Britain heavily in debt, and it imposed harsh taxes on its American colonies to raise funds. These provoked resistance that escalated to the Revolutionary War (1775-83).

By August 1776, the British were attempting to take back New York. After their success at the Battle of Long Island, British forces landed on Manhattan on September 15, 1776. Just a few days later, on the morning of September 21, a devastating fire broke out in Lower Manhattan, which destroyed more than 500 buildings. The British suspected that the fire had been set by revolutionary patriots; some Americans accused the British of starting the fire to plunder the city. A case for arson either way was never proved. But whatever the fire's origins, the city as shown on Ratzer's plan of New York ceased to exist.

▲ **The Great Fire of New York** raging through Manhattan in 1776

The streets **are paved**, and very clean, but in general they are narrow. There are two or three, indeed, which are spacious and airy, particularly the Broad-Way. **"**

REVEREND ANDREW BURNABY, *TRAVELS THROUGH THE MIDDLE SETTLEMENTS: IN NORTH AMERICA, 1775*

Visual tour

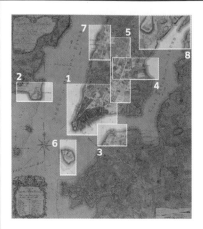

▶ **LOWER MANHATTAN** In the 1760s, New York extended as far north as present-day Chambers Street (also called Chambers Street on Ratzer's plan). The main "Broad Way Street" (now Broadway) led up to a triangle of land marked "Commons" on the map, a public space that is now the City Hall Park. In Ratzer's day, the largest building on the Commons was military rather than civic: the large "Upper Barracks."

KEY

▼ **NEW JERSEY** One of the few parts of what would become New Jersey shown occupied by Ratzer is a tract of land purchased by a Dutchman, Michael Pauw, in 1630 and thereafter known as Paulus Hook. In 1776, American patriots built a fort here to defend the western banks of the Hudson River.

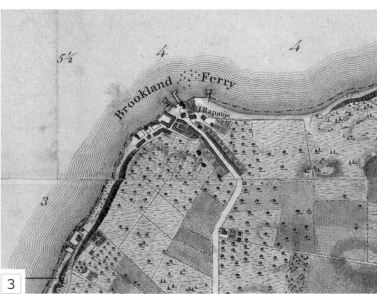

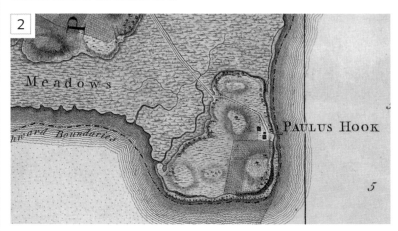

▲ **BROOKLYN** At this time, "Brookland," or Brooklyn, was still a rural area. The map shows it covered in orchards and plots of crop-growing farmland. The area's farmers—who were mainly of Dutch origin—supplied New York with produce, carried over on the Brookland Ferry and sold in the city's markets (the map's key lists five of these, identified as Fish, Old Slip, Fly, Pecks, and Oswego).

▲ **STUYVESANT FAMILY LANDS** Halfway up the east side of Manhattan are the three farmsteads and manor houses belonging to the descendants of Peter Stuyvesant, the last governor of New Amsterdam (New York's original name) before the British took over in 1664. An echo of these long-gone properties remains today in grid-breaking Stuyvesant Street on the Lower East Side, which follows the line of one of the old driveways.

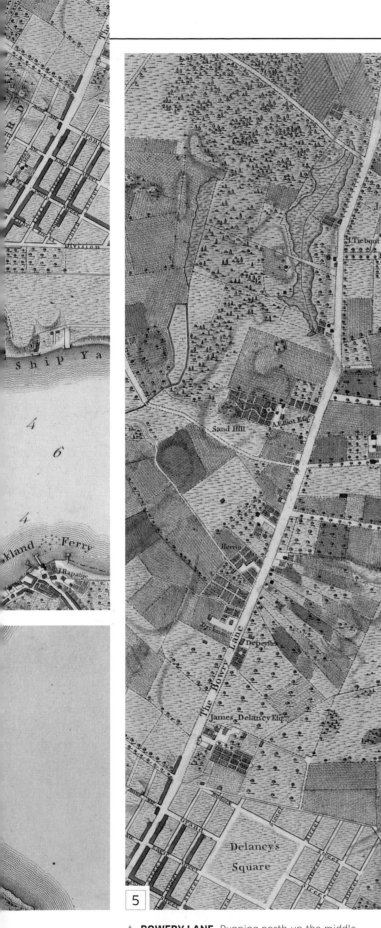

GOVERNORS ISLAND This tiny island was the landing place of the first Dutch settlers. It became known as Governors Island after the British took over in 1664. Ratzer's regiment was garrisoned here and the map, as issued in 1770, included a panorama of Manhattan as seen from the island across the harbor.

GREENWICH VILLAGE In 1767 this area was still an actual village, outside of the main city. The first outdoor monument in New York was commissioned by a private citizen of Greenwich, Oliver Delancey, for his farmstead. It was an obelisk dedicated to the memory of Britain's General James Wolfe for his part in the capture of Quebec from the French in 1759; it is simply labeled on the map as "The Monument."

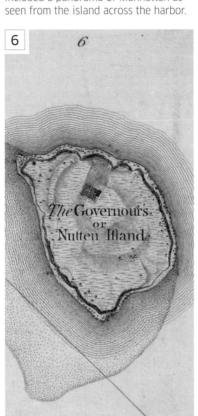

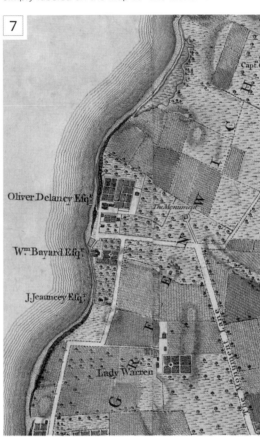

BOWERY LANE Running north up the middle of Manhattan, through fields and meadows, is Bowery Lane, whose name comes from the Dutch word *bouweries* (farms). At the southern end is a farm belonging to James Delancey, remembered today in Delancey Street on the Lower East Side.

KIPS BAY Labeled on Ratzer's map as Keps Bay, but more commonly written as Kips Bay, this is the site where, in September 1776, around 4,000 British troops landed to retake the island. They defeated a small American force and went on to capture Manhattan. To the north, beyond Turtle Bay, was the Beekman estate, which served as the British general's headquarters. Kips Bay survives today in name as a neighborhood between East 23rd and East 34th streets.

New York, 1875

PARSONS & ATWATER ■ SKETCHED AND DRAWN ON STONE ■
LIBRARY OF CONGRESS, WASHINGTON, D.C., USA

NEW YORK AND BROOKLYN

SCALE

City of glorious days, / Of hope, and labor and mirth, / With room and to spare, on thy splendid bays / For the ships of all the earth!!

RICHARD WATSON GILDER, AMERICAN POET (1844–1909), FROM HIS POEM "THE CITY" ABOUT NEW YORK

By the late 19th century, swollen by immigration, New York had grown considerably from its beginnings at the southern end of Manhattan. The site of the old fortress at the tip of the island had been repurposed to serve as an immigrant processing center, surrounded by a waterfront park. The city had expanded all the way north up the island in a ladderlike grid of city blocks, interrupted only by the great green space of Central Park, which was laid out in 1857–58. The most visible street running through the center of the map, Broadway, was the city's main north–south thoroughfare.

By the time this map was produced, the city had also grown to include more than just the island of Manhattan. Across the Hudson River, the areas of Hoboken and Jersey City were expanding, while over the East River a new bridge was under construction to link with the major manufacturing center of Brooklyn; a chunk of the Bronx had also recently been annexed.

Yet despite its growth, New York was still in its adolescence; apart from the heights of the new Brooklyn Bridge, the map depicts a completely low-rise landscape. The city's first passenger elevator had only been installed in 1870, and it was this innovation that would lead to the birth of the skyscraper.

IN **CONTEXT**

During the 19th century, immigration was actively encouraged by the youthful United States. Following the early Dutch, German, Irish, and English settlers came new arrivals from Italy, Russia, Poland, Austria, and Hungary. Of the roughly one million people squeezed into the burgeoning metropolis in 1875, some 40 percent had been born abroad. New immigrants were arriving in ever-greater numbers, brought in on the oceangoing steamships swarming the city's piers; by the end of the century the population of New York would explode to 3.5 million people.

▲ *The Bay and Harbor of New York* (c.1853–55) by US artist Samuel B. Waugh, depicting a typical scene of Irish immigrants arriving in New York by ship

Visual tour

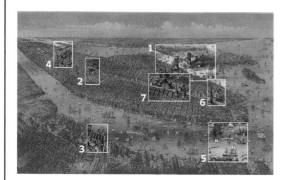

KEY

▶ **BROOKLYN BRIDGE** The construction of the Brooklyn Bridge, a major feat of engineering, began in 1869. It was not actually completed and opened for use until 1883, eight years after this map was drawn. The cartographers would have visualized the final result from the published plans, but they have made the bridge look shorter to bring it closer to the reader. At the time, Brooklyn was a distinct and separate city to New York; the building of the bridge brought the two areas closer together and in 1898 they merged.

1

2

3

4

▲ **UNION SQUARE** Situated at the junction of Broadway and the Bowery, this square was named for the union of these two principal north-south streets on Manhattan–rather than for the victory of the Union states in the recent civil war.

▲ **HOBOKEN STEAM FERRIES** As Manhattan filled up, immigrants crossed the waterways that bounded the island, east to Brooklyn, and west to New Jersey cities such as Hoboken. Starting in 1811, the world's first commercial steam ferry connected Manhattan to Hoboken, an area which through the 19th century developed a majority German population.

▲ **GRAND CENTRAL DEPOT** Immigrants to New York not only arrived by sea; some came overland by rail from elsewhere in America. Rail lines into Manhattan were brought together in one large station, Grand Central Depot, which opened in October 1871, just a few years before this map was drawn. It was later renamed Grand Central Terminal.

▼ **CUSTOMS HOUSE** The domed building on Wall Street was where all customs duties were collected. New York was the primary port of entry to the US for goods as well as people, so an immense amount of money passed through the customs house doors.

IN **CONTEXT**

In the mid-19th century, New York was of an almost uniform height and appearance: the four-storey, red-brick tenement was the basic, common building block of Manhattan. In response to ever-increasing numbers of immigrants arriving in the city, these tenements were designed to contain the greatest number of people in the least amount of space. They were generally planned on building lots measuring 7.5-by-30-m (25-by-100-ft) with four apartments to a floor. In theory, this was supposed to provide lodgings for around 64 people. In practice, hundreds were often squeezed into a single block, with shared toilets, poor ventilation, and little natural light.

▲ **An entire family** living in a single room of a late-19th-century New York tenement block

◄ **TRANSATLANTIC STEAMER** The map makes Manhattan and its facing shores appear like one great port. The two waterways are thronged with vessels, both sailing ships and the new steam vessels that were replacing them. Mass immigration to America drove many innovations in shipbuilding, particularly the need for bigger, faster, more efficient ships.

▲ **BROADWAY** The grandest civic buildings were on Broadway, including (from left to center) the civic court, city hall, and the central post office. To the right of the church spire is the tall, red Equitable Life Building, which had the world's first safety passenger elevator.

New York, 1963

HERMANN BOLLMANN ▪ COLOR PROCESS PRINT ▪
NUMEROUS COPIES EXIST

SCALE

MAP OF NEW YORK

Hermann Bollmann's "bird's-eye view" map of New York City has been called one of the greatest cartographic feats of all time and, while that is a matter for debate, it is undeniably enormous fun. The map shows Midtown Manhattan from East River to Hudson River and from Madison Square Park north to Central Park. It was prepared for the 1964 New York World's Fair, where it was sold at information and tourist kiosks. It was later reissued in further limited editions with various sponsors, such as Reader's Digest and American Airlines.

Axonometric projection

Bollmann used axonometric projection—in which parallel lines are used to show at least two sides of an object, but without any sense of perspective or distance—because, unlike a conventional ground plan, it could show comparative heights, perfect for skyscraper-filled New York. In order to make the map, Bollmann and his staff used special cameras to take 67,000 photos, of which 17,000 were shot from the air. These were used as a base reference for the cartographers to painstakingly hand-draw the city blocks. The level of detail and fidelity is extraordinary, although the avenues and cross-streets had to be artificially widened, and some of the heights of buildings were increased to aid readability. In addition to being a fine work of cartography, Bollmann's map also places the viewer above the city, peering down from on high—making it simply exhilarating to look at.

HERMANN **BOLLMANN**

1911–71

Originally a graphic artist, Hermann Bollmann was a native of Braunschweig, Germany. During World War II he served in a cartographic unit and there developed an interest in the 19th-century tradition of *Vogelschaukarten*, or "bird's-eye view" maps.

After the war, and faced with the devastation of many German cities, Bollmann had the idea of making a series of maps that would illustrate the rebuilding of certain urban areas, including his own hometown. He drew his first Braunschweig map in 1948 and repeatedly revised it over the years. He later mapped other German cities, as well as cities outside of Germany, and in a period spanning 25 years he produced more than 39 three-dimensional plans of places in Europe and North America. In many cases, he returned to these cities to update his maps, and in some cases he created as many as 15 revised editions of individual maps.

In the early days of his career Bollmann worked alone, sketching on a drawing board hung around his neck. Later he recruited assistants and purchased a Volkswagen, on the roof of which he mounted a camera with a wide-angle lens. For aerial views he used a light plane with special cameras. These innovations enabled him to work speedily, and his most ambitious project—this map of central Manhattan—was produced in just eight months.

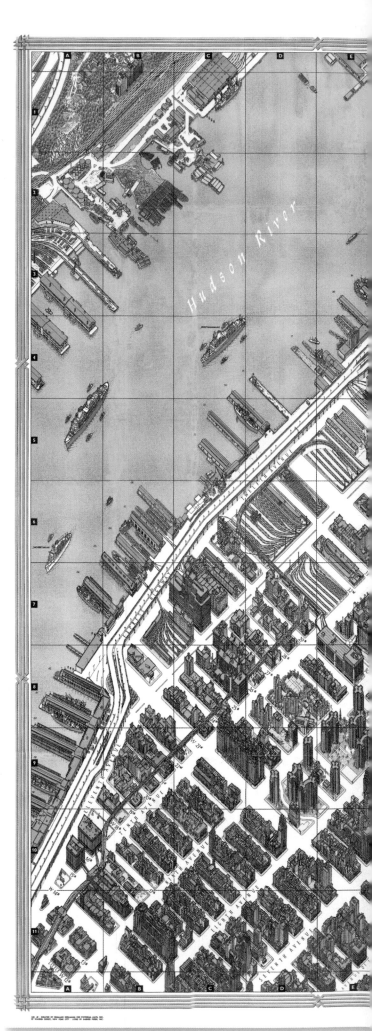

NEW YORK

Visual tour

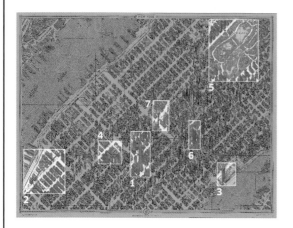

KEY

▷ **EMPIRE STATE BUILDING**
When Bollmann produced this map, the 102-story Empire State, with its spire height of 1,454ft (381m), was the world's tallest building. The cartographer acknowledges this supremacy by placing it almost on the vertical center line of the map. However, the building's height record would be broken just a few years after this map was produced, on completion of the North Tower of the World Trade Center in 1970.

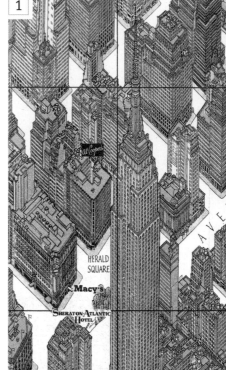

▽ **ELEVATED RAILROAD** Opened in 1934, the West Side Elevated Line was a raised railroad running from 34th Street down to Spring Street in Lower Manhattan. It ran through blocks rather than along roads, allowing trains to load and unload cargo inside buildings. Starting in 2009, sections of it have been transformed into the highly popular High Line public park.

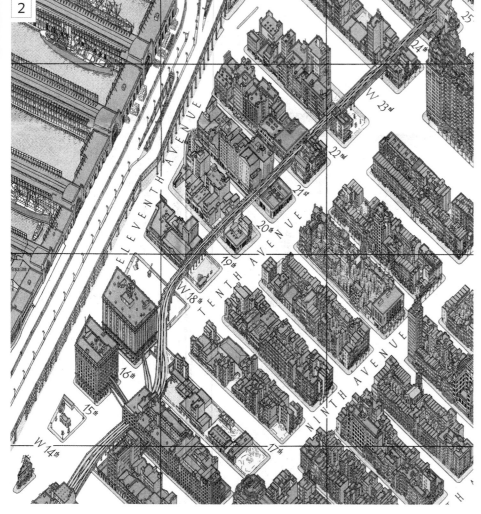

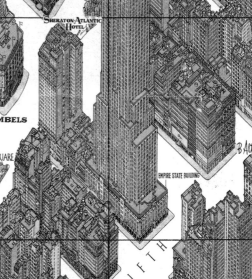

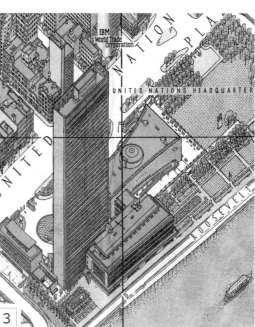

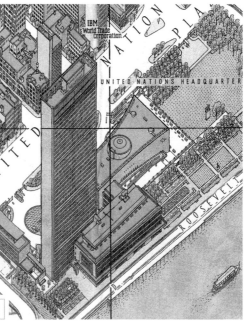

▷ **UNITED NATIONS HEADQUARTERS** Home to the global offices and facilities of the United Nations, the complex on First Avenue and East 42nd Street was constructed between 1948 and 1952. The 39-story slab of the Secretariat was the tallest building on the East River at this time. The modest block anchoring the site's southwest corner is the Dag Hammarskjöld Library, which had just been completed in 1961.

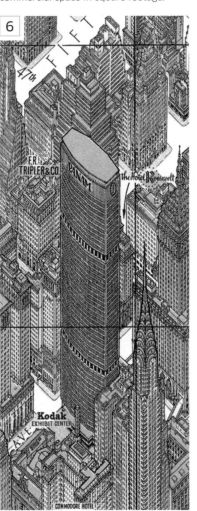

▼ PAN AM BUILDING One block west of the Chrysler Building and immediately north of Grand Central Terminal, the Pan Am Building opened in the same year that this map was made. At 59 stories, it was not the tallest building in New York, but it boasted the world's largest commercial space in square footage.

▼ TIMES SQUARE This map's version of Times Square presents it as a spacious and orderly plaza—an almost utopian vision of the area that also highlights how the mappers subtly distorted the street grid. In reality, Times Square was a cramped and canyonlike public space which was also one of the seediest and most dangerous places in New York at the time the map was drawn.

▲ CENTRAL PARK With its absence of any tall structures, there was little to be gained from a three-dimensional rendering of Central Park, so Bollmann chose to show no more than a fifth of its area. Recognizable monuments are few, but the sharp-eyed observer can pick out the Tavern on the Green beside Central Park West, and Central Park Zoo next to Fifth Avenue.

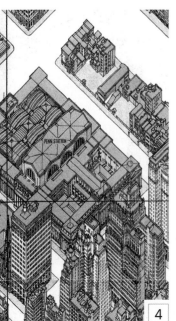

◄ PENN STATION The fast-paced rate of change in New York City caught out the mapmakers here: the map depicts the grand Pennsylvania Station, built from 1901–10 and demolished in 1963 in spite of high-profile protests. The new replacement commuter hub was built wholly underground. Above ground, the site would be occupied by the multipurpose Madison Square Garden arena, which opened in 1968.

IN **CONTEXT**

In the first 200 years of its development, the city that is now known as New York grew in a haphazard, organic manner. But with the population booming, some sort of controlled framework was considered necessary. In 1811 the city set out a grid stretching from its existing northern boundary to run for 155 streets. The east–west streets were intersected by a dozen north–south avenues.

The grid is not perfectly regular: some blocks are longer than others and some avenues are wider. Then there is Broadway, which, as can be seen on Bollmann's map, slashes diagonally across the city. In doing so it creates some of the few public spaces, including Columbus Circle, Times Square, Herald Square, and Madison Square.

The layout proved to be the perfect physical expression of what New York stood for, a democratic city in which all things were apparently equal, easy to comprehend, and that set out to absorb all.

▲ New York's grid layout as seen from directly above

New York, 2013

MAXWELL ROBERTS ▪ DIGITAL MAP

NEW YORK SUBWAY CIRCLES MAP

A new kind of city map came into being with the advent of complex city transportation networks. The job of these maps was not to portray the geography of the city, but to present a schematic diagram that showed how the elements of these networks related to each other logically. The freedom from precise geography that this entailed allowed mappers to investigate alternative means of presentation to make the networks of lines, interchanges, and stations easier for the viewer to comprehend. The most famous early example of these maps is probably the London Underground map drawn by Harry Beck (*see right*).

Psychologist Maxwell Roberts has spent over a decade studying global underground maps. He has redrawn many of these, including London, using his own system of concentric circles and spokes. New York, which has one of the oldest and most complex subway systems in the world, was the ninth of his circle maps. It differs from others in the series in that it is not a complete circle but a segment, and the central point is not on the land but in the harbor. Despite that, Roberts considers it to be the most powerful and orderly of all his designs to date. The map was devised for Roberts' own pleasure and is not in official use, but it has generated a positive response from New Yorkers online.

IN CONTEXT

Harry Beck's famous 1933 schematic map of the London Underground—which he based on diagrams of electrical circuits—was groundbreaking in its use of uniform 45-degree angles, evenly spaced stations, and geographic distortion. But like cities themselves, the transportation networks that support them are in a constant state of evolution, and the maps that explain them need updating regularly. The London Underground map in use today, while based on Beck's original schematic layout, bears little resemblance to its historic predecessor.

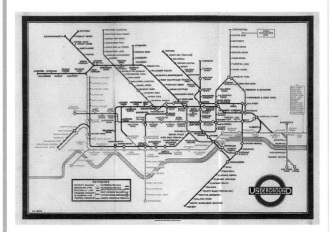

▲ **Harry Beck's schematic map** of the London Underground, which inspired generations of city transit maps

Visual tour

KEY

1

▲ **WORLD TRADE CENTER** One of the biggest challenges for Roberts was making sure that station names did not interrupt the lines and spoil the clarity of the map. To this end, he had to use an arrow to show the location of the World Trade Center Station.

2

▲ **SOUTH BROOKLYN** Because of the many stations on intertwining lines that appear in this area, Roberts had to start his design work in this portion of the map. Once everything fit in smoothly, the space he had used gave him the width and height of the overall map.

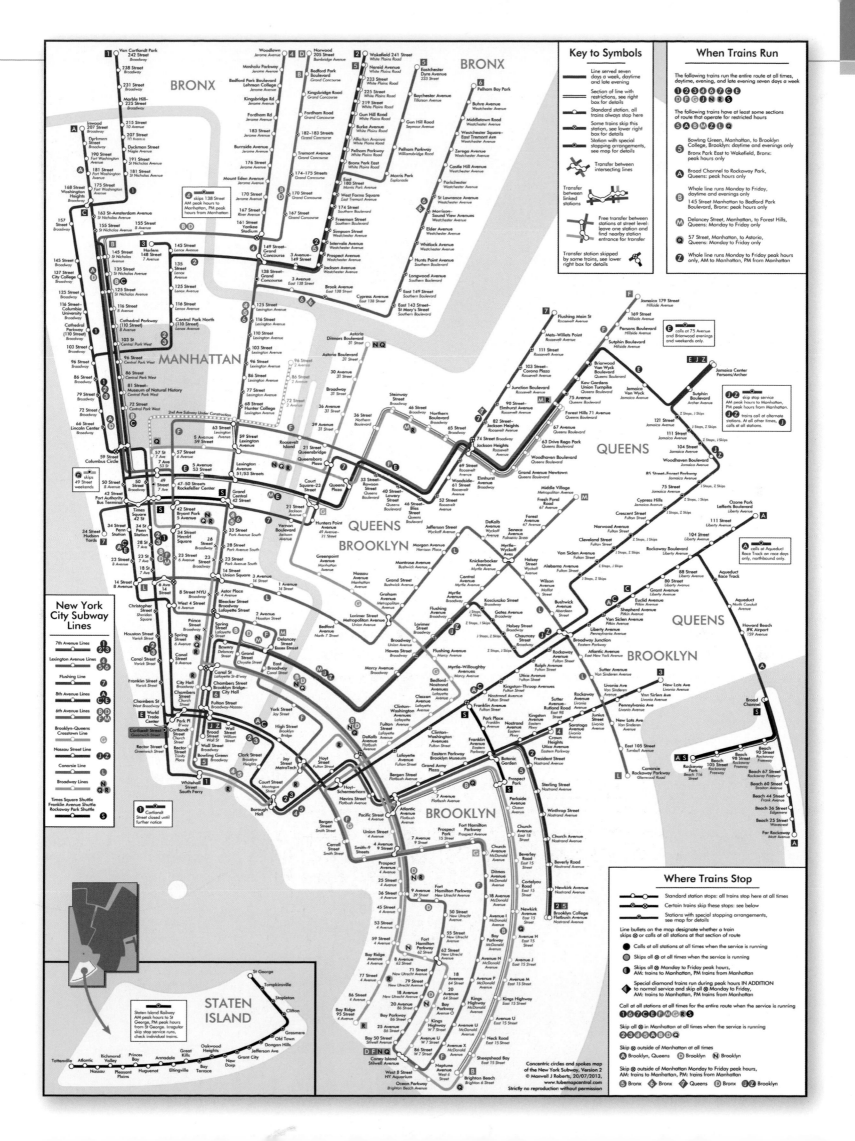

Tokyo, 2014

SOHEI NISHINO ▪ PHOTO COLLAGE ▪ PRIVATE COLLECTION

TOKYO 2014 DIORAMA MAP

SCALE

In the 21st century, the use of satellite photography has taken the art out of practical mapping. The combination of precise GPS (global positioning system) coordinates rendered through digital graphics, best exemplified by Google Maps, has taken away the element of human interpretation that contributed much individual beauty to many of the historic maps in this book. The Japanese artist–cartographer, Sohei Nishino, reverses that trend with his photography. He uses photographic collages to create highly detailed panoramas of some of the world's busiest urban centers. His work exists in the overlap between art and cartography, in a similar way to the photo-collages of David Hockney, but they are also reminiscent of ancient mosaic maps, such as the Madaba Map (*see pp.26–27*). To create his pieces, Nishino walks the cities on his own for a month to six weeks, shooting up to 10,000 images. From these, he selects and hand-prints approximately 4,000 photographs. He then cuts up and assembles the images on a large board, onto which the outline of the city has been sketched. The resulting collages are not precise geographic recreations, but an imperfect mix of landmarks and snapshots of daily life that constitute the artist's personal experience of a city.

SOHEI **NISHINO**

1982

Nishino was born in Hyogo Prefecture on Honshu Island. He developed his diorama technique while studying at the Osaka University of Arts.

Nishino takes his inspiration from the surveyor Inō Tadataka (1745–1818), who spent the final 17 years of his life surveying the islands of Japan by attempting to walk its entire coastline. Nishino's cartography is less scientific and more creative. Since producing his map pieces, he has participated in several international festivals, group shows, and solo exhibitions all over the world. He has also been producing works that are far more fantastical, such as i-Land, which depicts an imaginary Japanese city.

Visual tour

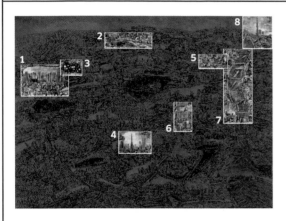

KEY

▶ **SHINJUKU** This is the main business district and home to the city's greatest concentration of skyscrapers. Several of the tallest buildings in Tokyo are shown here including the twin towers of the Metropolitan Government Building and the spired Empire State-like NTT Docomo Yoyogi Building. Unlike much of the rest of the map, here the artist has chosen to photograph the buildings from a distance in order to portray the distinctive skyline.

▼ **THE SUBWAY** The artist has said that what he is trying to capture in his "Diorama Maps" is a microcosm of the life and energy that comprises the city. Movement is an important element of this, and accordingly his Tokyo 2014 map is criss-crossed by speeding bullet trains, snaking subway cars, battalions of trolleys, and streaming traffic.

◀ **KABUKICHO** An interesting example of how the artist has imposed his own narrative on this work is in the entertainment and red-light district of Kabukicho, which is a part of Shinjuku (*see above*). Here, he uses photographs taken at night instead of in daylight because the neon street signs are the best-known characteristic of the area.

▶ **TOKYO TOWER** At first glance, it is hard to pick out many landmarks among the chaos of the map. Buildings loom and tilt, and it is easy to get lost, just as in the real city. However, Tokyo Tower, silhouetted against clear sky, provides a prominent navigation aid, both in the map and for visitors to Tokyo itself.

▼ **ASAKUSA** This district in the northeast of the city is famous for its large Buddhist temple, approached though an imposing outer gate (top right). Pilgrims and visitors flock here for the frequent festivals, and this is captured on the map in a busy collage of photographs of crowds and processions.

5

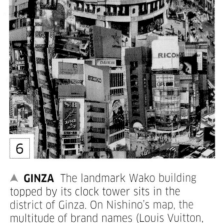

6

▲ **GINZA** The landmark Wako building topped by its clock tower sits in the district of Ginza. On Nishino's map, the multitude of brand names (Louis Vuitton, Chanel, and Bulgari) surrounding it immediately marks this area out as an upmarket shopping district.

▶ **SUMIDA RIVER** The river that flows through Tokyo is every bit as congested as the city's roads and railroad lines. During the three months Nishino spent in the fall of 2014 walking and taking photographs, he also made several excursions onto the river in canoes to capture the city from alternative angles.

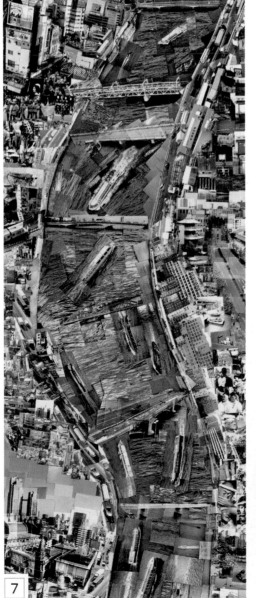

7

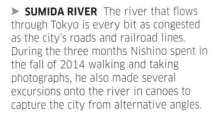

IN **CONTEXT**

Artists and designers continue to find new ways of mapping cities. Possibly as a reaction to the impersonality of GPS, these maps often take a personal or even humorous view of their subject. British ceramicist Grayson Perry (1960–) has made much use of maps in his work, often loading them with semiautobiographical details. British artist Stephen Walter (1975–) covers his maps with annotations offering commentaries exposing the prejudices relating to the mapped locations. American artist Saul Steinberg memorably did the opposite with a map he drew for the cover of *The New Yorker*, skewering the way Manhattanites viewed their own city and what lay beyond it.

▲ **Underground rivers**, pipes, and tunnels on display in Stephen Walter's *London Subterranea* (2012)

▼ **TOKYO SKYTREE** Nishino's 2014 map of Tokyo is the second photo collage the artist has created of the city—he made an earlier diorama in 2004. Nishino says that the city changed greatly in the intervening years. One notable difference was this broadcasting tower, completed in 2012. Reaching a height of 2,080 ft (634 m), it is the second tallest tower in the world.

8

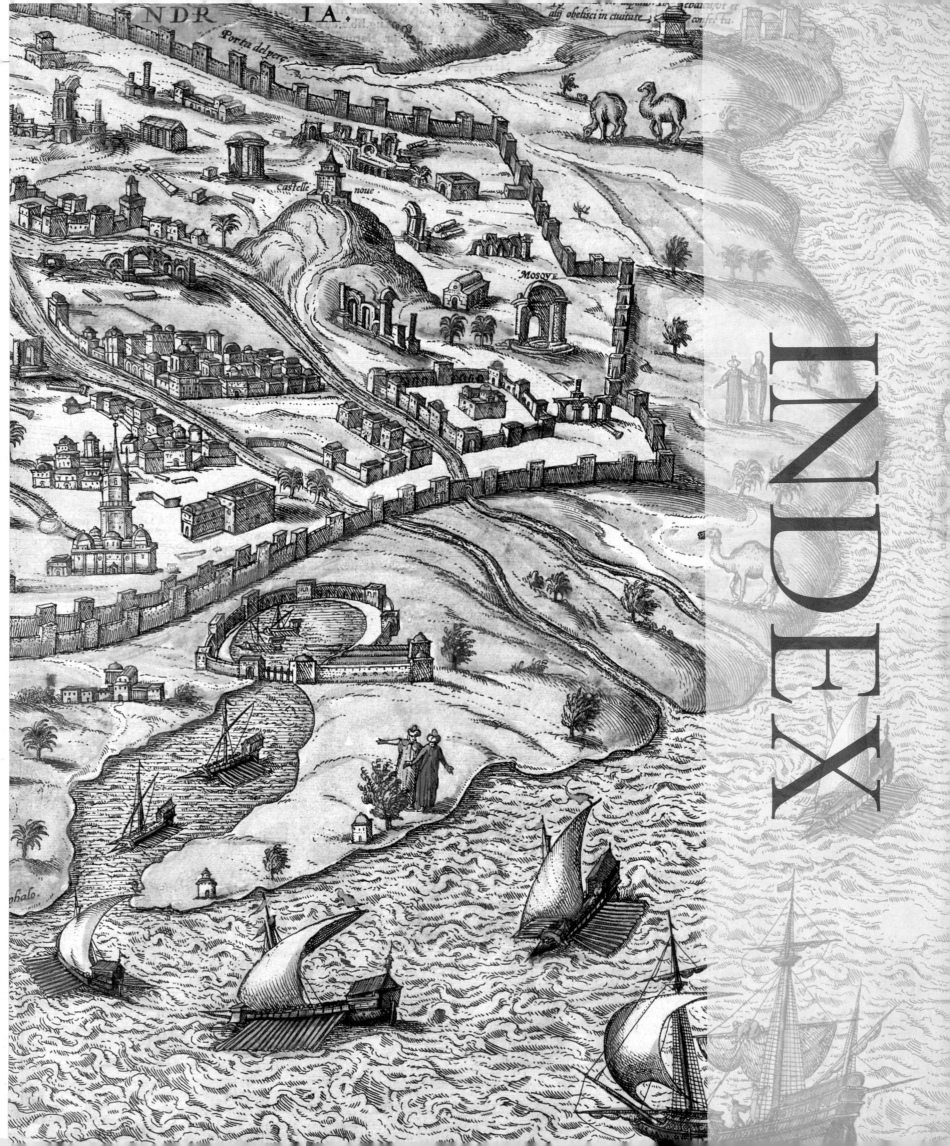

NDR   IA.   Porta del perg.
Castelle noue.   MOSQVE

alij obelisci in ciuitate   confecta.

INDEX

Acknowledgments

Dorling Kindersley would like to thank the following people for their assistance with this book:.
Smithsonian reviewer, Jim Harle, map curator volunteer, National Museum of Natural History; Sam Kennedy, Kate Taylor, and Anna Limerick for editorial assistance; Alex Beeden for proofreading; Margaret McCormack for indexing; Steve Crozier at Butterfly Creative Solutions; Megan Taylor for picture research.

The publisher would specially like to thank the following people for their help in providing DK with images:
Massimo De Martini at Altea Gallery Limited; Jorge Chavez at Barry Lawrence Ruderman Antique Maps Inc.; Kevin Brown at Geographicus Rare Antique Maps.

The publisher would like to thank the following for their kind permission to reproduce their photographs:

(Key: a-above; b-below/bottom; c-center; f-far; l-left; r-right; t-top)

1 Harvard University Library: (l). **Geographicus Rare Antique Maps:** (r). **Photo Scala, Florence:** (c). **2-3 David Rumsey Map Collection www.davidrumsey.com. 4-5 Library of Congress, Washington, D.C.. 6-7 Alamy Stock Photo:** Heritage Image Partnership Ltd (t). **National Library Of Scotland:** (c). **Sohei Nishino:** (b). **8 Corbis. 8-9 Getty Images:** SM Rafiq Photography (b). **9 4Corners:** Reinhard Schmid (br). **The Art Archive:** DeA Picture Library (tr). **10-11 Altea Gallery. 12 Photo Scala, Florence:** bpk, Bildagentur fuer Kunst, Kultur und Geschichte, Berlin (b). **13 Den Haag, Koninklijke Bibliotheek, 76 F 5.:** (tr). **Newberry Library, Chicago, Illinois, USA:** (b). **14-15 The Art Archive:** DeA Picture Library. **14 AF Fotografie. 16-17 Photo Scala, Florence. 18-19 Bridgeman Images. 20-21 Bridgeman Images. 22 Bridgeman Images:** Fitzwilliam Museum, University of Cambridge, UK (bl). **22-23 Majesty Maps & Prints. 24-25 Majesty Maps & Prints. 25-br Barry Lawrence Ruderman Antique Maps Inc. 26-27 akg-images:** Erich Lessing. **26 Alamy Stock Photo:** Robert Harding (bl). **27 Bridgeman Images:** (cr). **28-29 Den Haag, Koninklijke Bibliotheek, 76 F 5.. 29 The Bodleian Library, University of Oxford:** MS Araab. C. 90, fols. (cra). **30-31 Altea Gallery. 32-33 Altea Gallery. 33 akg-images:** Bible Land Pictures / WWW. BibleLandPictures (cr). **34-35 Geographicus Rare Antique Maps. 35 Barry Lawrence Ruderman Antique Maps Inc. 36-37 Alamy Stock Photo:** Heritage Image Partnership Ltd (t); Heritage Image Partnership Ltd (b). **38 Alamy Stock Photo:** Heritage Image Partnership Ltd (bl). **38-39 Alamy Stock Photo:** Heritage Image Partnership Ltd (t); Heritage Image Partnership Ltd (b). **39 Alamy Stock Photo:** Heritage Image Partnership Ltd (ca); Heritage Image Partnership Ltd (c); Heritage Image Partnership Ltd (bc). **40-41 akg-images:** Erich Lessing. **42-43 Photo Scala, Florence:** bpk, Bildagentur fuer Kunst, Kultur und Geschichte, Berlin. **42 Photo Scala, Florence:** Heritage Images (bl). **44-45 Photo Scala, Florence:** bpk, Bildagentur fuer Kunst, Kultur und Geschichte, Berlin. **45 Bridgeman Images:** Topkapi Palace Museum, Istanbul, Turkey / Dost Yayinlari (br). **46-47 Benaki Museum Athens. 48-49 Altea Gallery. 48 Getty Images:** DEA / R. MERLO / De Agostini (bc). **50-51 Altea Gallery. 51 Andrew Michael Chugg:** (br). **52-53 Newberry Library, Chicago, Illinois, USA. 52 The Bodleian Library, University of Oxford:** MS. Arch. Selden. A1, fol (bc). **54-44 Newberry Library, Chicago, Illinois, USA. 55 Corbis:** Michael T. Sedam (br). **56-57 National Museum of History, Mexico City, Mexico. 57 Alamy Stock Photo:** The Art Archive (br). **58 San Antonio Conservation Society:** (cr). **59 David Rumsey Map Collection www.davidrumsey.com. 60-61 David Rumsey Map Collection www.davidrumsey.com. 61 Alamy Stock Photo:** Jon Arnold Images Ltd (cr). **62-63 KIK-IRPA, Brussels (Belgium). 64 Rijksmuseum:** Koninklijk Oudheidkundig Genootschap, Amsterdam (br). **Photo Scala, Florence:** Courtesy of Musei Civici Fiorentini (bl). **65 Barry Lawrence Ruderman Antique Maps Inc:** (bl). **Kroll Map Company, Inc:** (br). **66-67 Stadsmuseet Stockholm / City Museum of Stockholm. 66 Alamy Stock Photo:** Universal Art Archive (cb). **68-69 Altea Gallery. 70-71 Altea Gallery. 71 Bridgeman Images:** Society of Antiquaries of London, UK (br). **72 Corbis:** Heritage Images (bl). **72-73 Library of Congress, Washington, D.C.. 74-75 Library of Congress, Washington, D.C.. 76-77 Altea Gallery. 78-79 Altea Gallery. 79 Bridgeman Images:** Museum of London, UK (tr). **80-81 Altea Gallery. 82-83 Courtesy of Dublin City Library and Archive. 84-85 Courtesy of Dublin City Library and Archive. 85 Bridgeman Images:** The Stapleton Collection (tr). **86-87 Rijksmuseum:** Koninklijk Oudheidkundig Genootschap, Amsterdam. **88-89 Special Collections, University of Amsterdam. 90 Stad Gent:** (bl). **90-91 KIK-IRPA, Brussels (Belgium). 92 KIK-IRPA, Brussels (Belgium). 93 KIK-IRPA, Brussels (Belgium). Photo Scala, Florence. 94 Bridgeman Images:** Vernet, Claude Joseph / Musee de la Marine (bc). **94-95 Kroll Map Company, Inc. 96-97 Kroll Map Company, Inc. 98-99 Bridgeman Images. 98 Photo Scala, Florence:** The Metropolitan Museum of Art (bl). **100-101 Barry Lawrence Ruderman Antique Maps Inc. 100 Alamy Stock Photo:** Jan Wlodarczyk (bl). **102-103 Barry Lawrence Ruderman Antique Maps Inc. 104-105 akg-images. 104 akg-images:** North Wind Picture Archives (bl). **106-107 The Map House. 108-109 Rijksmuseum. 108 Alamy Stock Photo:** Mary Evans Picture Library (bl). **110 Alamy Stock Photo:** Iakov Filimonov (bl). **110-111 Harvard University Library. 112-113 Altea Gallery. 112 Alamy Stock Photo:** The Art Archive (bl). **114-115 Altea Gallery. 115 Bridgeman Images:** Museo Correr, Venice, Italy (br). **116-117 Photo Scala, Florence:** Courtesy of Musei Civici Fiorentini. **118-119 Photo Scala, Florence:** Courtesy of Musei Civici Fiorentini. **119 Photo Scala, Florence. 120-121 akg-images. 122 Courtesy of Swann Auction Galleries:** (b). **123 Biblioteca Nacional Espana:** (br). **Altea Gallery. 124-125 Bridgeman Images:** Wien Museum Karlsplatz, Vienna, Austria / Ali Meyer. **124 Bridgeman Images:** Rafael Valls Gallery, London, UK (bl).

126-127 Bridgeman Images: Wien Museum Karlsplatz, Vienna, Austria / Ali Meyer. **128-129 Wien Museum. 128 akg-images. 130-131 akg-images:** The British Library. **132 Alamy Stock Photo:** Granger, NYC (cr). **133 David Rumsey Map Collection www.davidrumsey.com. 134-135 David Rumsey Map Collection www.davidrumsey.com. 135 Library of Congress, Washington, D.C.. 136-137 Biblioteca Nacional Espana. 138-139 Biblioteca Nacional Espana. 139-br Bridgeman Images:** Museo Municipal, Madrid, Spain. **140-141 Biblioteca Nacional Espana. 142-143 Courtesy of Swann Auction Galleries. 144-145 Geographicus Rare Antique Maps. 146-147 akg-images. 146 Bridgeman Images. 148-149 akg-images. 149 Alamy Stock Photo:** Agencja Fotograficzna Caro (br). **150-151 Harvard University, Yenching Library. 152 Alamy Stock Photo:** VPC Travel Photo (cr). **153 Barry Lawrence Ruderman Antique Maps Inc. 154-155 Barry Lawrence Ruderman Antique Maps Inc. 156-157 Altea Gallery. 158-159 Alamy Stock Photo:** Heritage Image Partnership Ltd. **160-161 Library of Congress, Washington, D.C.:** Geography and Map Division. **162 Princeton University Library:** (b). **163 Barry Lawrence Ruderman Antique Maps Inc:** (bl). **LucasAbstract:** (br). **164-165 National Library of Australia:** Francis Fowkes, Sketch & description of the settlement at Sydney Cove Port Jackson in the County of Cumberland. **166-167 Bridgeman Images:** National Library of Australia, Canberra, Australia. **168-169 Geographicus Rare Antique Maps. 168 akg-images:** historic-maps (b). **170-171 David Rumsey Map Collection www.davidrumsey.com. 170 Corbis:** (bl). **172-173 David Rumsey Map Collection www.davidrumsey.com. 173 Corbis:** Bettmann (br). **174-175 Princeton University Library. 174 akg-images:** De Agostini Picture Lib. (bl). **176-177 Barry Lawrence Ruderman Antique Maps Inc. 178-179 Library of Congress, Washington, D.C.:** Geography and Map Division. **180-181 LucasAbstract. 182-183 Altea Gallery. 184-185 Library of Congress, Washington, D.C.. 184 The Walters Art Museum, Baltimore:** (bl). **185 Library of Congress, Washington, D.C.:** Geography and Map Division (br). **186-187 Library of Congress, Washington, D.C.. 188-189 Library of Congress, Washington, D.C.:** Geography and Map Division. **190-191 Library of Congress, Washington, D.C.:** Geography and Map Division. **191 National Capital Planning Commission:** (br). **192-193 The Walters Art Museum, Baltimore. 194-195 Maris Anhalt / Oldprintart.com. 194 AF Fotografie:** (cb). **196-197 Maris Anhalt / Oldprintart.com. 197 Alamy Stock Photo:** Active Museum (br). **198-199 Majesty Maps & Prints. 200-201 Majesty Maps & Prints. 201 Alamy Stock Photo:** Brian Jannsen (br). **202-203 Library of Congress, Washington, D.C.:** Geography and Map Division.. **204-205 Library of Congress, Washington, D.C.:** Geography and Map Division.. **205 Corbis:** Yann Arthus-Bertrand (br). **206-207 National Library Of Scotland. 208-209 Altea Gallery. 210-211 National Library of Russia. 212-213 Alamy Stock Photo:** Images & Stories. **214-215 Library of Congress, Washington, D.C.:** Geography and Map Division. **216 Geographicus Rare Antique Maps:** (b). **217 Boston Public Library:** (bl). **Sohei Nishino:** (br). **218-219 Library of Congress, Washington, D.C.:** Geography and Map Division. **220-221 Collection of the National Library Foundation - Brazil. 220 TopFoto.co.uk:** ullsteinbild (bl). **222-223 Boston Public Library.**

224-225 New York Historical Society. 224 The New York Public Library: digitalcollections.nypl.org (bl). **226-227 New York Historical Society. 227 Bridgeman Images:** British Library Board. All Rights Reserved (br). **228 Bridgeman Images:** Musee Franco-Americaine, Blerancourt, Chauny, France (cr). **229 akg-images:** The British Library Board. **230-231 akg-images:** The British Library Board. **232-233 Library of Congress, Washington, D.C.:** Geography and Map Division. **233 Corbis:** Museum of the City of New York (br). **234-235 Library of Congress, Washington, D.C.:** Geography and Map Division. **235 Corbis:** Bettman (cr). **236-237 Geographicus Rare Antique Maps. 238-239 Geographicus Rare Antique Maps. 239 Corbis:** Cameron Davidson (br). **240-241 Maxwell J. Roberts, 2005-16. 240 TfL from the London Transport Museum collection:** Harry Beck (cr). **242-243 Sohei Nishino. 242 Sohei Nishino. 244-245 Sohei Nishino. 245 Courtesy of TAG Fine Arts:** Stephen Walter (cr). **246-247 Altea Gallery**

Jacket images: Front, Back and Spine: **San Antonio Conservation Society**

All other images © Dorling Kindersley

For further information see: www.dkimages.com